D1089923

Other Jossey-Bass Leadership and Nonprofit Management Titles:

IMPROVING LEADERSHIP IN NONPROFIT ORGANIZATIONS

IMPROVING LEADERSHIP IN NONPROFIT ORGANIZATIONS

Edited by
Ronald E. Riggio
Sarah Smith Orr

Foreword by Jack Shakely

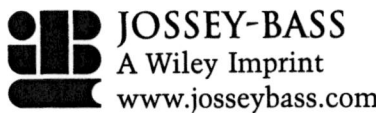
JOSSEY-BASS
A Wiley Imprint
www.josseybass.com

Published by Jossey-Bass
A Wiley Imprint
989 Market Street, San Francisco, CA 94103-1741   www.josseybass.com

Jossey-Bass books and products are available through most bookstores. To contact Jossey-Bass directly
call our Customer Care Department within the U.S. at 800-956-7739, outside the U.S. at
317-572-399386 or fax 317-572-4002.

Jossey-Bass also publishes its books in a variety of electronic formats. Some content that appears in print
may not be available in electronic books.   .

Cataloging-in-Publication Data available upon request.

CONTENTS

TABLES, FIGURES, AND EXHIBITS

Tables

Figures

Exhibits

FOREWORD

Even though he was never known as a wordsmith, President James A. Garfield gets my vote for having uttered one of the best, and most misquoted, entries in *Bartlett's Familiar Quotations.*

What he actually said was, "Give me a log hut, with only a simple bench, Mark Hopkins on one end and I on the other and you may have all the buildings, apparatus and libraries without him."

Hundreds of paraphrases abound; and Garfield's sentiments are remembered far more than his cumbersome phraseology. What usually comes out is something similar to what the wonderful writer John D. McDonald (1977) conjured up for his crusty romantic Travis McGee in *The Green Ripper:* "Meyer, you know what a perfect school is? A log, with Horace Mann at one end."

Garfield's thoughts remind us of two simple lessons we in the philanthropic field often seem hell-bent to forget: investments in leaders are seldom wasted, and no building ever taught anybody anything.

After more than thirty years of observing nonprofit organizations, I have come to the conclusion that, to paraphrase Tolstoy, failing nonprofits fail for many reasons, but successful nonprofits are successful the same. They all pay homage to a leader at the top, a person whose vision is so clear that it can be drawn on a napkin or talked through in a boardroom and the observer gets it—gets it so completely that checkbooks come flying out of pockets and grant contracts get written up on the spot.

Leadership is so clearly the deciding factor in nonprofit success, it seems surprising that it has taken us all this time to figure it out. But until recently, the words nonprofit and leadership went together like bicycle and fish. Nonprofit boards seemed intuitively to fear hiring leaders, giving them low-energy titles like executive director or executive secretary. Christine Letts suggested in an article in *Harvard Business Review* that successful candidates to head nonprofit organizations need to show leadership qualities in the job interview but practice them at their peril later. Maybe this is because boards of directors are made up of leaders. ("Imagine a football team made up of eleven quarterbacks, all asking for the ball," leadership scholar James Lawrence Powell once said to me.) The last thing a group of leaders needs is another one.

Whatever the reason, until the last decade, nonprofit leadership was discounted despite glowing examples to the contrary. As this wonderful book points out, an exhaustive study of leadership traits in the 1990s focused on the military, government, church, and business, failing to interview a single nonprofit CEO.

Perhaps one of the reasons nonprofit leaders were ignored for so long was because they were, and are, hard to spot. They don't fit the same mold. Marion Wright Edelman, founder of the Children's Defense Fund, is a small woman whose oratory is robust, crackling with clarity and power. Cesar Chavez was the quietest man I ever met, a mumbler perhaps, whose steely gaze could lift a thousand people out of their seats. Wendy Kopp, the woman who started Teach for America, would fidget like a graduate student as she outlined brilliant management strategies to keep her army of young teachers paid and in place.

I've met great nonprofit leaders you wanted to hug; others you wanted to punch in the nose. Being a leader is not synonymous with being popular, as any leader will tell you. But for all their differences, there are amazing commonalities. Each leader is endowed with great integrity, a moral, even spiritual, agenda that is practiced, never preached. This moral core of the leader inflames us; we are the missionaries to their mission.

They are also fantastic managers and, often, not the world's greatest delegators. They are transformers, and they get things done.

Leadership is, I think, a little like golf. It can be learned, but cannot be taught. This book will give the learner much to think about. We can learn to be a solutions broker. (Many great leaders don't necessarily have great ideas; they implement great ideas. Don't forget, Bill Gates never invented a thing in his life.) We can learn the power of charisma, and its dark side. We can learn to detect the dreadful founder's syndrome and its even more malevolent partner, successor's syndrome. Most of all, we can be reminded of the strengths we have within us, ready to come into play.

As a teenager, I was fascinated by atomic science. The electrons we studied were flying all over the place, but the protons and neutrons stuck together in a nucleus, and nobody knew why. Finally scientists suggested there was something called "cosmic glue" that held things together, something that couldn't be seen or whose existence couldn't be proven. I loved that phrase and the mysteries it encompassed.

Leadership is the cosmic glue of the twenty-first-century nonprofit organization. Without it, things fall apart and the center will not hold. With it, we can transform agencies, constituencies, whole communities.

Speaking about leadership, Margaret Mead, noted anthropologist, conveyed her optimism about the influence of people who are committed to change through this widely quoted statement: "Never doubt that a small group of thoughtful people could change the world. Indeed, it's the only thing that ever has" (Maggio, 1996).

Nonprofit leadership can be risky, lonely, scary, and almost always underfunded. But if you have it, give me a log with you at one end. Together we can hope to change the world.

September 2003   Jack Shakely
                                                     President
                                                     California Community Foundation

References

McDonald, J. D. *The Green Ripper.* Mattituck, N.Y.: Amereon, Ltd., 1977.
Maggio, R. *Quotations by Women.* Boston: Beacon Press, 1996.

DEDICATION

This book is dedicated, first, to those individuals who have made a career commitment to serve people and communities through their leadership of a nonprofit organization. It is your dedication that provides support to people and to society in countless ways. We thank you!

Second, we would like to recognize and thank Henry R. Kravis, business and community leader, whose vision and commitment to leadership has made the work and contributions of the Kravis Leadership Institute possible. It was Henry's suggestion that we explore nonprofit leadership, which eventually led to the twelfth annual Kravis–de Roulet conference and to assembling the important contributions contained in this book.

PREFACE

When we think about the leadership of nonprofits, an image of the organization's CEO or director first comes to mind. But leadership in nonprofit organizations can take many forms. While the director may draw the most attention, the supervisory staffs of many heavily volunteer-dependent nonprofits do most of the real day-to-day leading, particularly if one views motivation as a primary leadership task. Moreover, boards play an important leadership role in nearly every nonprofit organization. And let's not forget the volunteers—many of whom play key leadership roles in other organizations and bring this leadership experience with them. So leadership is loosely dispersed throughout the nonprofit organization, and it is all held together by shared purpose.

The intended audience for this book is these very leaders of nonprofit organizations. Although the authors may have focused the most attention on nonprofit directors, they are also speaking directly to the supervisors, to the board members, to the staff and volunteers—to all who contribute to the leadership of the organization.

This book began as a two-day conference, the twelfth annual Kravis–de Roulet Leadership Conference, held at Claremont McKenna College on February 22–23, 2002. The intent was to bring together leadership scholars, experts in nonprofit issues, and practitioners and leaders in nonprofit organizations to share information and learn from one another. The goal of the conference was straightforward—to focus on improving leadership in nonprofit organizations, the title of both the conference and this book. The scope of the conference was very broad, including such issues as the current and future challenges faced by nonprofit leaders, board management, motivation, compensation, leadership development, and program evaluation. Some issues (such as fundraising) were intentionally not addressed to make the content more manageable. Some individual papers were presented and panel discussions were held, along with discussions with the audience, which consisted primarily of nonprofit leaders, scholars, and students. Presenters and panelists later prepared the chapters that make up this book.

This book is intended to be a "guidebook" for leading nonprofit organizations rather than a "handbook" of nonprofit leadership or management. There are plenty of the latter. Usually, handbooks are written by experts in managing nonprofits and are "how-to" types of books. The chapters in this volume are more designed to stimulate a nonprofit leader's thinking and to point out new directions and new ideas for leading that are all well-grounded in theory, research, and practice.

Overview of the Contents

The book is divided into five parts. The first calls on nonprofit leadership experts— Frances Hesselbein from the Leader-to-Leader Foundation, Stephen Dobbs, coauthor (with Burt Nanus) of *Leaders Who Make a Difference* (Jossey-Bass, 1999), and Florence Green, executive director of the California Association of Nonprofits (CAN)—to discuss the leadership challenges and issues for nonprofit organizations.

Part Two focuses specifically on the leaders of nonprofit organizations. Drawing on his experience in initiating microcredit, self-help groups in rural Indian villages, K. M. Thiagarajan suggests that leading a service-oriented nonprofit is centered entirely on the organization's mission and that this should be the driving force in guiding the venture. Ronald Riggio, Bernard Bass, and Sarah Smith Orr suggest that transformational leadership should be a guiding model for nonprofit leadership, showing the "fit" between transformational leadership and the demands of leading the nonprofit organization and presenting some evidence that suggests that transformational leaders of nonprofits do lead more effective organizations but calling for more research on transformational leadership in nonprofit organizations. A chapter by leadership ethicist Joanne Ciulla points out some of the current and future ethical challenges that nonprofit leaders must deal with, and economist Kevin Hallock compares the compensation of for-profit and not-for-profit leaders and implications for their motivation and sustainability. Finally,

Georgia Sorenson presents new research that looks at issues of succession in the leadership of nonprofit organizations, paying particular attention to concerns to when an organization's founder steps down.

The two chapters in Part Three spotlight nonprofit board leadership. First, leadership scholar Jay Conger compares highly functioning for-profit boards with boards of nonprofit organizations; then nonprofit practitioner-consultant Susan Scribner analyzes dysfunctional and functional boards.

Part Four offers a different perspective, looking at issues related to the organizations that leaders lead. Gill Hickman begins with what she calls "organizations of hope"—for-profit companies that have a commitment to social action, establishing synergistic collaborations with nonprofit organizations and encouraging their employees to engage in community service. Hickman believes that these organizations of hope will provide important leadership for social change and responsibility in the future. Researchers Mark Snyder and Allen Omoto, renowned experts on volunteerism, discuss the motivations of volunteers and suggest strategies to assist nonprofit leaders in managing and motivating a volunteer workforce. A chapter by Craig Pearce, Youngjin Yoo, and Maryam Alavi completes this section. They discuss the notion of shared leadership and the important role it plays in leading nonprofit organizations, using a study of social workers to illustrate the point.

Part Five is the "nuts and bolts" section, offering nonprofit leaders some tools for both effective leadership and personal development. It begins with Tom Reynolds's chapter on leading the strategic planning and execution process. Victor Sohmen presents a model for leading nonprofit projects and discusses the kind of leadership needed to work in these decentralized units. Noted evaluation scholar Stewart Donaldson offers a very valuable model for program evaluation in nonprofit organizations, using examples from some wide-ranging programs that he and his associates have evaluated. Paul Arsenault focuses on the ongoing development of nonprofit leaders and suggests strategies nonprofit leaders can use to develop their leadership capacity. The book concludes with a chapter by Sarah Smith Orr, noting the common threads among many of the book chapters and offering a positive model for looking at leadership and life in the nonprofit organization.

Acknowledgments

We would like to acknowledge the assistance of Sandy Counts and Lynda Mulhall in helping to organize the conference, and Sandy's help in producing the final book copy. We would also like to acknowledge our editorial assistants, and Claremont

McKenna College students, Yoon-Mi Kim and Kate Oppenheimer, who helped with formatting, copyediting, and a variety of conference-related tasks.

September 2003   Ronald E. Riggio
                                                     Claremont, California

                                                     Sarah Smith Orr
                                                     Pasadena, California

THE KRAVIS LEADERSHIP INSTITUTE

The Kravis–de Roulet Leadership Conference

The Kravis–de Roulet Leadership Conference is an annual event sponsored by the Kravis Leadership Institute and dedicated to the discussion, promotion, and celebration of leadership. The conference brings recognized leadership scholars and practitioners to the Claremont McKenna College campus to explore current research and exchange ideas about leadership and the development of future leaders. The Kravis–de Roulet Leadership Conference is made possible through generous endowments from the Vincent de Roulet family and from Henry R. Kravis. Improving Leadership in Nonprofit Organizations represents the proceedings of the twelfth annual Kravis–de Roulet Leadership Conference, held at Claremont McKenna College on February 22–23, 2002.

The Kravis Leadership Institute

The Kravis Leadership Institute plays an active role in the development of young leaders via educational programs, research and scholarship, and the development of technologies for enhancing leadership potential.

THE AUTHORS

MARYAM ALAVI is the John and Lucy Cook Chair of Information Strategy and the senior associate dean of faculty and research at the Goizueta Business School, Emory University. Her publications have appeared in such journals as *Information Systems Research, MIS Quarterly, Academy of Management Journal,* and *Management Science.* Her research focuses on knowledge management and technology-mediated learning. Alavi served as the elected vice president of education of the Association of Information Systems (1995–1999) and was a Marvin Bower Faculty Fellow at the Harvard Business School.

PAUL M. ARSENAULT is an assistant professor at West Chester University in West Chester, Pennsylvania. He holds a Ph.D. from Temple University, an M.B.A. from the Babcock School of Management at Wake Forest University, and a master's in psychology from Vanderbilt University. Arsenault has held various positions in the profit and nonprofit sectors. He has been a marketing manager for consumer product companies, a program coordinator for a training program for unemployed people, director of a Head Start program, and a VISTA volunteer. Arsenault was awarded a grant from the James MacGregor Burns Center of Leadership to investigate assessment of the new leadership process. In addition, he has been actively involved in service learning, especially in the area of helping nonprofit organizations develop strategic plans.

BERNARD M. BASS is distinguished professor of management emeritus and founding director of the Center for Leadership Studies and Binghamton University, State University of New York. He is the author of more than three hundred articles and twenty-two books concentrating on leadership, organizational behavior, and human resource management, with his primary research focus for the past two decades on transformational leadership and management development. Over the past half century, he has been the principal investigator on numerous federal, state, and private foundation research grants. He was a founding editor of *Leadership Quarterly,* and he has consulted with and conducted training for many Fortune 500 firms and has lectured or run training workshops in more than forty countries. Bass is also a senior scientist for the Gallup Organization and a member of the board of governors of the Kravis Leadership Institute.

JOANNE B. CIULLA is a professor and Coston Family Chair in Leadership and Ethics at the Jepson School of Leadership Studies, University of Richmond. She has also held the UNESCO chair in leadership studies at the United Nations University International Leadership Academy in Jordan, where she directed and designed leadership development programs for emerging leaders from around the world. Ciulla has a B.A., M.A., and Ph.D. in philosophy. She publishes in the areas of business ethics, leadership studies, and the philosophy of work and is on the editorial boards of *Business Ethics Quarterly* and the *Journal of Business Ethics.* Ciulla is the editor of the New Horizons in Leadership series for Edward Elgar Publishing, Ltd., and is a member of the board of directors of the Desmond Tutu Peace Foundation. She is also a consultant who helps develop programs on ethics and leadership for universities, companies, and government agencies in the United States and abroad.

JAY A. CONGER is a professor of management at the London Business School and a research scientist at the Center for Effective Organizations at the University of Southern California in Los Angeles. He holds a D.B.A. from Harvard Business School, an M.B.A. from the University of Virginia, and a B.A. from Dartmouth College. Conger consults with a worldwide list of private corporations and nonprofit organizations. He serves as an adviser and coach to numerous executives and CEOs. Author of over seventy articles and book chapters and nine books, he researches leadership, boards of directors, organizational change, and the training and development of leaders and managers. His insights have been featured in *Business Week,* the *Economist, Forbes, Fortune,* the *New York Times, Training,* and the *Wall Street Journal.*

STEPHEN MARK DOBBS is currently executive vice president of the Bernard Osher Foundation and adjunct professor of humanities at San Francisco State University. He was educated at Stanford in philosophy, history, education, and the arts. Dobbs's first career included teaching arts and humanities at San Francisco State University, directing a humanities program at the Kennedy Center, and several visiting professor and scholar appointments. A second career has been in the foundation world as a program analyst for the John D. Rockefeller III Fund, senior program officer at the Getty Center, executive director of the Koret Foundation, and president and CEO of the Marin Community Foundation. Currently, Dobbs is pursuing writing interests, special projects, and community work. A recent special project was his role as coordinator of the California Nobel Prize Centennial, a program of the Consulate General of Sweden in San Francisco and Los Angeles.

STEWART I. DONALDSON is a professor of psychology, director of the Institute of Organizational and Program Evaluation Research, and dean of the School of Behavioral and Organizational Sciences, Claremont Graduate University. He has taught numerous courses and published widely on the topics of organizational psychology and program evaluation, including a recent book with Michael Scriven on evaluating social programs and problems. He serves as cochair of the Theory-Driven Evaluation and Program Theory topical interest group of the American Evaluation Association (AEA), is on the editorial boards of the *American Journal of Evaluation* and *New Directions for Evaluation,* and is or has been principal investigator on numerous evaluation grants and contracts. He is currently principal investigator of the evaluation of the California Wellness Foundation's $20 million statewide Work and Health Initiative.

FLORENCE L. GREEN is executive director of the California Association of Nonprofits (CAN). She has been a nationally recognized consultant and trainer for more than three decades. She has worked with foundations, nonprofit organizations, city and county governments, regional and national associations, colleges and universities, statewide and regional coalitions, and management support organizations. She has published several articles on fundraising, board development, strategic planning, collaboration, and nonprofit management and will soon publish a book on fundraising for public libraries. She is the past president of the Nonprofit Management Association (now known as the Alliance for Nonprofit Management) and is an associate to the National Center of Nonprofit Boards. Green is also a founder and member of the California Nonprofit Policy Council and a founder and board member of the National Council of Nonprofit Associations.

KEVIN F. HALLOCK is an associate professor of economics and of labor and industrial relations at the University of Illinois, Urbana-Champaign. He joined the faculty as an assistant professor in 1995, the same year he earned his Ph.D. in economics from Princeton University. He specializes in compensation of managers in for-profit and nonprofit organizations, the effects of job loss on firms, and the link between labor economics and corporate finance. His work has appeared in many journals, including the *American Economic Review*, the *Industrial and Labor Relations Review*, the *Journal of Economic Perspectives*, and the *Journal of Financial and Quantitative Analysis*. Hallock's work has been funded by the Alfred P. Sloan Foundation, the U.S. Department of Labor, the National Bureau of Economic Research, and the American Compensation Association, among others.

FRANCES HESSELBEIN chairs the board of governors of the Leader to Leader Institute (formerly the Peter F. Drucker Foundation for Nonprofit Management), where she served as its founding president and chief executive officer from 1990 to 2000. Hesselbein was awarded the Presidential Medal of Freedom, the United States of America's highest civilian honor, in 1998. Her contributions were also recognized by former President George H. W. Bush, who appointed her to two presidential commissions on national and community service. In 2001, Hesselbein was awarded the Henry A. Rosso Medal for lifetime achievement in ethical fundraising from the Center on Philanthropy at Indiana University. Hesselbein is editor in chief of the quarterly journal *Leader to Leader* and coeditor of a book of the same name. She is coeditor of the Drucker Foundation's three-volume Future Series as well as *Leading Beyond the Walls* and *Leading for Innovation, Organizing for Results*. Hesselbein was featured in a 2001 special issue of the *Harvard Business Review* as a member of a leadership roundtable of six leaders in an article titled "All in a Day's Work."

GILL ROBINSON HICKMAN is a professor of leadership studies in the Jepson School of Leadership Studies at the University of Richmond. At California State University, Dominguez Hills, she served as founding dean of the School of Health, dean of faculty affairs, director of staff personnel, and professor of public administration. She has also served as interim associate dean of the School of Community and Public Affairs at Virginia Commonwealth University, director of personnel for the Ontario-Montclair School District, personnel analyst for the California State University system, and administrative assistant for the city of Inglewood, California. She has been a presenter at the Salzburg Seminar in Salzburg, Austria, and at the University of the Western Cape in South Africa. She has published two books: *Leading Organizations: Perspectives for a New Era*, which she edited, and *Managing Personnel in the Public Sector*, written with Dalton S. Lee. In addition, she has published a number of articles and book chapters on leadership studies and is currently engaged in research for her third book, *Organizations of Hope: Leading the Way to Profitability and Social Action.*

ALLEN M. OMOTO earned his B.A. at Kalamazoo College and his Ph.D. at the University of Minnesota. He is currently an associate professor of psychology in the School of Behavioral and Organizational Sciences at the Claremont Graduate University in Claremont, California. He previously served on the faculty of the Department of Psychology at the University of Kansas, where he was also the director of the social psychology program. Omoto has an ongoing program of research on volunteerism and helping relationships, and his research has been supported by grants from the National Institute of Mental Health, the Fetzer Institute/Institute for Research on Unlimited Love, and the American Foundation for AIDS Research. He also has extensive public policy experience, including helping found and administer a community-based AIDS service organization and working in the U.S. Congress in 1995–96 as the American Psychological Association's inaugural William A. Bailey AIDS Policy Congressional Fellow.

SARAH SMITH ORR is an experienced coach for executives and organizations, with a specialty in the nonprofit field, as well as for women and men making a passage through a life transition. During her thirty years as a professional leader in the nonprofit sector, she has been a top executive of United Way organizations located in four states, has founded a statewide and several local community leadership organizations, and has served as a senior coach and trainer for the Hudson Institute of Santa Barbara. Orr obtained an M.B.A. through the Peter F. Drucker School of Management at Claremont Graduate University and is currently working on her Ph.D. in education at the same university, with her focus on adult development and leadership. Orr has received awards for her leadership of organizations and for her volunteer service. She is a founding member of the Kravis Leadership Institute board of governors. Orr is the owner of Smith Orr & Associates, a consulting firm located in Pasadena, California.

CRAIG L. PEARCE is an assistant professor of management at the Peter F. Drucker Graduate School of Management at Claremont Graduate University. He received his Ph.D. from the University of Maryland, his M.B.A. from the University of Wisconsin-Madison, and his B.S. from Pennsylvania State University. Pearce's areas of expertise include leadership, teamwork, and change management. He has won several awards for his research, including an award from the Center for Creative Leadership for his research on shared leadership. His research has appeared in dozens of professional journals, as well as other outlets. Prior to commencing his academic career, Pearce worked as an international management consultant in the area of process reengineering, organizational development, and turnaround management.

THOMAS J. REYNOLDS is formally trained in the areas of philosophy, psychology, and mathematical statistics. He received degrees from the University of Notre Dame and the University of Southern California. He is currently a visiting professor in the Mendoza College of Business at the University of Notre Dame. Reynolds has been conducting research on decision making with people of all ages and backgrounds and in all corners of the globe since 1976. The more than 250 research projects he has led have resulted in the development of a general choice model that details the key elements of decision making and how they interact to produce an individual decision. In addition to this applied research, Reynolds has written more than fifty scholarly articles dealing with decision making and, more specifically, with the role of personal values in the choice process.

RONALD E. RIGGIO is the Henry R. Kravis Professor of Leadership and Organizational Psychology and the director of the Kravis Leadership Institute at Claremont-McKenna College. He has served on the faculty of the University of California in San Francisco, Irvine, and Riverside, as well on the faculty of California State University in Fullerton. Riggio is the author of more than seventy-five books, book chapters, and research articles in the areas of leadership, organizational psychology, and social psychology. His research has included published studies on empathy, social intelligence, and the role of social skills and emotions in leadership potential and leadership success. His most recent books are *Multiple Intelligences and Leadership* and *The Future of Leadership Development* (both edited with Susan Murphy) and the fourth edition of *Introduction to Industrial/ Organizational Psychology*,

SUSAN M. SCRIBNER is the principal of Scribner & Associates and a consultant to nonprofit organizations. She is a member of the faculty at the University of California, Los Angeles, where she teaches courses in advanced financial policy and in board and organizational development. She has also taught at Cornell University and at California State University, Long Beach, and is the author of *How to Ask for Money Without Fainting, Boards from Hell*, and *Are You Chairing a Board by the Seat of Your Pants?*—all important resources for nonprofit leaders. Scribner has been a member of the National Association for Hospital Development, the President's Commission on the Employment of the Handicapped, and the National Association of the Deaf. Scribner is coordinating a special project in Ukraine to provide needed health care to the survivors of the Chernobyl nuclear plant disaster.

MARK SNYDER is a member of the faculty in psychology at the University of Minnesota, where he holds the McKnight Presidential Chair in Psychology and is the founding director of the Center for the Study of the Individual and Society. He received his B.A. from McGill University in 1968 and his Ph.D. from Stanford University in 1972. His research interests include theoretical and empirical issues associated with the motivational foundations of individual and collective behavior and the applications of basic theory and research in personality and social psychology to addressing practical problems confronting society. He has served as president of the Society for Personality and Social Psychology, as a member of the board of directors of the American Psychological Society, and on the Council of the Society for the Psychological Study of Social Issues. He is also the author of the book *Public Appearances/Private Realities: The Psychology of Self-Monitoring* and coeditor of the volumes *Cooperation in Modern Society: Promoting the Welfare of Communities, States, and Organizations* and *Cooperation in Society: Fostering Community Action and Civic Participation.*

VICTOR SOHMEN, a former globetrotting ship captain from India, obtained his M.B.A. in project management from the University of Calgary, Canada, and his master of international management degree from Baylor University in Texas. He is a recipient of the 1995 Canadian Governor-General's Gold Medal for academic excellence. His research interests include cross-cultural leadership and communication, transnational projects, acculturative stress, sociolinguistics, intercultural knowledge transfer, and international management. Presently he is doing Ph.D. research at the Umeå School of Business and Economics, Umeå University, Sweden, where he also teaches courses in cross-cultural studies, organizational strategy, and project management and leadership. Since 1990, he has contributed to international and regional conferences on project management, cost engineering, and international business.

GEORGIA SORENSON is the visiting senior scholar at the Jepson School of Leadership and founder of the James MacGregor Burns Academy of Leadership. A presidential leadership scholar, she is on the graduate faculty of the Department of Government and Politics at the University of Maryland and is an adjunct professor at Williams College in Williamstown, Massachusetts, and Ewa University in Seoul, Korea. She also serves as professor and adviser to the National School of Administration of the People's Republic of China and is on the international board of Tokyo Jogakkan University in Japan. Sorenson is on the board of directors of several leadership institutions, including Kellogg, the Asian Pacific American Leadership Institute, the Leadership Learning Community, LeaderNet, and New Voices. Earlier in her career, Sorenson was a senior policy analyst in the Carter White House for employment issues and later worked as a consultant to the Executive Office of the President. During her White House tenure, she served on the White House Productivity Council and on Vice President Mondale's Youth Employment Council. Sorenson has published in professional journals such as the *Harvard Educational Review* and the *Psychology of Women Quarterly*, and is author, with James MacGregor Burns, of *Dead Center: Clinton-Gore Leadership and the Perils of Moderation*, and is a frequent commentator on social issues in the popular media.

K. M. THIAGARAJAN is the founder of the Microcredit Foundation of India, a nonprofit company that provides small loans to underserved populations, especially in rural areas. He received his M.B.A. and Ph.D. degrees from the Graduate School of Business Administration at the University of Pittsburgh and worked as an assistant professor in the Graduate School of Management at the University of Rochester, where he worked with Bernard Bass developing training and research programs as well as cross-cultural comparisons of leadership behavior. Returning to India, he worked as a management trainer and consultant for various companies including IBM India and the Indian Oil Corporation. In addition, he was managing director of Loyal Textile Mills, Ltd., and chairman and CEO of the Bank of Madura. Thiagarajan has conducted executive training programs in the United States, Norway, Iran, Japan, and India. His work has been published in journals such as the *Journal of Applied Psychology* and *Management International.*

YOUNGJIN YOO is an assistant professor in the Information Systems Department at the Weatherhead School of Management at Case Western Reserve University. He holds a Ph.D. in information systems from the University of Maryland. He received his M.B.A. and B.S. in business administration from Seoul National University in Seoul, Korea. His research interests include knowledge management in global learning organizations, pervasive computing, and the design of sociotechnical information environments for large organizations. His work has appeared such journals as the *Academy of Management Journal, Information Systems Research, MIS Quarterly,* the *International Journal of Organizational Analysis,* the *Journal of Management Education, Information Systems Management,* and the *Korean Journal of MIS Research.*

PART ONE

CHALLENGES FOR NONPROFIT LEADERS

There are great untapped reservoirs of human energy and capacity awaiting leaders who can tap them and societies that deserve them.

JOHN GARDNER, *ON LEADERSHIP* (P. 74)

Thoughts about the challenges and opportunities that await nonprofit leaders in the social sector in the twenty-first century are presented in Part One. These authors challenge the status quo, raise questions about the role of leaders, and provide insights and recommendations for enhancing leader and nonprofit organization roles as the new century unfolds.

A key challenge shared by the three authors is that of change. They emphasize the need to increase the sustainable capacity of leaders and organizations to recognize change, embrace it, and make it work. The authors make the point that leadership does matter, especially in these times of uncertainty and challenge.

Gardner excerpt reprinted with the permission of The Free Press, a division of Simon & Schuster Adult Publishing Group, from *On Leadership*, by John W. Gardner. Copyright © 1990 by John W. Gardner.

CHAPTER ONE

FUTURE CHALLENGES
FOR NONPROFIT ORGANIZATIONS

Frances Hesselbein

We have come a long way since 1989 when Peter Drucker wrote an article for the July-August issue of the *Harvard Business Review* titled "What Business Can Learn from Nonprofits." Reading the title, many business leaders said to themselves, "That has to be a typo!"

There have been countless changes in the world as a whole and in the leadership models of nonprofit organizations. We are fellow travelers on a long journey toward an uncertain future, where the challenges will be exceeded only by the opportunities to lead, to innovate, to change lives, to shape the future. The mission, the star we steer by, will be our greatest protector; the values we live by, our greatest security; and innovation, the indispensable common imperative for leaders of change, leading in a world forever changed. I've traveled more than ever in recent years. I've felt a sense of urgency that there was a new openness that might not always be there; it could change. So two or three times a week I have been somewhere speaking: sometimes to corporations, sometimes to nonprofits, and many times on college and university campuses. I remember an incredible three days as a Distinguished Visiting Scholar at the University of Saint

Note: The editors asked Mrs. Hesselbein to open the 2002 Kravis-de Roulet conference presenting an overview of challenges for nonprofit leaders by pulling together her thoughts expressed on the topic from her many presentations and publications. The editors wish to express their gratitude for Mrs. Hesselbein's significant contribution to the conference and this text.

Thomas in Minneapolis and then later that year with Admiral Loy, then Commandant of the U.S. Coast Guard, in a leadership retreat with his sixty key officers. What was the title of the speech he chose? One word: "Transformation." I quoted Peter Drucker to these very different audiences: "If Peter Drucker were here, he would look at you and say, 'It is not business, it is not government, it is the social sector that may yet save the society.'" And then I would add, "Peter Drucker is not a pessimist, but he is very sober about the next ten years. He sees political turmoil in many parts of the world, including the United States. How sadly prescient are Peter's observations; and how helpful and powerful are his views on innovation, globalization, and collaboration in the next society. Peter Drucker calls this new century the century of the social sector . . . because he says, 'It is in the social sector that we find the greatest innovation, the greatest results in meeting human needs. And what we will do as a sector,' Peter tells us, 'will determine the health, the quality, and the performance of the twenty-first-century society.'"

Every day headlines and the airwaves remind us that we are, as Peter has told us so often, living and working in the vortex of the most massive social change since the American Revolution; and you and I are living and working in a world at war. This rapid transformation is hurtling us into a tenuous future. The questions we raise today and our response to these questions will determine whether or not our organization is present when the roll is called in 2010. The greatest challenge of this nonprofit century is to provide the leadership, the competence, and the management that will determine the quality and the performance of the twenty-first-century society. This is the big picture of our work and our challenge today and the significance of the social sector organization.

For all of us, I believe there are *three* great challenges, three *critical* challenges; and our response to them will define whether the organization, the enterprise, will be vigorous, relevant, viable, or even *alive* ten years from now. What are the three? The first challenge is directed specifically to the commitment, within the social sector, to leadership and the need to develop today leaders of change for the organization of tomorrow. A second great challenge, I believe, is to build a richly diverse enterprise. The third is the great challenge of (and opportunity for) collaboration, alliance, and partnership.

The First Challenge: Developing Leaders of Change

Some of the most significant work I have ever done, including my thirteen and a half years with the Girl Scouts and twelve years with the Peter Drucker Foundation, is the work, during the past six years, with the United States Army Chief of

Staff, first with General Reimer and now with his successor, General Shinseki, and his team. During some recent work together, General Shinseki brought together the three- and four-star generals of the Army in a command conference at West Point where I was to speak. My subject was leadership; and I am speaking *to* (you can imagine how intimidating) and looking *at* great heroes—great and quiet leaders. I reminded them that seven years earlier, General Reimer had invited me to come to the Pentagon for the first time to have a dialogue on two imperatives— diversity and leadership development in the new century—with forty-two generals and colonels. These are the men and women who are responsible for the leadership, development, recruitment, training, education, and care of the men and women of our United States Army. And when these people say, "Our soldiers are the Army's credentials," they mean it!

During a remarkably open dialogue about leadership, a distinguished general asked, "Mrs. Hesselbein, what is *your* personal definition of leadership?" I replied, "Leadership is a matter of how to be, not how to do." And I continued, "You and I spent most of our lives learning how to do and teaching others how to do, yet in the end, it is the quality and the character of the leader that determines the performance, the results."

Several years later I was part of a leadership roundtable in the *Harvard Business Review* (HBR) in which six of us—the CEOs of FedEx and Merck, a General Electric executive, two university professors, and I—engaged in a dialogue on leadership (Collingwood, 2001). I mentioned in that HBR roundtable that the 1999 *Army Leadership Field Manual* had only three words on the cover: "Be, Know, Do"—a fact I also mentioned in an article, "A Time for Leaders," on our Web site. I told the generals that ever since, the Drucker Foundation had been getting e-mail and faxes and phone calls. But the messages did not say, "My, what a wonderful roundtable!" They said, "Where can I get the *Army Leadership Manual?* How can I find out more about 'Be, Know, Do'?" Because the manual is unclassified, we reply, "Call (800) 553-6847 and ask for item number FM22-100ING." People are hungry for meaning, for significance, and it is remarkable that the *Army Leadership Manual,* an all-inclusive manual intended for everyone from generals, colonels, and noncommissioned officers to the newest civilian employees, is meeting that need. I also told that audience that I cheered when I read an article in the *New York Times* titled "Army Rethinks Priorities on Fighting and Spending." It closes with this quotation about the Army Chief of Staff: "Many foot-draggers are in the Army itself. But General Shinseki has a warning for them: 'If you don't like change, you'll like irrelevancy even less.'"

Warren Bennis of the University of Southern California, a colleague and friend of mine, did a study of one hundred male and female leaders for his book *On Becoming a Leader.* In his cross-sector study, only four common, powerful leadership characteristics emerged: commitment to mission, communicating vision, self-confidence, and personal integrity. Note that all of them are "how to be" qualities, not "how to do" qualities.

Now when we look at leadership, Peter Drucker reminds us that leadership is not rank, privileges, titles, or money; it is responsibility. And I would add that leadership has little to do with power and everything to do with responsibility, leading by example, and leading by voice, with language that illuminates, defines, and embraces. We are in a time of needed transformation. The future calls on our country and nations around the world for effective, ethical leaders in every sector, at every level of every enterprise—not "a" leader or "the" leader but many leaders, dispersing the responsibilities of leadership across every organization. Leaders with a moral compass that works full time; leaders who are healers and unifiers, who embody the mission and live the values, who keep the faith. This is the first great challenge: developing today leaders of the future, leaders of change.

The Second Challenge: Reflecting and Embracing Diversity

A second great challenge, I believe, is to build the richly diverse enterprise. If we are going to be relevant in 2010 and beyond, we begin today providing equal access. This is a very powerful term to use; it has no baggage. I regard providing equal access as a leadership challenge essential to achieving significance in the new century. Today, nonprofit and for-profit corporations know that they must be transformed into learning institutions if they are to succeed. Leaders must send a clear and powerful message that their goal is to provide equal access to opportunities for growth, learning, development, and participation to executives, faculty, students, management teams, workers, and customers from all segments of the nation's increasingly diverse population. And this is not a message or a function that can be delegated. The only way it works is for a vibrant message of equal access, in a richly diverse organization, with civility and good manners in the execution, to come directly from the president or the chairman, from the leaders of the organization, leading from the front, not pushing from the rear. And so I ask, inspired by the rapidly changing demographics, are we building today richly diverse organizations that reflect their communities with representation throughout the enterprise at every level?

When in positions of nonprofit leadership we look at our board, our management team, our faculty, our workforce, and our visual materials and then look out there at all the new customers we want to attract, we ask ourselves one critical question: "When they look at us, can they find themselves?" And we should celebrate the response. I shared that challenge several years ago with the officers at the Pentagon, and two days later, General Melton sent me a slide with a note: "We are now using this in our Army lectures." The slide was a color photograph of young Army recruits, men and women in fatigue uniforms—all those bright and wonderfully different faces—and the caption read, " 'When they look at us, can they find themselves?' Frances Hesselbein." That image is now my computer screen saver! It welcomes me every morning; it reminds me of that second great challenge: to build and reflect a diverse enterprise.

The Third Challenge: Collaboration, Alliance, and Partnership

The third great challenge is the challenge of collaboration, alliance, and partnership. We live in a world where governments, for a long time, have been abandoning the social services they once delivered, and business alone is unable or unwilling to provide services that governments at every level are relinquishing. And so the social sector, the third of the three critical sectors, is facing new and enormous expectations that somehow this sector, the nonprofit sector, will be able to provide, *alone,* the human services that the other two sectors are unable to deliver.

We look around us. Human needs are escalating not just in our own country but all over the world, while traditional resources are diminishing. Indeed, the day of the partnership is upon us. And the leaders of the social sector are called to take the lead, initiating partnerships with business and government leaders and their enterprises. A passionate focus of the Leader to Leader Institute is a common leadership imperative to encourage the leaders of the future to look beyond the walls of the nonprofit organization, the college, the corporation, the government agency, the foundation. When we look beyond the walls, we find partners and alliances to address the critical issues, the critical needs, as equal partners. Then we work together with those partners to build a cohesive, inclusive community that embraces all of its people. If you and I share a vision, and our vision of the future is a country of healthy children—all children—strong families, good schools, decent housing, work that dignifies, all embraced in this diverse, cohesive, inclusive community, then leaders of the future, leaders of change, need to move beyond the walls and together build the healthy community as energetically as they built the corporation, the university, the enterprise within the walls. Indeed, corporate enlightened self-interest indicates that there is no hope for a productive corporation within the walls if the community outside the walls cannot provide the healthy, energetic, competitive workforce essential to the corporation of the new century.

Today we find a new openness among the best-managed and best-led corporations to forming partnerships with nonprofits that do address critical issues and critical needs where the corporation and the nonprofit share a common bottom line—changing lives. In these new partnerships, the people of the corporation find new significance in their lives. And as Peter Drucker says of them when they enter these partnerships, they "move from success to significance." So today our small Leader to Leader Institute has remarkably energetic partners, and I'll mention just a few: Mutual of America, General Electric, the Claremont Colleges, Bright China Management Institute, Chevron/Texaco Management Institute, and the Mandel and Kellogg foundations. All work with us on significant, specific projects that change lives. Gone is that old "I write the check; you do the work" approach to corporate philanthropy. Today the people of the corporation and the people of the nonprofit live a shared vision, shared commitment, shared people, shared resources, and shared performance. We change lives together beyond the walls.

The twenty-first century's social sector organizations, colleges, communities of faith, and health and human service and youth organizations are called to lead from the front and to see ourselves life size. This is a new challenge, a new imperative—taking the lead as an equal partner with government and corporations—as all three sectors, for the first time in history, acknowledge that alone they cannot meet the burgeoning needs of the American society and of many parts of the world, a world to remain in turmoil for years to come. Indeed, the day of the partnership is upon us. Sometimes, in the social sector, we do not see ourselves life size. There are a million and a half social sector organizations in this country alone, and the number is growing every day. There are twenty million social sector organizations around the world, growing even faster as the emerging democracies realize that they cannot sustain democracy without this third sector. Twenty million around the world—only 5 percent adequately funded. Yet together we generate one trillion American dollars in revenues each year. The social sector is hardly a junior member; it is the equal partner of business and government.

Toward the end of 2001, a Drucker Foundation team, in partnership with the Bright China Management Institute, conducted leadership and management seminars in Beijing, Shenzhen, and Dongguan. This is how I opened each seminar in those Chinese cities:

> Today leaders speak a common language. Across the three sectors, business, government, and the social sector, around the world, we speak this common language. The language of leadership and management, where mission, goals, vision, and strategy travel easily from East to West. And managing for the mission has the same power wherever there are leaders who hold out to their people the mission—why they do what they do, their reason for being, the purpose of the organization. So today for business, government, and social

sector leaders of change, the principles of leadership and management are basic, they are fundamental, they are generic to all organizations in all three sectors, and they are global, as true in Beijing as in Boston.

That was always my opening message, and it remains my message today.

The day we arrived in Beijing, we climbed the Great Wall of China, and the Great Wall became our metaphor for leading beyond the walls—building partnerships that change lives. Today in this global society, there is a sense of urgency, a sense that perhaps at this moment in the world's history, we all have a rare opportunity, all three sectors together, to create a new kind of world, linked by ideas. And that can be the real legacy of globalization: changed lives and cohesive communities.

Long ago in another century, George Bernard Shaw wrote a message that calls across the years. He wrote, "I am of the opinion that my life belongs to the community. And as long as I live, it is my privilege to do for it whatever I can. I want to be thoroughly used up when I die. For the harder I work, the more I live. Life is no brief candle for me; it is a sort of splendid torch, which I have got hold of for a short moment, and I want to make it burn as brightly as possible before handing it on to future generations."

Ten years from now, when the history of all of your organizations is being written, may they write of you: "For a little while, they held a splendid torch. The future called; they responded; they kept the faith."

References

Army Leadership Field Manual. [http://www.adtdl.army.mil/]. Document #FM 22-100, Aug. 31, 1999.

Collingwood, H. "All in a Day's Work." *Harvard Business Review,* Dec. 2001, pp. 55–66.

Drucker, P. F. "What Business Can Learn from Nonprofits." *Harvard Business Review,* July-Aug. 1989, pp. 1–7.

Shanker, T. "A Nation Challenged: The Military Budget; After Terrorist Attacks, Army Rethinks Priorities on Fighting and Spending." *New York Times,* Nov. 8, 2001, p. B6.

CHAPTER TWO

SOME THOUGHTS ABOUT NONPROFIT LEADERSHIP

Stephen Mark Dobbs

In Lewis Carroll's *Through the Looking-Glass*, Humpty Dumpty says to Alice, in a rather scornful tone, "When I use a word, it means just what I choose it to mean, neither more nor less." "The question is," replies Alice, "whether you can make words mean so many different things." "The question is," said Humpty Dumpty, "which is to be master, that's all! Anyway, when I make a word do a lot of work, I always pay it extra."

Leadership is a word that we make do a lot of work, and we ought to pay it extra. Leaders shoulder heavy burdens and responsibilities for service in our society. We look to our leaders to make decisions that affect us both as individuals and as members of a large and complex world. This promotes a dependence on leadership at every level and in every setting—family, work, community, social life—to provide direction and guidance. Leaders help us face and meet challenges of all kinds and guide us toward the future.

Leadership is also a word much beloved by politicians, pundits, and professors, who fill the bookstore shelves with treatises about it and invoke such exemplars as Napoleon, Lincoln, and Churchill. The leadership lessons for these and other historical figures are on sale now (Asprey, 2000; Johnson, 2002; Williams, Pederson, and Marsala, 1994; Hayward, 1997). Leadership has also long been a favorite study of the behavioral and social scientists, who dissect the leader personality and compile long lists of its desirable characteristics. Decades of such studies have yielded an unsurprising inventory of attributes and qualities that contribute to leadership effectiveness.

Traits validated in the literature include, in no particular order, high energy level, ability to tolerate stress, self-confidence and self-control, emotional maturity, integrity, physical stamina, intelligence and judgment in action, willingness to take risks, task competence, being honest, ability to articulate and move toward a vision, understanding of followers and constituents, need to achieve, loyalty, having a caring spirit, capacity to inspire, capacity to motivate, courage and steadiness, the winning and holding of trust, assertiveness, and flexibility of approach. And that's only a partial list.

But this list of desirable characteristics, which is somewhat overwhelming, may cause us to ponder whether or not we are simply expecting too much from our leaders. The list reminds me of the search committee of a nonprofit organization seeking a new executive director. The typical position description often includes a well-intentioned but likely impossible set of expectations. In one case, after the committee agreed to settle for no less than someone with messianic attributes, I recommended that we adjourn to the water's edge at San Francisco's Ocean Beach, face west, and hire the first person who came walking toward us.

In fact, all personality traits are not equal. Some are more important for leadership than others. For example, one characteristic that I believe is indispensable to good leadership is what psychologists call "tolerance of ambiguity." This is the ability to encounter, and even embrace, what is not well-defined or not subject to obvious resolution. The individual who is tolerant of ambiguity is not threatened when the environment is problematic and even obscure but rather seizes the opportunity to define it. Ambiguity reflects the way the world often is: open to interpretation and multiple courses of action. Tolerance of ambiguity is therefore essential for leaders who confront challenges that are not clearly defined or neatly posed. Leaders do not always function in arenas of clear choice. Nonprofits, which may lack the stability and financial cushion of other types of organizations, are especially vulnerable to ambiguity and the consequences of unproductive leadership decisions.

Successful leaders are not deterred by contradiction, classification, doubt, or uncertainty. In fact, to fulfill the leadership role, an individual must not only tolerate ambiguity but perhaps even prefer it. An open future offers more opportunity for shaping. Just a single trait like tolerance of ambiguity can cue a broad discussion of leadership effectiveness. In fact, leadership is a member of that special category of big concepts (love, creativity, and justice are others) that are subject to excessive platitudes, especially in speeches.

But I choose to treat leadership not as a holy grail but rather as a phenomenon engaged in by otherwise ordinary human beings who struggle with the leadership task. Whether their gifts are divinely inspired, the outcome of a nurturing environment and training, or just good luck, we ought to reflect on the experiences of our leaders to better understand how we can be supportive and live with the consequences of their actions. This includes challenges running from the personal and intimate, such as bringing up children and developing a healthy family life, to the macro leadership challenges of bridging the deep divides that exist among people of different cultures and nations.

We've seen such chasms of understanding here in America. Our society is, in fact, desperate for leadership in a world that may be changing too quickly for us to adapt. We are in the middle of a severe leadership crisis. The widespread cynicism and disinterest in public affairs and civic life that now afflicts millions of Americans is dangerous in a democracy, where everyone's contributions are needed to maintain an egalitarian ethos.

Think of the citizens of Eastern Europe, who lived for half a century behind the tyranny of the Iron Curtain and are only now enjoying the fruits of an open society. Imagine what they must think about America when they learn that less than half of our adult population regularly exercises its precious right to vote for political leaders. That is perhaps evidence of the American freedom to choose— or not to choose. But there are other features of our system that are undeniably to be emulated. America is a nation of pragmatists, with practical concerns and results. We demand action from our political leaders, although sometimes movement alone is enough. We can vote our leaders out of office when they do not meet our expectations or fulfill their promises or when they fail to lead.

Accountability is a little more complicated in some other leadership settings. For example, when leaders of the popular culture fall off the pedestals we put them on—such as when sports heroes or movie stars get in trouble with the law—we don't "unelect" them, but we demonstrate our disappointment by withdrawing our interest and our loyalty. We cease to treat them as role models.

Leadership is a fundamental motif in American culture, as important as motherhood and apple pie. It carries emotional baggage rooted in the aspirations for success, fulfillment, and deliverance. Americans are sometimes obsessed with their leaders in various sectors, including politics, commerce, communications, technology, entertainment, and the popular culture in general. They simply cannot read too much about George Lucas, Bill Gates, or Hillary Clinton. We shower accolades on leaders ranging from Jack Welch to Tiger Woods. They come from very different places but share Olympian standing as leaders and role models.

The "leadership culture" is one in which leaders become celebrities. The media obligingly cover their personal and professional lives for an audience that appears to have an insatiable appetite for information about, exposure to, and contact with these leader-celebrities. In addition, high honors are awarded to those who define, direct, and deliver leadership in their particular domains. Which are the leading business corporations? We have the annual Fortune 500 list to weigh all of the contributing factors and assign rankings. Who are the leading actors and actresses? Watch the Oscars, Emmys, and Tonys to validate the pecking order.

But what do we do when we have difficulty coming up with names for a list? Perhaps in politics, the mantle of leadership is most conspicuous by its absence. Ironically, we sometimes end up awarding the largest prize of all, the presidency of the United States, to the lesser of two leaders. Think back to how the two major candidates in the quadrennial White House sweepstakes tried to act and look like leaders during the 2000 campaign—and how they both failed miserably. With years of Bush life facing us, we have some time to ponder the impacts of electoral judgments.

Lest you think this is a bit unfair, throwing a brickbat at our president, whose distinction in office is based on a disputed election and a disputed war, he does have remarkably high polls right now. Is this because Americans are so smart and savvy that they understand the importance in the post–September 11, 2001, environment of maintaining a united front? Or is it the result of wishful thinking, with Americans hoping to see their aspirations miraculously converted to reality?

As a society, we are united in the sympathetic sense that we realize that no person would desire such a crisis thrust upon him. But frankly, I believe that the polls mask deep divisions of doubt and ambivalence. Citizens might ask, where in our hour of great need are the Thomas Jeffersons, the Abraham Lincolns, the Franklin Delano Roosevelts? So many current politicians' names are also floated as presidential timber, but that commodity is about as rare as old-growth Redwood near a lumber mill.

We have what I believe is a leadership gap. John Kennedy in 1960 drove home the "missile gap." We now have a leadership gap, a leadership crisis, and perhaps no single story in the news has underscored this fact more than the revelations about the Enron Corporation. The saga revealed a world in which large business corporations falsify their records, overstate their profits, and cheat their investors. Is there anyone on this planet who does not think that a massive failure of leadership brought about this mess?

What is so sad about this is that the public distrust is spreading like a malaise from one sector to another, from politics to commerce. The cynicism is likely to run very deep and for a very long time. Directors in boardrooms are second-guessing and asking questions they have never asked before. How do we know we are getting the straight scoop? Is someone at the table hiding information that's going to come back to haunt us or, indeed, bury our organization altogether?

Consider how an entire profession has been tarred by the scandal. Whether it turns out to be massive corruption or the malfeasance of a few, accountants now risk being perceived in a category with used-car salesmen. There is a very large disaffection and disillusionment in this country right now, and not just among people whose retirement savings have been eviscerated by corporate misconduct. Repairing the damage will fall on the next generation of business leaders. Incidentally, the nonprofit world has had its own shameful episodes of ethical chicanery as well—the scandals of the United Way, New Era Foundation, and others.

What is the casualty of all of this for leadership? It's the issue of trust. Americans have always been self-satisfied that we do things aboveboard and only in other countries are dealing under the table and bribery considered part of doing business. Welcome to the American campaign finance system. It hits home, and it hurts to realize that our actions are not always so pure.

Despite the bad apples in the barrel, the leadership culture is constantly evolving. An excellent example of this is reported in the January 28, 2002, cover story of *Newsweek* magazine, on the "new black power" (Cose, 2002). It reports a major shift regarding who may be presumed to be speaking for the African American community. The new leaders are not political figures but members of the Fortune 500, an unprecedented achievement for blacks in America.

African Americans such as Richard Parsons at AOL Time Warner, Kenneth Chenault at American Express, and Stanley O'Neal at Merrill Lynch lead some of the nation's largest and most respected companies. It is a profound change that figures like Jesse Jackson and Al Sharpton no longer monopolize spokesmanship for African Americans. There are now business leaders in the black community who are taking their deserved place at the table.

But it still hasn't happened for women. It's a scandal that there are so few women running Fortune 500 companies, like those at Hewlett-Packard, eBay, Autodesk, and a handful of other corporations. The glass ceiling is still in place, and leadership from men will be required to deconstruct it.

I think one way in which the leadership culture has been strengthened is through the more positive and less sensational attentions of the mass media, which remind people in high places of the pressures under which they must lead. It has been suggested that leaders in war and recession have to stand and deliver. Crisis can be a political godsend, as seen with George W. Bush and the very public side of decision making covered by the media in the congressional debate about Iraq in the fall of 2002 ("Congress Approves Bush's Request for Resolution on Use of Force").

The leadership culture also provides rewards that are widely taken to be the equivalent of being anointed as at the top of one's field. This includes Oscars and World Series rings. On the other hand, even being named *Time* magazine's Man of the Year has not prevented Jeff Bezos of Amazon.com from a long fall from commercial preeminence.

Although money, fame, and adulation are familiar rewards in the leadership culture, they exist primarily in the for-profit sector, including business corporations, professional sports, and the entertainment industry. The rewards in the nonprofit world, what Peter Drucker and Frances Hesselbein call the social sector, are more modest, reflecting the fact that the expectations in these sectors are different. Go out and ask ordinary people in the street whether they think teachers and social workers ought to get better pay, and they'll almost always answer yes. What do you think of teachers earning $100,000 a year? That's only a fraction of the compensation bestowed on industrial tycoons and many of their minions.

But when it comes time to pay the taxes or assessments that raise teacher wages, many citizens become reluctant. They share the expectation that people who teach their children receive, after all, a great deal of "psychological income." They don't just get a paycheck, they get real satisfaction and self-worth, an income that the IRS doesn't even ask them to declare. There is a disconnect here between the importance of the work and the reward.

Of course, the nonprofit or social sector really depends on volunteers to get its work done. Many agencies are staffed largely by volunteers. It is a wonderful thing, the generosity of the American people. But an invidious perception may exist that work that one has to pay to get done is important work, while work that people do not get paid for is less important. Volunteer energies must be worth something less.

When I was president of the Marin Community Foundation, I read reports about the tens of millions of Americans engaged in some type of volunteer activity in their respective communities. But my question is, what about the others? Where are they? Literally millions of citizens don't show up on anyone's radar screen. They don't give their time or talent, and often they don't even write a check. They don't help at all. That's one big difference between for-profit and nonprofit groups. The executive director of a social sector organization has to deal with volunteers. These are people who are not working for an employer in the conventional sense. There's no paycheck to serve as a carrot.

The other big difference between for-profits and nonprofits is fundraising. Fundraising is the necessary task of providing the fuel that runs the agency engine. It is also the preoccupation and bane of many nonprofit leaders' existence, to meet "development" goals. Their lives would be a lot different and simpler if they didn't have to constantly cultivate donors and raise money. I assure you that Kenneth Lay of Enron never had to go out and raise money for his organization. He found it in the most marvelous offshore places and didn't even have to leave his desk.

But the most distinctive attribute of nonprofits, and the one of greatest consequence for the leader, is that nonprofits have a different bottom line. The criterion for success in the for-profit sector is increased sales, market share, and return to investors. These are all important outcomes, and these "profits" are integral to a capitalist system in an open society. But we don't judge our success in the social sector by such criteria. We don't assume that an organization is necessarily better because it's bigger or has a fatter budget. On the contrary, the bigger it is, perhaps the more difficult it is to find out what's going on with it.

What is the bottom line for a nonprofit, social sector organization? It's change and transformation; it's doing something that matters and the progress that may flow from it; it's creating social good. In *Leaders Who Make a Difference,* the book I wrote with Burt Nanus (Nanus and Dobbs, 1999), we maintain that the creation of social good is the whole point of the exercise. The mission of the social or independent sector is to change society, to change ourselves, and to change the world.

Unfortunately, our society does not give much attention or recognition to that ambitious task. This is startling when one realizes that, as Peter Drucker has repeatedly pointed out, government has proved incompetent at solving large problems and that virtually every success we've had has been achieved by nonprofits. Recognition is sometimes available, but hardly of the same magnitude as in other sectors. Such recognition includes the Carnegie medals, Kennedy Center honors, and the first President Bush's Points of Light awards. But these hardly compare in glitz, glamour, and materiality with the payoffs in commerce and the popular culture.

In a way, this is puzzling because of a fundamental disconnect. I see people appreciating and agreeing that the social sector is important, once one defines and identifies it. At the same time, there is a curious lack of social concern for the people who work in it. I applaud grant applications in which nonprofits request a decent amount of money for their staff costs. We should not require or expect nonprofits to operate on the proverbial shoestring.

I think that nonprofits are so used to being budgeted to the bone for the labor-intensive things they do that they are afraid to ask, for example, for a six-figure salary for an executive director (even though the average corporate chieftain counterpart routinely receives seven-figure compensation). Foundations need to take the initiative in enabling nonprofits to pay their people well, lest the best and brightest go elsewhere when their idealism proves insufficient to pay the rent.

I want to share with you my philosophy of good leadership. In the Nanus-Dobbs book, we define the principal function of the leader as building relationships in order to strengthen the organization. This has a community consequence through the services that the organization delivers. In the process, social capital is created, which makes it possible to address other problems. This emphasis on relationship building puts a premium on the leader's political and communication skills. Making contacts, seeking advice, and cultivating support are never-ending quests because relationship building is literally never completed. Relationships need be maintained, strengthened, and expanded.

I have also composed a little mantra about leaders that is easily remembered, although it requires substantial effort to be carried out: "Good leaders do three things. They inspire. They perspire. And they retire." First, they inspire and lead by the force of their mission, their ideas, and their personality. Leaders are people with superb sensitivity to what other people think, feel, and want. They exhibit the flexibility that enables them to shift and adjust as the situation requires. Inspiration is a product of both meeting on common ground and pressing the right buttons.

Second, good leaders perspire. They lead by the example of their high energy and productivity. They work hard and immerse themselves in their duties. Perhaps no single generalization is more apt about nonprofit organization leadership than this willingness to make an enormous investment of time, talent, and energies. Nonprofit leadership is persistence to get the job done.

Finally, good leaders retire. They lead by mentoring others to follow; then they stand down when their day is done. When is that? It can't be determined by a formula or a calendar. Some people have the vitality to continue to lead well beyond "retirement age," while others may elect and deserve early retirement. Leaders should be watchful for the cues that indicate it's time for a leadership change.

Too many leaders, sometimes including the charismatic founding director, see themselves as indispensable to the organization they created and shaped. But such an organization has a questionable future unless it can emancipate itself from even a successful, long-term leader. In the Nanus-Dobbs book, we profile Harold Williams of the J. Paul Getty Trust as a leader who let his staff know what he intended to do and by when it would be accomplished. After meeting his goals over his eighteen years at the helm, Williams stepped down to ensure an orderly succession.

Humpty Dumpty was right, you know. The meaning of a word is about who is to be master, that's all. We define the essential strategies for successful leadership by the examples we set, by the practices we follow, and by the expectations we hold for those whom we entrust with society's major agendas.

References

Asprey, R. *The Rise of Napoleon Bonaparte.* New York: Basic Books, 2000.

"Congress Approves Bush's Request for Resolution on Use of Force," *Iraq Debate: NPR Special Coverage.* [www.npr.org/news/specials/iraq]. Oct. 11, 2002.

Cose, E. "Rethinking Black Leadership." *Newsweek,* January 28, 2002, pp. 42–55.

Hayward, S. F. *Churchill on Leadership: Executive Success in the Face of Adversity.* Roseville, Calif.: Prima, 1997.

Johnson, P. *Napoleon.* New York: Viking, 2002.

Nanus, B., and Dobbs, S. M. *Leaders Who Make a Difference: Essential Strategies for Meeting the Nonprofit Challenge.* San Francisco: Jossey-Bass, 1999.

Williams, F. J., Pederson, W. D., and Marsala, V. J. *Abraham Lincoln: Sources and Style of Leadership.* Westport, Conn.: Greenwood Press, 1994.

CHAPTER THREE

TEN THINGS NONPROFITS MUST DO IN THE TWENTY-FIRST CENTURY

Florence L. Green

In the past fifteen years, the California nonprofit community has had to respond to a dramatically new social and political landscape. This landscape includes a new and constantly evolving mix of people and cultures; growing use of technology in all aspects of our work; the downsizing and devolving of government; mind-boggling budget shortfalls; a volatile economy; the movement of the business community into areas that have traditionally been the turf of the nonprofit community in a way that threatens the nonprofit community's ability to remain focused on its public service missions; growing criticism about nonprofit accountability; the inability or declining interest of state and local government to effectively address the social, economic, cultural, and environmental issues in our state; and the ability or inability of the nonprofit community to successfully fulfill its role as "the civil society."

Management guru Peter Drucker refers to this time as the "age of social transformation," in which old rules are being turned upside down and a new social order is being created. These new realities bring a complex mix of opportunities and challenges for nonprofit organizations. In the coming decades, it will no longer be enough to update the mission, develop new programs, or improve problem-solving skills. Nonprofit success now depends on an organization's ability to respond to real change with new thinking, new structures, new management, and new linkages to resources.

Here are ten ideas for how an organization can survive, adapt, and thrive in the new reality.

1. Become a Learning Organization

With change happening at a rapid pace, it will be essential for nonprofits to develop the capacity to renew themselves continuously in response to the changing environment. In Peter Senge's seminal work *The Fifth Discipline: The Art and Practice of the Learning Organization,* he describes "learning organizations" as organizations where people continually expand their capacity to create the results they truly desire, where new and expansive patterns of thinking are nurtured, where collective aspiration is set free, and where people are continually learning how to learn together.

What It Entails

The tools of the learning organization are observation, assessment, design, and implementation. Although these activities might not sound new, it is how they are implemented that distinguishes the learning organization. Learning organizations do not seek absolute truths. Instead, through a process of dialogue and inquiry—not the usual discussion process where one point of view finally dominates—learning organizations seek profound understandings and new interpretations of the current reality.

Rather than judge or blame individuals for failures, learning organizations deeply examine the tangible and intangible "systems" that give rise to particular situations or behaviors. Systems are forces that continually affect each other over time, often with the intent to achieve some kind of purpose or outcome. They can be human systems, information systems, decision-making systems, or systems that are less visible, such as values, policies, and norms. They are the basic interrelationships that control behavior in our organizations, and they sometimes produce unintended consequences. By exploring the interrelationships of organizational systems and how they affect each other, learning organizations discover patterns and factors that help them identify causes and effects in the ways they are dealing with change or problems.

Learning organizations also rigorously examine deeply held beliefs, habits, images, and assumptions about how the world operates and what is required for effective action. These "mental models" can be generalizations ("everything happens for the best," "you can't fire volunteers") or complex theories (how childhood traumas shape our behaviors, assumptions many nonprofits make about how board members are to behave). Learning organizations understand that unexamined practices and assumptions can keep us from understanding how to respond to the new reality and can even perpetuate counterproductive behavior and situations.

Unfortunately, there are many examples of organizations and individuals that would rather fail than let go of core beliefs. (A prime example is the fairly consistent belief in most organizations that board members should be fundraisers even though year after year most board members do not bring in money and barely make their own contributions. Yet the organization continues to believe it is the role of the board to do fundraising.) Excavating and exploring entrenched assumptions can result in enormous learning when done with honesty and openness. The process can be very upsetting. However, when left unquestioned, assumptions and beliefs can be formidable obstacles to organizational growth and progress.

Our assumptions and beliefs usually overlook critical interactions, patterns, and systems because our beliefs are so deeply ingrained in our thinking. By recognizing our assumptions and inviting others to challenge them, we can begin to observe how things really are. Since our ability to observe and analyze the environment is only as good as our ability to see objectively, getting past our beliefs and assumptions is crucial to finding the best path to our future.

Once we recognize how our assumptions and beliefs shape our thinking, we can see that neither problems nor solutions are "out there." Rather, they are inside of us and in the tangible and intangible systems that make up our organizations. Most of the learning organizations' experts tell us that problems cannot be solved, nor can the future be addressed, independently of what our organization is and how it behaves. So rather than blaming funders, government, board members, volunteers, donors—all the people that we think don't support us— we must first look at our internal operations and beliefs and see how they keep us from understanding and then responding to the new realities of today.

Learning organizations experiment with different responses to the new reality. They create a "safe failing" environment in which new ideas, mental models, action strategies, and other lessons can be tested. As they develop alternative responses to the new reality, they ask themselves, "As I look at this system, what do I want to change over time?" or "What would cause this system to change over time?"

How Action Happens

Once the learning organization has an alternative approach in mind, it can create the conditions for action. Bringing staff, volunteers, board members, clients, and others into a shared vision of the future is extremely important. Unlike the traditional vagueness of most nonprofit vision statements, the shared vision of a learning organization must be very explicit. It should outline a specific destination or a clearly defined future—"we will have seven job training programs in these three cities that successfully place 250 program graduates in living-wage jobs each month by a specific date"—and it should be owned throughout the organization.

Creating conditions for renewal requires identifying and letting go of the practices that stand between the organization and its vision. Staff and managers will need to build new skills and devise fundamental activities that will lead to the new vision. The important task is to stay focused on the shared vision: what do you have to do each day, every day, to achieve the shared vision? Without that kind of commitment, transformation and renewal are not likely to occur.

Finally, a learning organization evaluates and judges its alternative approach by the results it actually achieves. It also looks beyond outcomes to consequences; in particular, it looks for unintended consequences that can have both positive and negative impacts. What happened or didn't happen in your community and with your clients because of the actions of your organization? Learning organizations also publicly evaluate the consequences of their actions.

What It Really Means

Being a learning organization is, in the end, about being able to remove or redesign systems in organizations, and in the nonprofit sector, in a way that responds to the changing environment with creative and effective approaches. It does not assume that the same theory or practice will be equally effective over time or space. And although it involves every staff and board member in the process, it does not assume that everyone can or should exert equal leverage or play an equal role in changing the organization.

Being a learning organization requires a basic shift in how we think and interact. It requires change that goes beyond organizational culture and management practices. It requires personal transformation and community building. It requires incredible commitment, without which the required hard work could never be done.

Being a learning organization is not about examples you can copy. Each organization must build its own learning organization. The purpose of a learning organization is not the survival of the organization but rather its renewal. Definitions, maps, processes, and procedures are permanently open to revision. The learning organization is in a continuous state of becoming as it continuously seeks to find the best constructs for organizing and implementing its role in the world.

2. Become a Transformational Leader

The major new reality we face today is that change occurs more and more frequently. Consequently, the time we have to adjust to change has greatly decreased. We tend to think of change as something we can control or something we have to do, yet for the most part, change usually happens without us. Although we speak of managing change or being change agents, a more helpful way to think about change might be that we have to go through an internal process to come to terms with, adjust to, or take advantage of change. To do that well, we need someone to guide us through that transition. That person could be called a "transformational leader."

Learning organizations need a transformational leader at the helm. In *Breaking Free: A Prescription for Personal and Organizational Change*, David Noer suggests that the skill that organizational leaders who really make a difference have is the ability to "facilitate transition." He suggests that the transformational leader intervenes in underlying structures to remove or reduce the constraints that prevent response to change. The transformational leader's role is to facilitate transformation: his or her own, the board's, the staff's, and the organization's.

The old adage "You can't help others until you help yourself" is particularly true of the transformational leader. Once we accept that the new reality means we can't continue to do things in the same way (and that discovery will not be a flat, straight road but rather a winding tour of hills and valleys as we go through the necessary processes), we understand that some kind of transformation is needed so that we can adapt or respond to the new reality. Dean Anderson and Linda Ackerman Anderson, in their book *Beyond Change Management: Advanced Strategies for Today's Transformational Leaders,* suggest that transformation demands new strategies and practices. It requires first that the transformational leader change his or her own mind-set, behavior, and style. So continually building personal skills (also called "personal mastery") is the first step the transformational leader takes.

Personal mastery—building personal skills—is the foundation of the transformational leader. Like the learning organization, the transformational leader must have a very specific vision of what he or she wants to achieve. It can't be vague ("we want to improve the quality of life for our clients"); it must be specific. It should spell out a specific destination or desired future that is either personal—to run a mile in four minutes, for example—or tied to the organization's shared vision. It is the gap between the reality of today and the personal vision for the future that shapes the skill building and learning of the transformational leader. For such a leader's primary task is to move the organization from where it is now toward the shared vision of what it could be.

Like learning organizations, transformational leaders must also scrutinize their own deepest-held beliefs, practices, and assumptions. Here, too, objectivity is essential. The goal is to let go of judgment and of ingrained assumptions, generalizations, and other beliefs that prevent us from seeing reality objectively. Gaining personal insight and awareness involves continuous learning and maybe even breaking from the organization's current management and leadership paradigms.

The job of the transformational leader is to focus on closing the gap between reality and vision. Transformational leaders understand that superficial changes can leave larger problems unsolved, hampering the progress of day-to-day activities and weakening the organization's ability to achieve a new future. Transformational leadership is not about acquiring a title or a position. It is about soul searching, focused energy, lifelong learning, and continual refining of the vision. It is about building skills and learning over time.

3. Form Strategic Alliances

The health and sustainability of a community are the products of the whole community working together, not just the result of isolated interventions by a single organization. As we begin to see the interconnectedness of so many issues in our community, it makes sense to pool resources like expertise, knowledge, money, and connections. Nonprofits that forge strategic alliances are more likely to succeed at effecting broad social change than organizations that try to do it alone. At the same time, because our traditional structures emphasize the solitary organization, many nonprofit leaders are not comfortable with the diffuse and sometimes slow-moving nature of collaborations.

My dear friend Arthur Himmelman, a collaboration consultant to nonprofit organizations, has defined strategic alliances as serving one of two purposes: betterment or empowerment. A betterment alliance seeks to produce a specific, identifiable outcome, usually related to public policy, communication, or relationships between groups. After that outcome is achieved, the betterment alliance usually disbands. An empowerment alliance, by contrast, seeks to transform how communities or groups of nonprofits do their work. They usually stay together for a very long time and often formalize their relationship. The most effective alliances, particularly for empowerment, include the nonprofit, government, and business sectors. Empowerment alliances usually result in some kind of transformation that permanently alters how organizations operate or how communities function.

In the new reality, it is important that strategic alliances be flexible so that participating organizations can move in and out as needed to achieve their own vision. In addition, leaders must build the auxiliary skills that are necessary to a successful alliance in order to create flexible and effective structures. Results are usually more effective if the alliance grows out of an internal process of learning how to serve communities most effectively than if it is driven from the outside by funders.

4. Give Accountability and Ethical Behavior Top Priority

Recent scandals in business, government, nonprofits, and other types of organizations have turned the spotlight on ethical conduct and accountability. In response, nonprofit organizations have a growing interest in ethics, and several umbrella groups have developed codes of ethics and performance standards for nonprofit organizations. No longer is there the assumption that people who work in nonprofits always do what is right. The requirement for future nonprofit executives, managers, and board members will be not only to manage and lead well but also to manage and lead ethically.

Accountability includes three basic requirements:

- The mission and purpose of the organization must be carried out.
- The organization must continually be productive and moving toward a specific goal or outcome.
- There must be no improper use of resources or conflicts of interest.

The past few decades have brought additional requirements:

- Form 990 must be filed if income is over $25,000 in any given year.
- Form 990 must be made available to the public when requested.
- The organization must not engage in unfair competition with privately owned businesses.

In spite of these requirements, criticism of the nonprofit community has grown over the past few years.

Nonprofits have always lacked meaningful ways to demonstrate the value of what they do. In a sense, calling the nonprofit sector the "independent sector" is a misnomer because in fact the nonprofit sector is accountable at all times to a variety of publics: donors, grantmakers, government, clients, boards, business, the community, the general public, and perhaps most of all, one another. The conflicting demands of these differing audiences and the organization's own ability to achieve certain goals and outcomes sometimes make it difficult to demonstrate accountability or to really engage in ethical decision making.

The role of nonprofits in society is profoundly shaped by how they are perceived by the public. It may be that the actions of a few have harmed all nonprofits, but further loss of public trust would be catastrophic for the nonprofit sector. In truth, there is actually very little meaningful oversight of the nonprofit sector, causing many critics to believe that no one is "minding the store." Although everyone agrees that nonprofits must be more accountable, additional government regulations would not be beneficial: nonprofits don't need more restrictions or more reporting.

Nonprofit organizations must take responsibility for their own accountability and ethical behavior. Accountability is often seen as a measure of efficiency—that is, the cost per client to produce the outcome. But efficiency is not enough. Accountability also includes information on the effectiveness of the service. Effectiveness should be measured in terms of the impact on the individual, but it should also measure deep and broad changes that occur beyond the organization's doors:

- As a minimum obligation to the public, report honestly and accurately about finances, missions, client numbers, and outcomes.
- Fill out Form 990 accurately, file it in a timely manner, and display it on the organization's Web site, because the public has the right to see it.
- Have regular external audits and public annual reports that show if and how the organization has achieved its purpose and mission.
- Identify lessons learned so that they can be applied later and shared with others.
- Examine any unintended consequences, and determine the ways in which they helped or hindered the organization's progress.
- Be willing to make changes if current programs are not getting the results you hoped for.
- Let go of programs that do not achieve the desired results.
- Evaluate whether and how the core problem, need, value, or underlying cause has changed since the issue was first addressed.

Accountability is a process of public disclosure of how the organization contributes to the public good—a safer, healthier and fairer society—through its programs and services. Accountability is about results: it is about the consequences of actions or lack thereof.

Accountability begins with values and ethics. Values and ethics are about what is good or bad, what is right or wrong, what is important or not important. Ethical decision making is the practice of doing what is good, what is right, and what is important. Ethical choices, particularly when they are tough choices, are essential to maintaining our tax-exempt status and rebuilding the image of the non-profit sector.

Nonprofit executives are rightly frustrated by the image problems that ripple throughout the sector when scandals erupt. Doing everything you can to make sure your organization operates with integrity is an important step. But accountability is bigger than one organization. So we must be concerned not only about the accountability of our own organization, through our own actions, but about the accountability of the entire nonprofit sector as well.

The California Association of Nonprofits has developed a statement of ethics and values that can be helpful in shaping your internal ethical discussions (see Exhibit 3.1).

5. Develop Indicators That Measure the Consequences on the Community

Nonprofits have traditionally depended on board expertise, strategic planning, staff knowledge, advisers, reports to funders, meetings with stakeholders, evaluation results, occasional research, and professional associations for information. Although this information is valuable, it tells the nonprofit very little about the actual consequences of its services. While the for-profit sector looks to sources like Wall Street and the consumer price index for information on price fluctuations, consumer trends, and public mood swings, each nonprofit organization goes to different sources that often give divergent information about social trends and effective methods for addressing problems.

Nonprofits must link their in-house assessments to broader social indicators that could both demonstrate an organization's impact on the community and promote a more accountable approach to what nonprofits do. When tied to a shared vision of improving certain aspects of community life or some aspect of clients' lives, indicators are an effective way of understanding how closely an organization's actions are aligned with its vision and mission.

Clearly, other community issues and players have a role in an organization's success. That is why it is so important to form strategic alliances that include a variety of players so that all of the critical players have a shared vision and are seeking the same general outcomes. To document changes in our communities and to discover whether or not those changes are the consequences of our organizations' actions, nonprofits must partner with other major community organizations and institutions to set key indicators and track real-world trends and information over time. The indicators should help organizations determine whether the consequences of their actions add to the health, well-being, or quality of life of their community.

EXHIBIT 3.1. CALIFORNIA ASSOCIATION
OF NONPROFITS STATEMENT OF ETHICAL PRINCIPLES.

- As organizations, nonprofits must continually reflect upon and evaluate their organizational relevance to society in light of changing conditions—even when it means considering the option of going out of business.
- When using public funds to provide services, nonprofit organizations must distinguish themselves from and improve upon what government might otherwise offer by understanding and responding better to constituencies; intelligently governing themselves; and maintaining a superior, front-line knowledge of the community, its assets, and its needs.
- Nonprofits must conduct their business with the highest possible degree of transparency, openness, and inclusiveness, scrupulously avoiding becoming mechanisms through which private interests masquerade as public purpose.
- Nonprofit leaders should comply not just with the letter of state, federal, and local laws that affect their organizations but with the full spirit and intent of the laws.
- Nonprofit leaders should engage in vigorous efforts to monitor themselves, their colleagues, and the work of the sector, identifying and correcting abuses of the sector and calling for appropriate governmental action when necessary.
- Nonprofits must effectively demonstrate that their organizations are managed with integrity and commitment to maintain the trust that has been placed in their hands.
- Nonprofits must evaluate programs, measure results, and communicate the consequences of their work to the client, community, and core cause levels as an ongoing process, not as a single event.

Several organizations have done a great deal of work over the past ten or fifteen years to develop both indicators and outcome measurement processes. The Bay Area Alliance for Sustainable Communities provides an excellent example of how a community can measure itself to determine if the various programs, services, trends, and government processes are moving the community toward sustainability.

Indicators can include outcome measures, such as how long clients keep jobs after completing a certain level of training, or context measures, such as the number of child care slots per thousand preschool children. The John S. and James L. Knight Foundation has initiated the Community Indicator Project in Long Beach and San Jose, California, to determine whether the $126 million the foundation spent in twenty-six communities over nine years produced any improvement in community life. The Community Indicator Project has also helped the foundation become more responsive to community needs and better positioned to create grant initiatives.

Nonprofits do not have to reinvent the wheel in order to use indicators. Indicators are a very effective way to reflect outcomes, and they can be used to help organizations understand why certain outcomes have not been achieved.

6. Adopt Results-Based Budgeting Tied to Indicators

Asking, "Did it make money or not?" and "Did it pay for itself?" are essential to nonprofit's budgeting process. But the answers to these questions can skew the process in favor of programs that are financially stable. Unfortunately, it is not always a given that the program making the most money is the most effective at fulfilling the organization's mission. We must also ask the hard question about whether the money we are spending is worth the results we are achieving.

Results-based budgeting ties the budgeting process to the indicators noted in item 5. Results-based budgeting recognizes that there is a relationship between how an organization spends its income and the results that are achieved. The results-based budgeting question is, "Are the consequences achieved by this program or activity worth the price?"

In other words, program and service outcomes must benefit the constituents or the community in a meaningful way, and the organization must be able to demonstrate that benefit in a manner that justifies the expenditures—even if the budget balances at the end of the year. A balanced budget is not a sufficient measure of whether or not the organization is successful.

It is natural for nonprofits to be troubled about placing a tangible value on their services; after all, the real value is attached to intangible processes like behavioral changes, improved quality of life, and increased knowledge or skills. But nonprofit organizations' stakeholders—funders, volunteers, community supporters, and partners—need to know that their gifts of time, funds, and energy are making a measurable difference. Results-based budgeting allows nonprofits to measure and demonstrate the "return on investment" to members, clients, communities, and funders.

Nonprofits will add more value to such a measurement by disseminating the results widely. Donor reports, newsletters, annual reports, press releases, and word of mouth should all promote the value of an investment in the organization by advertising the results achieved. Providing full and frequent results-based information will impress both current stakeholders and others whom the organization wishes were more involved.

7. Financially Empower the Organization So That It Can "Do More Mission" over Time

Author and consultant Peter Brinckerhoff promotes the concept of financial empowerment as a long-term strategy to give nonprofits the flexibility and power to "do more mission" over the long term in a more focused and timely manner. The concept is more than just financial stability. It is a long-term strategy to use every technique you know to generate money for your organization.

Brinckerhoff's measurement criteria suggest that a financially empowered nonprofit should have all of the following:

- More revenue than expenses in at least seven years out of ten
- A cash operating reserve of at least ninety days
- At least 5 percent of its revenue from an endowment
- At least one nontraditional source of revenue, such as earned or business income

Don't be discouraged if these can't be achieved right away. These are long-term goals that, much like an individual savings or retirement account, must be worked on and built up over many years. The first step is to make a long-term commitment to achieve financial security in the nonprofit. The second step is to devise a long-range plan for getting there. And the third step is to carry out the first task of the long-range plan.

One practice Brinckerhoff advocates is the widespread sharing of financial information with staff. Information sharing, he claims, helps build ownership and competence throughout the organization. It is achieved by training all staff members thoroughly and continuously in budgeting and finance issues. The goal is to delegate budget development responsibility and spending authority to more staff while retaining oversight and feedback among management. As part of this process, the organization can build commitment to deferred gratification by putting some money aside each year—even as little as $100 or $500—for a "mission reserve account." When it becomes large enough, let the agency's staff decide collectively how it will be used; the only criterion is that it must somehow forward the agency's mission. This sort of inclusion and diffuse decision making is a wonderful way to empower staff and your organization to build financial stability.

An equally important goal is to begin an endowment. A Boston College Social Welfare Research Institute report argues that in spite of the economic crisis in this country, we will nevertheless experience over the next several years one of the largest transfers of wealth in our nation's history (Havens and Schervish, 2003). Depending on the rate of economic growth in the country, this transfer will be at least $41 trillion! Instead of wishing, the organization could benefit from this phenomenon by identifying prospects, putting a program together, and carrying through on asking for bequests and other estate-related gifts.

Remember, "doing more mission" over time is a long-term strategy. The goal is to invest each year, to build staff capacity each year, to build the endowment each year, to improve income generation each year, and to get better each year at managing the income the organization has.

8. Creatively Rethink Resource Development, Governance, and Management Styles

In a hectic and complicated world, our behavior tends to default to the simplest, safest, or most traditional path. However, if organizations are going to adopt the recommendations outlined in this chapter, nonprofit leaders must also rethink almost every aspect of organizational management—and take proactive steps to revitalize or reform the aspects that are not working.

One of the most difficult tasks for nonprofits today seems to be getting boards to perform better. Much of the current approach to fixing "broken boards" is on "fixing" the people who serve on boards. Given that there are hundreds of board training programs and even a national organization that focuses on building board skills, why are the same problems still being identified after two decades of effective board development programs and training?

Perhaps we are fixing the wrong thing. Rather than focusing on fixing board members, maybe it is now time to look at how the world has changed and see if the current model for boards still makes sense for the organization.

The first challenge in solving this problem is finding people who have the time and energy to serve on boards. With so many telling us that they do not have time to give to board meetings or do not want long-term commitments, maybe it is time for nonprofits to rethink our beliefs about governance. What can an organization do to reduce the time commitment required for board members? Perhaps board members need to participate only in designated responsibility areas and do not have to attend all meetings. Perhaps they can meet by telephone or debate issues back and forth over a several-day period on an Internet site or meet once a quarter for a full day that includes committee meetings as well as a meeting of the board. Perhaps every board member does not have to serve the same length of time.

The demands of family and work life may require that nonprofits change how boards meet, how members serve, and how they give time. We also need to face the fact that far too many board meetings are boring and cause people to feel that their time is not being used effectively. How can your organization make board meetings more interesting and purposeful? What can be done to accommodate prospective board members who have the required skills or access but limited time to give? Don't let bylaws be a barrier to your thinking: bylaws can be changed.

Another issue that has emerged in recent years is the hierarchical structure of our workaday world. In many organizations, it no longer makes sense to have one leader at the top if the organization is to engage in constant renewal in response to changing conditions. Nonprofits of the future will need leaders at all levels of the organization, and they will need staff members who can quickly respond to the changing environment. Look for ways to flatten the management structure. Invest in building the decision-making and collaborative skills of staff. Look for ways to reduce the burden of top-level staff by increasing the ability of line staff to make decisions and implement change.

Another arena in need of new life and creativity is fundraising. Most nonprofits would like to boost or revamp their fundraising efforts but either lack the know-how or believe they have tried all possible approaches. But a fundraising makeover could be as basic as gathering more information about the types of new donors on the horizon or updating information about existing donors. Most of the traditional fundraising knowledge comes from data on how older white men make contributions. But women, people of color, and young and successful entrepreneurs are also potential donors. As a sector, nonprofits still know very little about how these publics want to give. Any good fundraiser will tell you that the pursuit of charitable donations is not a "one size fits all" activity: nonprofits must have multiple approaches, tailor-made for multiple audiences.

Finally, ask yourself whether the organization needs to bring its stakeholders closer to the mission. Don't wait until the funding report is due to keep the grant-makers updated on what the organization is doing. Instead of asking them to help, ask them what your organization can do to help make their job easier. Look for new ways to communicate to funders about what the organization does and the impact it has. For example, when was the last time a longtime funder toured your facility? And, of course, never miss a deadline: it signals not only disorganization but also a lack of respect for the grantmaker's part in the mission.

If many nonprofits are to survive in the new reality—with shrinking support and changing communities—they must develop new ways of managing and new ways of developing resources. Whether it is technology, policy, procedure, fundraising, management, or governance, nonprofit agencies must forge new ideas and attitudes about what works, what does not, and what they can afford to try.

9. Adopt a Vision and a Mission That Incorporate Diversity

In California, we often talk about the "Big One," the massive earthquake we have been warned about for decades. Well, the Big One has already hit California: it is called diversity, and it is a change of cataclysmic proportions. People of color now constitute more than half of California's population.

The American myth of the melting pot promotes the belief that newcomers assimilate, learn English, leave their culture behind, and adopt American ways and institutions—and perhaps worst of all, too many of us believe that this is how it should be. But the desire of immigrants to maintain their own culture, language, and national heritage is not only natural, it adds vitality and strength to our society as well. New beliefs, knowledge, and traditions can infuse new life into our organizations and lead us to the very policies, ideas, and practices we need to be truly effective. But the process does not come naturally or easily: experimenting with and adopting new ways to include others must be another priority for nonprofit organizations.

Nonprofit organizations are largely based on old European models, and it is doubtful that those designs will have maximum effectiveness as our communities become more and more diverse. True diversity goes far beyond the number of ethnic or racial groups represented on an organization's staff and board: nonprofits' diversity goals need to provide for new ways of thinking about problems, relating to the community, and approaching people for support or mutual benefit.

Diversity is forcing us—or should force us—to question some very basic assumptions about the sector. If we are going to be truly inclusive as a sector, nonprofits must actively figure out how to make programs, staff, operations, and management more inclusive—to be both a service and a place where the expertise and knowledge of diverse communities are used.

10. Be at the Table

One of the great themes of American history is the expansion of political participation to include the propertyless, women, descendants of slaves, and immigrants. History has seen the steadily expanding number of those seated at the table of public debate. My organization, the California Association of Nonprofits, strongly believes that broad nonprofit involvement in the development and implementation of public policy is at the heart of building a healthy and robust civil society. Nonprofits must claim their rightful role as political participants at every level of government.

First, do not believe the myth that nonprofit organizations are barred from lobbying! The federal government has supported lobbying by nonprofit charities since 1976 when Congress enacted liberal provisions under the lobby law. The same message came from the Internal Revenue Service in regulations issued in 1990, which support both the spirit and intent of the 1976 legislation.

The bottom line is, nonprofits can lobby lawmakers at all levels of government for legislation, regulations, and policies that would benefit the sector or organizations' own constituents. What nonprofits cannot do (and this is where the confusion often lies) is contribute money to or officially support or oppose a particular candidate running for office. It is imperative that nonprofit agencies stay abreast of measures that would hurt or help them and their constituents—and make their voices heard when such legislation comes up for debate.

Some of the most profound social changes of the past half-century have been spurred by nonprofits engaging in lobbying. Civil rights organizations, environmental groups, Mothers Against Drunk Driving, antismoking groups, women's rights groups, the antiabortion movement, and many others have used research, public education, advocacy, litigation, legislation, lobbying, and direct action to focus public attention on their issues and to produce change. However limited, the right to lobby and advocate is a right nonprofits must protect and a practice all nonprofits must adopt.

Another way we can be at the table is to support creative new ways for nonprofits to get their voices heard. Many years ago, the Filer Commission—one of the first national efforts to explore the value nonprofits bring to their communities—called for representation of the nonprofit sector within the federal government in the form of a special office, an assistant to the president, a congressional subcommittee, or all three of these. The idea is to position a liaison who would act as a bridge between the nonprofit sector and the political leaders who create, enforce, and interpret the laws. Such representation can only heighten the strength of the sector within our government offices by helping nonprofit voices be heard. Nonprofits can also increase their political clout by speaking with a united voice representing the entire nonprofit community.

Finally, organizations in the nonprofit sector must run their own people for public office. There is no question that nonprofits' ability to effect change runs wide and deep within their own defined spheres. But the best way to secure advocates in the wider circle of public policy is to put those advocates where they can make decisions. To meet the challenges of the future, the nonprofit sector needs strong political leaders who actively seek a role in developing and implementing policies that affect the sector and its constituencies. Such leaders are best recruited from among the organization's own ranks.

Conclusion

Becoming a learning organization and engaging in transformation is not a linear process. Adapting to change can be slow and frustrating. Be willing to fail—and be willing to learn from your failures. Understanding how things are connected and how they shape and influence success and failure is critical. One can learn how to be a transformational leader by doing the work and by continuing to learn from one's own experiences. Learning from mistakes is part of the process.

In some cases, the most successful and meaningful responses to change will be small, pragmatic improvements: having some board meetings by conference call or creating shared decision-making opportunities for staff so that there is an increased sense of ownership for organizational outcomes. Survival of nonprofit organizations should not be the end point. The end point should be organizational renewal. Being all things to all people and believing that "if you build it, they will come" will surely undermine the transformational process. Failing to develop or follow through on action steps will also undermine progress.

This is not about a quick fix. It took your organization a long time to get to where it is today; it will take time to move it in a new direction. Success lies in transforming each individual, each day, each week, each month. Know the key results you want to achieve. Measure performance against the key results. Create an environment where people feel they can practice and experiment with complex issues and complex solutions. Make skill building a priority. Welcome all ideas and points of view. Develop new ways of thinking, new structures, new linkages to resources. You have to see and understand the whole organization and how the parts affect one another before you can focus on individual parts.

The work of the nonprofit sector includes public radio and television, food banks, youth sports leagues, environmental cleanup groups, art museums, free clinics, health research, colleges and universities, theaters, homeless shelters, community organizations, job training programs, and everything in between. Its beneficiaries are elderly people, infants, mothers, fathers, families, people with and without disabilities, and people of all ethnicities, sexualities, and political persuasions. All nonprofits have in common a mission to somehow improve and enhance the quality of life in their communities. They can do so only if they successfully meet the challenges of the new realities.

References

Anderson, D., and Anderson, L. A. *Beyond Change Management: Advanced Strategies for Today's Transformational Leaders.* San Francisco: Jossey-Bass, 2001.

Brinckerhoff, P. C. *Financial Empowerment: More Money for More Mission: An Essential Financial Guide for Not-For-Profit Organizations.* New York: Wiley, 1998.

Havens, J. J., and Schervish, P. G. "Why the $41 Trillion Wealth Transfer Estimate Is Still Valid: A Review of Challenges and Questions." *Journal of Gift Planning,* Jan. 2003, *7*(1), 11–15.

Himmelman, A. T. *Communities Working Collaboratively for a Change.* Minneapolis: Himmelman Consulting Group, 1992.

Noer, D. M. *Breaking Free: A Prescription for Personal and Organizational Change.* San Francisco: Jossey-Bass, 1997.

Senge, P. M. *The Fifth Discipline: The Art and Practice of the Learning Organization.* New York: Currency Doubleday, 1990.

PART TWO

A FOCUS ON THE
NONPROFIT LEADER

Leadership can never stop at words. Leaders must act, and they do so only in the context of their beliefs. Without action or principles, no one can become a leader. They have already embroiled themselves in the good work of being and becoming leaders. They are eager to equip themselves to do their jobs better.

MAX DE PREE, *LEADERSHIP JAZZ* (P. 6)

This part raises for the leader important questions about actions, beliefs, and principles. It examines how leaders develop and equip themselves to provide extraordinary leadership through which they, together with other constituents, can achieve great works.

The subjects range from theoretical and real-life examples of transformational leadership, including what it looks like when the leader does not engage in continual renewal, to the importance of mission as the driving force behind successful programs and the ethical and personal decisions one must make as a leader. Also included is a comparative study of compensation between the nonprofit and for-profit sectors.

CHAPTER FOUR

MISSIONARY LEADERSHIP

Harnessing the Power of the Mission

K. M. Thiagarajan

Nonprofit organizations often come into being to serve social causes that are not deemed to be profitable or viable in a market economy. Empowering poor rural women and providing them small loans, helping the disabled, educating the poor, preventing the spread of HIV, protecting the environment, upholding human rights, and the like are social causes that attract nonprofit organizations. The "mission" of such organizations is embedded in the "cause" that is sought to be served by them.

In the case of for-profit organizations, even when they have lofty ideals as their chosen mission, it is implicitly understood by all parties concerned—management, employees, shareholders, and the public—that the mission is subservient to the basic goal of maximizing shareholder wealth. It is only natural that the primary concern of an organization set up to earn profits should be precisely that: to earn profits and enhance shareholder wealth or market capitalization. Like all human endeavors, such organizations also serve various public purposes, such as producing goods and services needed by the society and providing employment, in the process of achieving their primary goals.

The social causes served by nonprofit organizations have the power to attract a special group of highly committed individuals who seek satisfaction from serving those causes. The mission also has the power to unite all those who subscribe to it and to unleash tremendous energy. Missionary leadership is the process whereby a leader uses the inherent power of the mission to attract highly committed individuals who want to serve the cause and then enables them to derive satisfaction from such service.

If this distinct character of a nonprofit organization that has a genuine, embedded mission is not understood, and if one deals with leadership in nonprofits in the same manner as in for-profit organizations, we would lose a crucial and powerful advantage that is unique to nonprofits. The consequences can be serious, not only for nonprofits but also for society as a whole.

The concept of "missionary leadership" evolved from my experience in initiating a program to extend microcredit to poor women in Indian villages. Ironically, this project was the result of my attempt to rejuvenate the loss-making rural branches of a commercial bank—a for-profit organization. A brief description of the project follows.

Case Study: Microcredit to Rural Women

In 1993, I became the chairman and chief executive of Bank of Madura, a commercial bank in the private sector in India. It was a tradition-bound, moderately profitable, regional bank with low levels of technology and productivity. In response to the economic liberalization initiated by the Indian government at that time and rapid changes in the market, a major restructuring effort was undertaken. Loss-making branches were merged with other branches or closed. New branches were opened across the country in cities with good profit potential. The operations were computerized and automated. New products and services were introduced. Profitability improved substantially.

The chink in the armor was the vast network of rural branches (102 out of a total of 275 branches) located in villages with small populations and low levels of economic activity. The rural branches were started more due to government policies and regulatory pressures than out of commercial considerations. Whereas the policy allowed closure of urban branches, closure of rural branches required various permissions, which were difficult to obtain. Gradually, after obtaining the necessary approvals, some of the branches were merged and the number reduced to seventy-seven. When the option of closure no longer existed, we had to deal with the real issue of how these branches could be revitalized.

At this point I learned about the tremendous work done by the Grameen Bank of Bangladesh, founded by Muhammad Yunus, a pioneer in the field of microcredit. Following his example, in November 1995 we established the Rural Development Division to provide microcredit to poor women in the villages where our branches were located.

In the Indian version of microcredit, which has evolved its own group formation and credit delivery models, self-help groups (SHGs) are the basic unit to which the loan is given. Each SHG is composed of twenty women who voluntarily form the group and choose one another in the knowledge that they have to jointly guarantee the loan. During the first six months, they save a small amount each month (they determine the amount, based on their earnings), pool the savings, and deposit these funds in the bank. The monthly deposit is normally in the range of 50 cents to one U.S. dollar at the official exchange rate (although in buying power it is worth much more in India, especially in rural areas). They meet twice a month and receive training on how to organize their group meetings, start a bank account, and calculate interest and also learn about women's rights and other general issues. During the second six months, besides continuing to save, they begin to lend their savings to group members. The group decides the amount, rate of interest, priority of needs, and other procedures for lending. During this one year, the women become quite proficient in handling finance, understanding the implications of cooperating and pooling their savings, and the importance of repayment. They also gain self-confidence, become articulate, and understand the need for joint social action. At the end of the first year, the group becomes eligible to receive credit from the bank, subject to regularity in savings and repayment of internal loans by every group member. Normally, the loan is about U.S.$50 per person, but in the case of Bank of Madura, an individual could receive up to U.S.$200 to undertake small business activities like raising a milk cow, setting up a tailoring shop, or producing food items. Repayment is made every month, and the group collects the amount due and pays the bank. The loan is given without any collateral but is guaranteed by all of the SHG's members. The initial training, peer group pressure to be responsible, and mutual monitoring by the members all help considerably in the repayment rate, which is about 99.5 percent.

Normally, the self-help groups are formed by NGOs (nonprofits), and banks extend the loans. However, we decided to form the groups ourselves through our branches. This was an unusual move for a commercial bank, and to understand the process, we need to take a look at how banks work in India.

Rural branches are managed or administered by the head of a geographical division, which has many metropolitan, urban, and rural branches. Since the volume of business is very low in rural branches, the division heads do not pay attention to them. The executives and staff in banks, who are better educated and highly paid relative to those in many other segments, do not like to live in villages. Lack of modern amenities, good schools, health care facilities, and entertainment make villages unattractive to them and their families. To illustrate, many government banks have a policy of making the promotion of managers from grade I to grade II contingent on a stint in a rural branch. Such transfers are commonly known as "punishment postings." Most often, staff live in nearby towns and commute to the village. They spend very little time at the branch and do not interact with the villagers, who are poor, uneducated, and socially not their equals.

When the Rural Development Division was started, it became obvious that unless this issue was faced squarely, the division could not take off. As a first step, the management of all the rural branches was brought under the division irrespective of the branch locations. This move made rural branches gain legitimacy and gave a sharp focus to their activities. Next we decided to "attract" people from within the bank who wanted to get involved in rural development work on a voluntary basis instead of compelling people to work in these branches. Although the personnel department was skeptical, people did come forward. Instead of selecting all those who volunteered, we decided to select people on the basis of their commitment to the project and their willingness to live in the village. The candidates were also told that they should relate to people in the village, especially the women, as equals, without any gender, caste, class, or other biases.

Those who showed any hesitation in the interview were not selected. This move sent strong signals throughout the bank that senior management was committed to the concept of rural development through microcredit. Many individuals who were already in the division opted to stay; however, not all were retained. A thorough review of each person's background was made to ensure that he or she could be part of the new project. Those who were considered unsuitable were transferred out. The personnel policy was also amended to provide automatic transfer to an urban branch to anybody in the Rural Development Division, at any time, who requested this. Within a few months, a team of about 325 highly motivated individuals, from a total of 2,600 employees, was assembled.

The core team of senior executives, headed by the divisional manager, studied various microcredit projects in detail, visited many nonprofits involved in forming SHGs, received training from experts in the field, and met frequently to decide on a strategy. After an intensive two-day residential workshop without anybody from outside the division, the core team decided to form SHGs themselves without linking with nonprofits. This was a big surprise, but the decision was accepted.

This led to the birth of a "nonprofit" within the for-profit bank. The cost of starting, training, and monitoring SHGs, which is called "capacity building," is an expensive and time-consuming process. This cost is even higher when a bank promotes groups through its own personnel, whose salary levels are much higher than salaries in the nonprofit sector. Besides, the overheads of the bank are also high. This is why banks rely on nonprofits to undertake capacity building and only come in to provide credit.

The decision to directly promote SHGs was based on the reasoning that there would be no additional cost, since the cost of fixed overheads and salaries of individuals in the rural branches was already being incurred. A decision was also made that no increases in staff or overhead costs would be allowed in the Rural Development Division. The capacity of the division to promote SHGs without additional costs was pegged at fifteen hundred SHGs. It was also agreed by the core team of executives in the division that new methodologies to promote SHGs at lower cost would be found when the capacity of fifteen hundred groups was reached.

The new division was organized around five clusters of branches with a project manager heading each cluster. A training center was started that trained all the staff in the division on promoting, training, and monitoring SHGs. To begin with, the core team decided to go slow: start a few groups and evaluate the process. Since it takes one year before a group becomes eligible for a loan, it took time to evaluate the process. Thereafter, groups were started in larger numbers. Initially, the team faced hardships in working in the villages, promoting groups, and training women who were either not very educated or illiterate. These hardships vanished when they saw the difference they were making in the lives of the village women and the hospitability, friendship, and gratitude received from them.

In the year 2001, Bank of Madura merged with ICICI Bank, which is the second-largest financial institution in India. I continued with the bank for one year as adviser for the microcredit project before I went on to found the Microcredit Foundation of India in 2002. During the time I was adviser to the project, we selected two hundred women who were members of the SHGs promoted by the bank to start SHGs on their own. These women were well versed in the concept and had demonstrated leadership qualities. They were further trained by the bank personnel before they started forming groups. They were also remunerated for this work, but this cost is considerably lower than the cost of promoting groups by the bank. Now there are five hundred village women who are promoting groups under the supervision of bank personnel and linking them with the bank for credit. At last count, there were eight thousand SHGs, with a membership of 160,000 women. When this number and the credit portfolio grow further, the activity has the potential to become profitable.

Key Elements of Success

The employees of the bank who worked in other divisions and visitors to the Rural Development Division, especially from other banks, were amazed at the level of commitment, hard work, and satisfaction in their achievement shown by the employees of this division. Four key elements in this process can be identified:

1. *Presence of a powerful mission.* Although we never had a separate "mission statement" for this division, the mission became quite obvious. "Empowering poor women in villages through self-help groups and microcredit" was the unstated but obvious mission. It might be added that even though we had a "mission statement" for the bank that was widely publicized and also printed on pocket-sized laminated cards that were distributed to every employee, few could remember it. The employees' true commitment was to the mission of the SHG program, not to the bank's "manufactured" mission.

2. *Commitment to the mission.* The mission of this division did strike a chord in many individuals, and they were willing to work in villages, to be part of it, despite hardships and personal inconvenience. They had left a job and joined a mission.

3. *Motivation from within.* During my many interactions with people in the division, it was obvious that the source of motivation was coming from within and not from external stroking or rewards. The zeal they exhibited could be legitimately characterized as missionary. Once the key elements were in place, the members of the division were working for themselves and not for me, the divisional manager, or the bank.

4. *Cohesiveness as a team bound by a common cause.* There were fewer disputes in the division compared to the rest of the bank, and those that arose were easier to resolve. All that was needed was to answer the question, "What is best for this project, this cause?" There was an implicit understanding that the cause was greater than the individual.

I did not play an active day-to-day leadership role in this process as one might expect of the executive leader of an organization. My main contributions were the following:

- Identifying the activity or the "cause."
- Thinking of the idea of attracting "volunteers," rather than assigning work to people based on their educational qualifications, experience, or past performance, as is usually the case, and then thinking of ways to motivate them. These mission-driven workers provided their own motivation.
- Acting as a "gatekeeper" to ensure that individuals committed to the mission were selected and that others were not chosen.
- Giving everyone a lot of freedom.

The experience I have just described can be viewed as an instance of "transforming leadership" as conceptualized by James MacGregor Burns (1978) or "transformational leadership" as conceived by Bernard Bass (1985), and in fact, it can be made to fit into the framework of these theories. However, if one were to do that, much of the learning that can be gained from this experience would be lost. If the process can be looked at afresh, it might reveal significant differences that can perhaps add additional insights into leadership processes that transform organizations.

Missionary Leadership

The term *mission* is now commonly used in all organizations, and mission statements have become mandatory. However, the word *missionary* is still associated with people who seek the propagation of a faith. In the present context, the term *missionary leadership* is used in its generic sense to highlight the fact that nonprofits would require leaders who are themselves deeply committed to the mission and strive to fulfill it.

Concept of a Mission

The term *mission* is overused and therefore overburdened to the extent that the underlying concept itself may become trivialized. The idea of a mission whose votaries become missionaries and exhibit uncommon zeal and are willing to go to any length to uphold and fulfill the mission even at the cost of personal deprivation needs to be restored to its rightful place. Despite the devaluation of the term *mission*, as in the term *mission statement,* the power of the concept to motivate people is real.

The concept of "missionary leadership" is predicated on the presence of a genuine mission. The relationship between the leader and followers is based on their common, shared desire to serve the mission and is not purely relational. This would distinguish missionary leadership from leader-member exchange theory (Graen and Scandura, 1987), for example, or even transformational leadership, which focus primarily on the relationship between leader and follower.

Assembling a Missionary Team

Leadership theories tend to assume that the followers are a given and leaders proactively transform them or elevate followers from lower to higher levels of needs. However, a missionary leader is one who understands the power of the mission to attract committed individuals and deliberately assembles a team of dedicated people to fulfill it.

All individuals, at some level of their being and at different stages in their lives, respond to their inner needs, even if they do not always actualize them. This is true even when they are transactional in the context of their work, business, or other spheres. Thus at any given time, some individuals are more ready to serve causes and join a mission than others. They might do this by volunteering their services, joining the effort full time or part time, or supporting the cause from the outside by raising resources and giving moral support.

The success of a leader in a nonprofit organization will depend on the extent to which he or she can identify, attract, and retain individuals who can become missionaries for the cause the leader espouses. Conversely, success will also depend on the person's ability to avoid engaging contractual or transactional workers who have no commitment to the mission, even as unpaid volunteers.

In assembling the mission team, in addition to commitment, the team members also need competence, and the selection process has to be conscious of this. The ideal scenario would be to have a team that is highly committed and highly competent. Compared to for-profit companies, nonprofits can be weak in the areas of accounting and finance, administration, and management. However, it would be easier to provide training and support to a team of highly motivated missionary followers than to try to get a group of qualified and competent people who pursue their own personal agendas instead of being fully committed to the mission. Today, many managerial functions, including payroll, accounting, database management, external communication, and even fundraising, can be outsourced to professional firms who specialize in them. Nonprofits can consider this option so that they can focus their energies on the main purpose of the organization.

This aspect of carefully selecting and assembling a team of people who are committed to the cause is perhaps the most critical element in the success of missionary leadership. The alternative is the time-consuming and difficult process of getting a group of employees to buy into the vision or take ownership of the mission and trying to transact with them through rewards and punishments or transform them by raising their levels of motivation.

Motivation

The source of motivation of missionary followers is at the sublime level and not at the mundane, need-fulfillment level, which is often the case with contractual workers. Motivation at the mundane level is based on satisfying the material or ego needs of individuals in return for their work and contribution to the organization. Material needs based on desire are hard to satisfy because fulfillment creates new desires. Ego needs also expand with fulfillment. An important component of material and ego needs is the desire for differential gains, where satisfaction is obtained not only from what one gets but also from how much more one gets in relation to others. This leads to competition between members of a team, lack of trust, and a breakdown in communication and makes team building a difficult hurdle.

Motivation at the sublime level addresses issues that are internal to the individual—the need for personal growth and the desire to derive satisfaction from serving a cause. Serving a common cause binds individuals and promotes cooperation. The energies are focused on serving the cause.

The distinction between the two types of motivation—need fulfillment at the mundane level and inner fulfillment at the sublime level (see Exhibit 4.1)—does not mean that people fall into either one category or the other. All individuals have material and ego needs, and they seek ways to satisfy these needs from their workplace, family, friends, and community. It is also true that all individuals have deeper, inner needs at a sublime level, where they seek satisfaction from serving a cause that benefits society and not themselves individually. Some people are more aware of this need in themselves than others. People may respond to these needs at different times in their lives. Typically, college students and retirees are keen to work with nonprofits. Many individuals pursue both types of needs at the same time.

The missionary leader has to be conscious of this distinction and respond to the inner needs of followers to seek satisfaction from serving the cause. In the process, the leader has to ensure that the other needs of the individuals, such as financial security and emotional support, are satisfied so that they do not detract these people from their goal of serving the cause.

Role of the Leader

Leadership theories generally revolve around the leader's qualities, such as charisma, and his or her ability to motivate followers. The theme of this chapter is that in nonprofits with a mission, the real source of motivation is the power

EXHIBIT 4.1. TYPES OF MOTIVATION.

Mode	Level	Focus	Needs	Outcome
Normal	Mundane, surface, physical	Outside the individual	Material or corporal needs, ego recognition, differential gain	Dissipation of energy, high transaction costs, divisiveness
Mission	Sublime, inner, metaphysical	Within the individual	Inner rewards, personal or spiritual growth, desire to serve social causes	Focused energy, binds individuals, cohesiveness

of the cause being served and the inner need of individuals to seek personal satisfaction at a sublime level from serving the cause. The leader is the medium that enables this process. The leader does not modify or transform the needs or motivational level of the followers but recognizes the deeper needs in the individuals that attracted them to the mission and offers them the opportunity to fulfill these needs.

The missionary leader also has to ensure that the powerful energies that can be unleashed are directed toward serving the cause and not dissipated on internal organizational issues such as communication, problem solving, or conflict resolution, which soak up organizational energy. If the leader can establish a culture where each member subscribes to the idea that the cause is greater than the individual or the team and builds consensus on how the team should work together focused on the achievement of the cause, the energies will be unified.

The leader of a nonprofit organization has the unique opportunity to focus the collective energy of a group of committed people on the cause instead of dissipating this powerful energy on motivational and organizational issues.

Conclusion

Missionary leadership can transform a nonprofit in pursuit of a genuine mission. The concept of missionary leadership proposed in this chapter is based on my own personal experience; it is not a theory based on data collection or research. If this chapter prompts discussion, analysis, and further study, my purpose in writing it will have been well served.

References

Bass, B. M. *Leadership and Performance Beyond Expectations.* New York: Free Press, 1985.

Burns, J. M. *Leadership.* New York: HarperCollins, 1978.

Graen, G. B., and Scandura, T. "Toward a Psychology of Dyadic Organizing." In B. Staw and L. L. Cummings (eds.), *Research in Organizational Behavior.* Vol. 9. Greenwich, Conn.: JAI Press, 1987.

CHAPTER FIVE

TRANSFORMATIONAL LEADERSHIP IN NONPROFIT ORGANIZATIONS

Ronald E. Riggio,
Bernard M. Bass,
Sarah Smith Orr

Leading a nonprofit organization is quite different from leading a business in the private sector. Some (but not all) of the fundamental differences that are illustrated in the chapters of this book are the nonprofit organization's focus on a cause as opposed to profits (Chapter Four); its reliance on a voluntary workforce (Chapter Twelve); its governing board, which may include individuals who help fund the organization (Chapters Nine and Ten); its less attractive compensation packages for management and staff (Chapter Seven); and the requirements of external agents, such as government entities, for ongoing performance assessment as a prerequisite for funding (Chapter Sixteen). Although there are also similarities between leading nonprofit and leading for-profit organizations (as well as similarities with government organizations, the military, and others), it is important to consider the special nature of nonprofits when applying theories and principles of effective leadership to organizations in the nonprofit or social sector.

Applying Transformational Leadership Theory to Nonprofit Organizations

In many ways, the theory of transformational leadership has roared onto the scene (see Dumdum, Lowe, and Avolio, 2002). Beginning with James MacGregor Burns's conception of the "transforming leader" (1978) and continuing with the research of other leadership scholars (Bass, 1985, 1998; Avolio and Yammarino, 2002), the essence of transformational leadership is the leader who not only inspires commitment to a vision or cause but also develops, or "transforms," followers to reach their highest potential and to take on the responsibilities of leading the organization toward its mission. This notion of "mission-driven" leadership, introduced in Chapter Four, is also at the heart of transformational leadership, and it is this focus on the central mission or purpose of the organization that makes the theory of transformational leadership a particularly appropriate one for nonprofit organizations.

Transformational leadership is often contrasted with "transactional leadership," which is the more "traditional" notion of leading via some sort of social exchange between leaders and followers. In transactional leadership, leaders offer fulfillment of certain follower needs (pay, chances for promotion, developmental opportunities, and so on) in exchange for the follower's loyalty, dedication, and hard work. In many ways, transformational leadership "transcends" transactional leadership because it is built around the notion that leaders and followers are held together by some higher-level, shared goal or mission, rather than because of some personal transaction.

We will argue that transformational leadership theory, as inspired by Burns but formulated by Bass (1998), is a very good model for guiding leadership efforts in nonprofit organizations. We will first look at the elements of transformational leadership and apply these to leading nonprofit organizations. Next, we will review research on transformational leadership applied to the nonprofit sector, to see whether there are data to support its application. Finally, we will provide some case study illustrations that portray transformational leaders who have been successful at leading their organizations to achieve mission-driven success and conclude with some guidelines for nonprofit leaders that are suggested by transformational leadership theory.

Transformational Leadership Theory

Transformational leaders are leaders who develop positive, rich, emotional relationships with followers that build commitment to a common purpose or cause and contribute to their development as individuals and as future leaders. Typically, this common cause contributes to the "greater good," so there is an obvious "moral" overtone to transformational leadership (Avolio and Yammarino, 2002). Transformational leaders also lead groups and organizations that attain performance levels that often far exceed expected standards (Bass, 1985). Transformational leaders are charismatic and inspiring. They serve as positive role models for followers, who are inspired to emulate these leaders. Transformational leaders challenge and stimulate their followers intellectually and encourage them to "stretch" and improve their competencies. Finally, transformational leaders develop supportive, mentoring relationships with followers, but these relationships are also designed to challenge followers to develop their own leadership competencies and potential.

Bass's conceptualization of transformational leadership (1998) views it as composed of four factors, each of which begins with the letter *I:* idealized influence, inspirational motivation, intellectual stimulation, and individualized consideration.

Idealized influence (also known as *charismatic leadership*) involves leaders serving as idealized role models for followers. Transformational leaders "walk the talk." They demonstrate high standards of moral and ethical conduct, as well as commitment to the cause. As a result, followers admire and respect these leaders and imbue them with extraordinary qualities and capabilities. Followers personally identify with their transformational leader, using the leader as a model for their own behavior (see Shamir, House, and Arthur, 1993). This component of transformational leadership is particularly relevant to leaders of nonprofit organizations because it helps build follower commitment to the cause. Followers emulate the leader's commitment and may view the leader as the embodiment of the organization's values and mission (Shamir, Zakay, and Popper, 1998).

Inspirational motivation is the component of transformational leadership that arouses followers' enthusiasm and sense of team spirit. Transformational leaders articulate a shared vision and inspire followers to strive toward challenging goals. This element is often associated with inspirational leadership and is particularly important for leaders of nonprofit organizations when inspiring and motivating volunteer workers and staff.

Intellectual stimulation involves the leader's encouraging followers to be innovators and creative problem solvers. Often this stimulation occurs through a process of empowering and intellectually challenging followers to take initiative—similar to some elements of shared leadership, as suggested in Chapter Thirteen. Transformational leaders challenge followers to think in new ways and are not critical of strategies or opinions that differ from the leaders' own. This component of transformational leadership is particularly important in nonprofit organizations, where volunteers and paid staff members are often attracted to the organization precisely because they can have a direct impact. In addition, some volunteer or low-paid staff members may be primarily motivated to work for nonprofits because of the opportunity to gain high-level work experience or responsibilities that will build their skill sets for their future careers—experiences that may not be available in lower-level positions in for-profit companies. Transformational leaders provide these skill-building opportunities.

Individualized consideration reflects the transformational leader's ability to focus on each individual follower's particular needs and goals by acting as a coach or mentor to develop each follower's leadership potential. Transformational leaders are effective listeners, but they are also sensitive to the emotional needs and concerns of followers. Again, this element of transformational leadership should be particularly important in nonprofit organizations, where a leader needs to be particularly sensitive to the various motivations that cause volunteers to be affiliated with the organization (see Chapter Twelve).

These "four *I*s of transformational leadership can be measured by the Multifactor Leadership Questionnaire (MLQ) (Bass and Avolio, 1995), an instrument that has followers rate their leaders on items that represent each of the four components of transformational leadership. The MLQ has been widely used in research on transformational leadership and has helped spur interest and studies using the theory.

The individual components of transformational leadership have clear applications to leading nonprofit organizations, but in many ways, the sum of the theory is greater than its parts. As Bass states, "Transformational leadership does not stop with the successful elevation of followers (from lower levels to higher levels). . . . A shared agreement is developed that bonds leader and followers in a moral commitment to a cause that goes beyond their own self-interests" (1998, p. 26). True transformational leadership is what Bass refers to as "socialized"—it transcends self-interest. Socialized transformational leaders are both more oriented toward serving others and more focused on the leader's and group's shared goals. It is the sense of moral good and a passionate commitment to the cause that make transformational leadership theory particularly appropriate for understanding leadership in nonprofit organizations. This is not to say that transformational leaders are not effective in the for-profit sector, in government, and in the military. However, transformational theory seems a particularly good fit for nonprofits, where commitment to the cause and contributing to the greater good of society are overriding themes.

Another reason that transformational leadership may be particularly appropriate for nonprofit organizations stems from Bass's assertion (1985) that whereas transactional leadership is more common in mechanistic, bureaucratic organizations, transformational leadership should be more effective in flexible, "organic" types of structures. This notion is suggested by Den Hartog, Van Muijen, and Koopman (1996), who suggest that nonprofits tend to be, but are not always, less bureaucratic than for-profit organizations.

Research on Transformational Leadership in Nonprofit Organizations

Before discussing research that examines the role of transformational leadership in nonprofit organizations, it is important to briefly review research on the validity and efficacy of transformational leadership theory. In recent years, there has been so much interest in and such a large volume of studies of transformational leadership that there have been two separate meta-analytic reviews investigating how transformational leadership relates to both leader effectiveness and follower satisfaction with the leader. The earlier review (Lowe, Kroeck, and Sivasubramaniam, 1996) found solid evidence that transformational leadership had strong and consistent relationships with both leader performance and satisfaction with the leader, with follower satisfaction with the leader having stronger relationships to transformational leadership than leader performance did. Interestingly, none of the studies used leaders from a nongovernmental nonprofit organization. The researchers did, however, compare leaders in public versus private organizations. Contrary to their expectations, but consistent with our notion that organizations that are mission-driven[1] are a good fit for transformational leadership, these researchers found that transformational leadership effects were stronger in the public organizations (primarily educational institutions and the military) than in the private, for-profit companies. The second meta-analytic review (Dumdum, Lowe, and Avolio, 2002) found essentially the same results using studies published after the earlier review. However, these researchers found no significant difference in transformational leadership between leaders in the private and those in the public sector. In summary, strong and consistent evidence supports both the theory of transformational leadership (see also Antonakis and House, 2002), and the relationship between transformational leadership and leader performance and follower satisfaction.

As mentioned, there has been surprisingly little empirical research into transformational leadership in nonprofit organizations, particularly in contrast to the large number of studies that have investigated transformational leadership in for-profit companies and in government, military, and educational institutions. One Australian study compared two CEOs of nonprofit organizations with two CEOs from similarly sized for-profit companies (Egan, Sarros, and Santora, 1995). Despite the authors' claims that nonprofit organizations should be more conducive to transformational leadership, there did not appear to be any differences in the transformational leadership qualities of the CEOs in the two sectors. It is important to note, however, the extremely small sample size of four leaders.

The most direct test of the fit between transformational leadership and nonprofit organizations was a study by Egri and Herman (2000) in which thirty-three nonprofit leaders were compared to thirty-eight leaders in for-profit companies in the United States and Canada. All of the companies were in the same industry, providing environmental products or services (recycling, manufacturing nontoxic cleaners, environmental cleaning services, and so on). The majority of both groups were the heads of the organizations, but all participants were in management or leadership positions. The results suggested that compared to managers and leaders in general (comparing their results with normative data), leaders in environmental organizations seemed to have values more consistent with transformational leadership. Although there were no significant differences in the transformational leadership qualities of leaders in for-profit and nonprofit environmental organizations, nonprofit environmental organizations appeared to be highly receptive to transformational leadership and for-profit environmental organizations only moderately open.

Clearly, there is a need for more research on the role of transformational leadership in nonprofit organizations. One obvious reason is that for-profit organizations, with their large numbers of employees, easy access to leadership consultants, and large leadership development budgets, are more likely venues for scholars to study transformational leadership quantitatively. Yet there is also a shortage of qualitative research on transformational leadership in nonprofits. Bass observes, "Leadership is as much emotional as rational in effect. We need to appreciate what the nonquantitative scholars . . . have to say about charisma and transformational leadership" (1998, p. 166). In this vein, we will explore qualitatively the fit between transformational leadership and the nonprofit world.

Transformational Leaders in Nonprofits: Three Positive Examples

In an effort to provide a better understanding of the model of transformational leadership and to illustrate its application to nonprofit leaders, we will focus on three particularly effective leaders in very different sorts of nonprofit organizations.

Father Rocky Evangelista of the Tuloy sa Don Bosco Street Children Project

Father Marciano Evangelista, a Catholic priest, founded the Tuloy sa Don Bosco Street Children Project to help some of the estimated 100,000 homeless male street children in Manila, Philippines, turn their lives around through a residential program of education and vocational training. Father Rocky, as he is known to the boys, embodies many of the elements of transformational leadership and has incorporated the notion of "transformation" into the youth program itself. He believes that the youth in his program are transformed through being allowed to make the choice to join the program and follow its rules and the demanding schedule required of students (Sherman, 1999). One would think that the opportunity to receive room, board, and an education that leads to employability would be enticing. However, the program is rigorous, requiring self-discipline and adherence to rules—something with which the street children are quite unfamiliar.

Before being admitted to the formal educational program, Father Rocky and his team invite street children to the program's "free zone," where they can receive basic shelter (they are allowed to sleep on the floor), free food, clothing, and bus fare, with no strings attached. Boys in the free zone interact with boys in the school, and the boys enrolled in the school program serve as positive role models for the newcomers. Any boy in the free zone has access to the school program. However, Father Rocky believes that the children must make the free choice to join the program, rather than being required by an authority figure or leader, so the eventual choice to join the program is left solely to the boys themselves.

The residential program provides a general education along with technical training in a variety of trades from woodworking to auto repair and provides children formerly consumed with basic survival on the streets with a chance to experience childhood activities, such as sports, television, and regular outings. In addition to paid staff, Father Rocky has dozens of volunteers involved, many of them professional people who help him scour the back streets of Manila, encouraging children to join the program. The program has been extremely successful for a decade, and more than seven hundred boys have benefited from the program.

Father Rocky Evangelista is strongly committed to the mission of his program, working tirelessly as a leader, administrator, and fundraiser. Although he characterizes his involvement as "divinely inspired," he also acknowledges that Philippine President Gloria Macapagal Arroyo challenged him to make the Tuloy sa Don Bosco program a model for similar youth programs when she was the secretary of social welfare. Father Rocky typifies the transformational leadership component of idealized influence. He demonstrates strong commitment to the cause and has created a model—both a model program and a leadership role model—that can be followed by others working to save Filipino youth.

Another important element of transformational leadership displayed by Father Rocky is individualized consideration as he and his staff act as mentors to develop each child's potential. He carries this focus on individual development over to his staff, who display unusual loyalty and dedication to both Father Rocky and to the Tuloy sa Don Bosco program.

John Bryant of Operation HOPE

Another transformational leader who founded an innovative nonprofit organization is John Bryant, CEO of Operation HOPE, Inc., the United States' first nonprofit social investment banking organization. Following an outbreak of civil unrest in Los Angeles in April 1992, Bryant developed a strategy, and adopted as his mission, to provide economic development to the devastated area of South Central Los Angeles. Organizing a "bankers' bus tour" one week after the riots, Bryant persuaded a multiethnic group of bankers, investors, and government officials to tour the South Central community to survey the devastation but to also realize that this was a community with potential for recovery that was worth investing in.

Operation HOPE provides both economic education and access to capital to low- and middle-income families in Los Angeles, and its economic education program has moved beyond Los Angeles to a nationwide focus. In its first half dozen years, Operation HOPE's Banking on the Future Program reached more than one hundred thousand students in over 350 schools nationwide, teaching young people in inner cities about banking and personal finance. The vision of Operation HOPE is to "convert" lower-income and financially underserved residents into more economically knowledgeable and economically stable members of society. This is done through an integrated program of financial education and assistance, encouraging residents to become bank customers and to learn the value of saving money, by turning renters into homeowners and workers into business owners via loans, and by developing the employable skills of minimum-wage workers through computer literacy programs. Operation HOPE has helped produce nearly one thousand new homeowners and new business owners in the Los Angeles area.

John Bryant personifies the transformational leadership component of inspirational motivation. After spending just a few minutes with him, it is hard not to be "infected" by his enthusiasm. He is very good at articulating his vision of the enormous impact financial assistance and financial education can have on low-income individuals and families. One colleague says, "John is extremely dynamic. He completely embodies what he is trying to do. He is very genuine."

Moreover, Bryant is known as an exceptional mentor and is very high on the transformational leadership dimension of individualized consideration. Rachael Doff, the current executive vice president of Operation HOPE who originally applied for a receptionist position, tells the story of how Bryant mentored her over the years in both her professional and her personal growth and development. "John is all about excellence in what he does, and he wants you to do the same. He provides daily feedback and challenges. He demands that you increase your level of creative thinking. He challenges you to set the next level for yourself. By working with John Bryant, you become a positive, solution-oriented professional."

Jan Levy of Leadership Tomorrow

Jan Levy is executive director of Leadership Tomorrow, a regional civic leadership program located in Seattle, Washington. For more than twenty years, Leadership Tomorrow has been encouraging citizens to become more involved in community issues and thereby furthering the development of the region's leadership capacity. Leadership Tomorrow is distinctive because it is a large program, with well over a thousand graduates, and program participants work in groups to tackle serious regional and community problems and issues. Moreover, the program actively involves over 150 volunteer alumni annually in recruitment efforts for future classes, in sponsoring and delivering elements of the program, and in program governance. Levy says, "Typically, in a given year, more than 60 percent of all of Leadership Tomorrow's standing committee members and board members are alumni. There is a continual effort to recruit a mix of alumni and non-alumni volunteers in every volunteer aspect of the program, in order to keep the perspectives fresh."

Levy, herself an alumna of Leadership Tomorrow, has directed the program since 1989. In addition to her work in making Leadership Tomorrow a truly challenging and top-notch leadership development experience, Levy has aided the formation of a number of new civic leadership programs in the Pacific Northwest and has contributed greatly to community-based leadership by virtue of her positions on the board s of the Community Leadership Association and the Robert K. Greenleaf Center for Servant-Leadership.

Jan Levy relies heavily on the transformational leadership components of intellectual stimulation and individualized consideration. She challenges followers to take on tasks that are true "stretch" experiences and is very good at getting them to take ownership and responsibility for their projects. Failures become learning experiences. "I try to get both the teams and individuals to focus on their strengths—to use these to take on challenges." She particularly values the diversity of backgrounds and opinions of her volunteers and paid staff. "I encourage them to express their opinions, to question the status quo."

As illustrated by these three successful leaders of nonprofit ventures, transformational leadership seems to be a fitting model for application in the nonprofit sector. However, there may be instances where transformational leaders lose their way. True transformational leaders are partly defined by the notion of the socialized leader, oriented toward the greater good. What happens when a formerly socialized transformational leader begins to focus more on personal outcomes than shared, socialized outcomes? This is the subject of our final case study.

Transformational Leadership—Falling from Grace

What does it look like when a leader, who manifested all the characteristics and outcomes of a transformational leader, goes to the dark side of leadership? What are the signs that the leader is slipping away from the model that propelled his or her assent to a prominent and admirable position and the organization to a high level of performance?

There is sufficient evidence in the nonprofit sector, through some high-profile public reports, that leaders who are known for their leadership ability to transform complex organizational systems can occasionally fall from grace. In Chapter Six, Joanne Ciulla cites the dramatic and powerful example of visionary leader William Aramony, president of the United Way of America (UWA), and the profound impact and repercussions of his fall from grace, not just on the entire United Way system but on the nonprofit sector as a whole.

Few United Way professionals, if any, would dispute the fact that when Aramony assumed the presidency of the United Way of America and for more than a decade thereafter, he manifested all the characteristics of a transformational leader. He transformed the national organization and the national system. Aramony took the reins of UWA during very challenging economic times for nonprofits. He had the skills and competencies essential to the transformation of an outdated model of national outreach, supporting member nonprofit organizations, bringing energy, standards, visibility and new levels of accountability to the system. He was able to formulate, articulate, and communicate a compelling vision that motivated all to make a commitment to the organization and its mission and support it—nationally.

There are some fourteen hundred local autonomous United Way organizations across the United States and abroad. The United Way system is not a top-down organization; it is a network of independent local organizations, each with its own governing board and staff, with the same basic mission, similar structure (depending on size), and processes. It is a complex system of thousands of skilled (and some not so skilled) professionals and high-profile volunteers representing all sectors of our diverse communities nationwide. To gain and retain the commitment and support of the local United Way organizations was an enormously time- and energy-consuming process.

It was Aramony who energetically led the charge to establish standards of excellence that each local United Way would adopt and adhere to. He led the creative and branding process to adopt and use a single logo image. He directed the pooling of resources through a dues assessment agreed on by each local United Way. He crafted a national and international presence (through such means as airing high-profile United Way television spots in partnership with the National Football League, featuring NFL players) via materials and messages. During Aramony's early years, the National Academy for Voluntarism was formed, providing leadership and functional skill development for United Way professionals nationwide. A powerful and prestigious UWA board of directors was created. Aramony positioned the United Way system on the cutting edge of philanthropy—drawing a new map and fashioning new tools to expand the impact of philanthropy beyond local, regional, and even the national walls. As Bass describes it, as a transformational leader, Aramony was able to achieve "a new consensus, a new balance of power, and a changed allocation of the organization's resources . . . achieved by the transformation of cognitive maps of how and what is to be done" (1998, p. 28). Aramony had charisma and was the personification of idealized influence. New leaders in the system proudly sought to emulate Aramony (garnering them the affectionate nickname "Aramony's clones")—to seize the concepts he put forth to challenge the leadership of local United Ways to think and climb their way out of the "old model of doing things" box.

What happened? The public account is covered effectively in Chapter Six, especially with respect to the moral and ethical issues. Ciulla offers insight beyond the surface appearances of the Aramony scandal and his fall from grace, noting that on the surface, it "looks like a case of arrogance, abuse of power, greed, and excess." She notes the differences between what the public expects from nonprofit leaders versus business leaders (although that is now questionable, given the Enron and other recent scandals). Ciulla comments on the danger of acting like for-profit leaders; certainly there was just cause for Aramony to fall prey to that trap.

In a recent conversation between the current president of the United Way of America, Brian Gallagher, and Sarah Smith Orr, a former executive director and top executive in the United Way system, it was affirmed that although the members of the United Way of America's board of directors in place during Aramony's tenure were engaged, they apparently weren't focused on their role and their responsibility for governance and operations. And yes, the UWA board members did treat him like a peer, enabling him to see himself on a par with—and to be treated on a par with—the business CEOs with whom he worked.

Gallagher provided additional insights that did not make the public record. Aramony, upon reflection, slipped into a more transactional leadership mode, expecting loyalty and unquestioning followership despite the fact that changes were occurring in the corporate and community environments that required modifications in the ways United Way organizations conducted their business. It seemed as though he lost his ability to see the signs of change around him, to stay in touch with fairly dramatic changes in the philanthropic environment. He was drifting behaviorally; he had no answer for the changes. Gallagher emphasized the importance, for the transformational leader, to create formal ways of staying in touch with the organizations in the field—to stay on top of external and internal issues that might affect or impede the organization's ability to perform and fulfill its mission. Gallagher also stressed the importance of establishing governance measures for the board of directors to clarify roles and expectations and for evaluating performance that provide the organization with greater safeguards without suffocating the leader and the organization.

What clues foretold Aramony's fall? At least three are now clear. Let's look at these clues and how they relate to the theory of transformational leadership.

1. *Development of egocentric behaviors: arrogance, abuse of power, and excess.* As Ciulla points out in Chapter Six, "There are moral issues associated not only with how nonprofits raise money but also with how they reach their goals. . . . Power poses one of the distinctive ethical challenges to leadership. It does not always corrupt, but it creates temptations that leaders must understand and overcome." Power is heady—power perverts. Arrogance can be interpreted as an inability to listen, demonstrating a lack of sensitivity and caring. And excess is clearly demonstrated in very visible ways through behaviors, relationships, and physical settings. According to transformational leadership theory, the leader moves from a focus on the shared mission to a personal agenda.

2. *Establishment of a "circle of loyalists" to protect and inform.* The circle of loyalists may consist of top staff members who have been recruited, not to challenge the status quo but to maintain it. This is contradictory to the essential nature of the transformational leader as the person who develops followers, via intellectual stimulation, into creative problem solvers who are not afraid to challenge the leader. Brian Gallagher, the current UWA president, was hired by Sarah Smith Orr out of an interns program at UWA. He stood out because he was one of these types of followers, getting noticed because of his omnipresent challenging and prodding—pushing to get out of the box. A transformational leader needs to be surrounded with people who move beyond the walls—people who question "why?" in an attempt to get to a level of higher effectiveness.[2]

3. *Being increasingly out of touch.* As Gallagher notes, when the leader is unable to see and respond to the signs of change in the external and internal environment, the organization begins to slip-slide away. The leader needs to stay focused on the mission. The leader needs to continue to stay visible in order to continue to be a role model for followers (idealized influence) and to keep them

engaged and moving forward (inspirational motivation). One of the most important leadership characteristics for a nonprofit leader in the twenty-first century, according to Gallagher, is the ability to articulate a concrete future destination that is overarching and that inspires—with the ability and the responsibility to effectively manage change and transformation.

Conclusion

This chapter has attempted to use transformational leadership as a model to provide a better understanding of successful leadership in nonprofit organizations. Although a great deal of research suggests that transformational leadership is related to success in the for-profit sector, very little similar research has been conducted in the nonprofit sector. Using case study examples, we have tried to increase understanding of how the specific components of transformational leadership play an important part in leading nonprofit organizations in an effort to stimulate future research in this area.

Notes

1. This is not to say that for-profit organizations cannot be "mission-driven," merely that public institutions are more likely to focus around missions that involve providing service to the general populace without expecting financial returns; in other words, they are not "profit-driven."
2. In a nonprofit organization, the board of directors can constitute a circle of loyalists. The chief executive officer, who has a prominent role in the identification and selection of the incoming board members without sufficient input from board members and outside community leaders, will eventually establish a majority of loyalists who will serve as a protective shield and tend to neglect their governance responsibilities. Bowen (1994, p. 38) provides this challenge to business leaders as they join a nonprofit board: "Don't give in to the temptation to check your toughness at the door."

References

Antonakis, J., and House, R. J. "The Full-Range Leadership Theory: The Way Forward." In B. J. Avolio and F. J. Yammarino (eds.), *Transformational and Charismatic Leadership: The Road Ahead.* Greenwich, Conn.: JAI Press, 2002.

Avolio, B. J., and Yammarino, F. J. (eds.). *Transformational and Charismatic Leadership: The Road Ahead.* Greenwich, Conn.: JAI Press, 2002.

Bass, B. M. *Leadership and Performance Beyond Expectations.* New York: Free Press, 1985.

Bass, B. M. *Transformational Leadership: Industrial, Military, and Educational Impact.* Mahwah, N.J.: Erlbaum, 1998.

Bass, B. M., and Avolio, B. J. *MLQ: Multifactor Leadership Questionnaire for Research: Permission Set.* Redwood City, Calif.: MindGarden, 1995.

Bowen, W. G. "When a Business Leader Joins a Nonprofit Board." *Harvard Business Review,* September-October 1994, pp. 39–43.

Burns, J. M. *Leadership.* New York: HarperCollins, 1978.

Den Hartog, D. N., Van Muijen, J. J., and Koopman, P. L. "Linking Transformational Leadership and Organizational Culture." *Journal of Leadership Studies,* 1996, *3,* 68–83.

Dumdum, U. R., Lowe, K. B., and Avolio, B. J. "A Meta-Analysis of Transformational and Transactional Leadership Correlates of Effectiveness and Satisfaction: An Update and Extension." In B. J. Avolio and F. J. Yammarino (eds.), *Transformational and Charismatic Leadership: The Road Ahead.* Greenwich, Conn.: JAI Press, 2002.

Egan, R.F.C., Sarros, J. C., and Santora, J. C. "Putting Transactional and Transformational Leadership into Practice." *Journal of Leadership Studies,* 1995, *2,* 100–123.

Egri, C. P., and Herman, S. "Leadership in the North American Environmental Sector: Values, Leadership Styles, and Contexts of Environmental Leaders and Their Organizations." *Academy of Management Journal,* 2000, *43,* 571–604.

Lowe, K. B., Kroeck, K. G., and Sivasubramaniam, N. "Effectiveness Correlates of Transformational and Transactional Leadership: A Meta-Analytic Review of the *MLQ* Literature." *Leadership Quarterly,* 1996, *7,* 385–425.

Shamir, B., House, R. J., and Arthur, M. B. "The Motivational Effects of Charismatic Leadership: A Self-Concept-Based Theory." *Organization Science,* 1993, *4,* 577–593.

Shamir, B., Zakay, E.E.B., and Popper, M. "Correlates of Charismatic Leader Behavior in Military Units: Subordinates' Attitudes, Unit Characteristics, and Superiors' Appraisals of Leader Performance." *Academy of Management Journal,* 1998, *41,* 387–409.

Sherman, S. "The Power of Choice." In F. Hesselbein, M. Goldsmith, and I. Somerville (eds.), *Leading Beyond the Walls.* San Francisco: Jossey-Bass, 1999.

CHAPTER SIX

THE ETHICAL CHALLENGES OF NONPROFIT LEADERS

Joanne B. Ciulla

When I think of nonprofit leaders, community leaders, and leaders of social movements, I am reminded of an ethnographic study of Ongka, a "big man" from the Kawelka, a tribe of about one thousand people in the western highlands of Papua New Guinea (Nairn, 1989). Ongka has no formal power or authority as a big man. He is not elected, and he has no job per se, no employees, and no resources to barter. All that Ongka has is an idea and his ability to persuade people to contribute to this idea. His goal for the tribe is to put on a large moka for the neighboring tribe. A moka is a feast of pigs and presents. He says it is the most important thing in his life. Tribes in this part of New Guinea engage in a kind of competitive feasting, in which each tribe tries to outdo the other to enhance its own prestige. Ongka's goal is to collect between five and six hundred pigs, five cassowaries, one truck, cash, and maybe some cows for his feast.

Planning for such a feast takes five years. During that time, Ongka walks from village to village trying to convince people to donate their pigs. Ongka's leadership challenge is striking because he not only has to convince people to donate their most valuable possessions, but he also has to enlist those same people as volunteers to feed and care for the pigs for several years prior to the feast. The narrator of the study says, "With no authority, he can only push, and if he pushes too far, he loses

The author thanks Cassie King for her research and editorial assistance.

their cooperation." Ongka embodies a pure form of leadership, one that comes from his ability to persuade people to buy into his vision and values.

Whereas nonprofit leaders who run organizations with paid employees have positional power and the power of reward and punishment over their paid employees, when they work with volunteers or they solicit funds, they have only the power of the organization's ideas and values. With the exception of large, well-established nonprofits, most nonprofit leaders do not enjoy the status of their political and business counterparts, and they work long hours for little pay and sometimes little thanks. Leaders in nonprofits rely heavily on personal power, which can include expertise, friendliness, charisma, and the ability to elicit admiration. However, the most important source of power for a nonprofit leader is the ability to gain the respect, trust, and loyalty of others. Although this is important for leaders in all contexts, it is of particular importance for nonprofit leaders because, like Ongka, they often do not have other sources of power, such as rewards, punishments, control over resources and information, and status or authority (Yukl, 1994).

The Moral Dynamics of Charity

In a simple black-and-white world, the nonprofit leaders would be the altruistic ones in white hats who "do God's work," and business leaders would be the self-interested ones in black hats who are only out to make a buck. The term *nonprofit* or *not-for-profit* describes an organization in economic terms. Nonprofits include a wide variety of organizations, ranging from environmental, community, political, policy, and arts groups to those that aid the poor and the needy. The very idea of a nonprofit is that the organization doesn't profit but that some individuals, groups, or societies benefit from the work of the organization. The word less used these days to describe a nonprofit is *charity*. Not all nonprofits think of themselves as charities. Most of us think of charity in the narrow sense of giving to the needy. For example, a nonprofit think tank would not regard itself as a charity, yet it could be funded by voluntary donations. Nonprofit funding may come from one individual, a number of individuals, or other funding institutions. The word *charity* is a moral term. Its root comes from the Latin *caitus* or *carus*, meaning "dear." One dictionary defines *charity* as "Kindness: benevolence; a giving voluntarily to those in need; leniency or tolerance in judging others; institution or organization for helping those in need. Help so given; love of fellow men" (*Oxford Pocket Dictionary*, 1984, p. 117).

All major world religions reserve a special place for charity as a form of moral action. Catholics are required to do "good works." In Buddhism, charity is part of compassion, which is the core value of the Buddhist's moral system. One of the five pillars of Islam is *zakat,* a tax levied to benefit the poor and needy. Throughout history, people have recognized that charity is good not only for those who receive it but also for those who give. Giving to charity makes us better human beings and provides a way to show love or care for others.

The moral dynamic of charity is often obscured because we increasingly use the language of business and economics to describe the work of charities and the moral qualities of their work. *Nonprofit* is an economic term that seems to contrast the organization with one that makes profits. When you think of it, the term is really off the point. The real contrast between a charity and a business is far broader than whether it makes a profit or not. In a society that often uses economic values such as profits as norms against which all is measured, the term *nonprofit* makes sense. However, it masks the moral difference between a business and a charity. Another example of this is the term *social capital,* which is an economic term for moral concepts such as goodwill, loyalty, and commitment. The term *social capital* not only hides these moral goods but also dilutes their moral import. Moral goods usually have the quality of being intrinsically good. Under the term *social capital,* these moral goods are instrumentally good—they allow you to get things done. While goodwill is clearly useful if you want to implement a community project, it is also simply a morally admirable quality in human beings. It is ironic that the terms *nonprofit* and *social capital* have been embraced by scholars and practitioners in part because the language makes their work sound more legitimate than fuzzy moral terms such as *charity* and *goodwill.* I would argue that all nonprofits have the moral virtue of charity as their basis because their implicit or explicit mission is in some way to aid or improve individuals, society, culture, the environment, or the world. People may disagree with a nonprofit's notion of the good—for example, pro-life nonprofits have a different view of the good than pro-choice groups. Nonetheless, we recognize that these organizations focus on a moral cause or other social goods as their goal.

Leaders have to be mindful of three distinctive qualities of nonprofits. First, all nonprofits have an underlying moral cause, some notion of the good for a group, society, or humanity. Second, they use these moral aspirations, goals, and values to serve as a basis for eliciting moral action from volunteers and financial support from outside constituencies. These constituencies can be either other nonprofit funding agencies, such as the Kellogg or Ford foundations, or individuals. Third, the act of giving to a nonprofit group by an institution or an individual has a moral dynamic to it that is different from the act of buying a product. When we buy a car, we expect it to work for us. If we get a lemon, we either return it or get the dealer to fix it. It's annoying, but a bad car is nothing personal. When we give to charity, we expect others or a cause to benefit. Charity provides a path between self-interest and altruism—not all giving is altruistic, nor is it all self-interested. When the target group or cause doesn't benefit, it's personal. We may feel betrayed and sometimes foolish because our act of generosity has been denigrated. Donors are denied the satisfaction of giving monetary expression to their empathy and concern for the less fortunate when the money they contribute for starving children pays for something else. Consider the outcry when the American Red Cross failed to distribute promptly the funds raised for victims and families of the September 11, 2001, terrorist attacks. In response to criticism, the Red Cross vowed to become more transparent. Red Cross chairman David T. McLaughlin stated that the organization had an obligation to respect the intent of its donors. He said, "Whenever we respond to a disaster and solicit funds, donor intent will be very clear, very documented and confirmed in the faxed receipts that go back to the donor" (Strom, 2002).

Philosophical Consistency

The moral challenges distinctive to leaders in nonprofits stem from their role as the ones in the white hats in pursuit of some noble cause. While we want leaders in all sectors to be ethical, leaders in the nonprofit sector face a distinctive set of concerns because of the nature of their power and of their work. People often say that leaders should be held to a "higher moral standard," but does that make sense? If true, it would mean that it is acceptable for everyone else to live by lower moral standards. I don't think adherence to higher ethical standards is the real moral issue for leaders. The difference between the morality of leaders and everyone else is that the ethical failures and successes of leaders are magnified by their role, visibility, power, and the impact of their actions and behavior on others. History is littered with disastrous leaders who did not think they were subject to live by the same moral standards as everyone else. Hence leaders should not be held to higher moral standards than everyone else; they should be held to the *same* standards. We want leaders who will succeed more often than most people at meeting those standards and being morally consistent. Nonetheless, because of the distinctive moral qualities of nonprofits, the moral failure of a nonprofit leader elicits a somewhat different reaction than the moral failure of a business or political leader.

People often have different expectations of how nonprofit leaders should behave. We expect leaders of moral causes and organizations that espouse morality, such as religious organizations, to be "like Caesar's wife"—beyond reproach. Most people are also more sensitive to the level of moral or philosophical consistency in nonprofit leaders. For example, consider the case of Tim Eyman, leader of a citizens' group called Permanent Offense. This group sponsored a number of successful ballot initiatives that were aimed at holding politicians accountable for how they spent taxpayers' dollars. In February 2002, the *Seattle Post-Intelligencer* revealed that Eyman had paid himself $45,000 of the money raised for one of his ballot initiatives. Although this is not illegal, the politicians whom Eyman had often called "corrupt" seized on the issue to undermine his credibility and the credibility of the causes that his organization supports. Eyman must have realized how hypocritical he looked, because when confronted with the allocations, he denied that he had paid himself the money. He later confessed, saying, "I was in lie mode" (Ammons, 2002). Despite appearances, Eyman was probably not a complete hypocrite. People who are complete hypocrites express strong moral values and then act against them. What is most odd about some hypocrites is that they are not always liars. Some believe in and know they should live up to the values they talk about, but they fail to do so, either intentionally or unintentionally (Ciulla, 1999). This may have been Eyman's problem.

Leadership scholars sometimes use altruism as a measure of morality in leaders (Kanungo and Mendonca, 1996). It is tempting to do this with nonprofit leaders. In Eyman's case, we could say that he was not a good leader because he let his self-interest get in the way of the organization's interests. Altruism and self-interest are motives for acting. While we admire people who act from altruism, it is not in and of itself a normative principle (Nagel, 1970). A leader may do a wonderful job of ethically serving his or her constituents and organizations and not be motivated by altruism at all. For instance, a leader might act on what Immanuel Kant called "a good will," meaning the rational desire to do one's duty. According to Kant, this is not altruism. Moral action is not a matter of self-interest or the interest of others; it is a matter of rationally choosing to do what is right because it is right. Kant tells us that a good will "is not good because of what it affects or accomplishes, not because of its fitness to attain some proposed end; it is only good through its willing" (1993, p. 7).

Altruism is behavior that is generally done for others at some cost to oneself. It stands in contrast to selfishness, which is behavior that benefits oneself at some cost to others (Ozinga, 1999). Leaders such as Mahatma Gandhi and Nelson Mandela behaved altruistically, but what made their leadership ethical was not their altruism but the means they used to achieve their ends and the morality of their causes. The actions of both Gandhi and Mandela would not be diminished if they had done the same things out of self-interest; however, perhaps our emotional response to them might be. A terrorist leader who becomes a suicide bomber might have purely altruistic intentions, but the means that he uses to carry out his mission—killing innocent people—is not considered ethical even if his cause is just. The ends do not justify the means, regardless of whether the suicide bomber is self-interested or altruistic. We tend to admire people who are altruistic and sacrifice themselves for a cause, but their altruism does not guarantee that their actions are ethical.

Robin Hoodism

We are all familiar with the story of Robin Hood and his merry men who stole from the rich and gave to the poor. Robin Hood is the nonprofit version of Machiavelli's prince, because both men seemed to believe that the ends justified the means. While Machiavellian ends were wealth and power, Robin Hood's ends were feeding the poor and pursuing his own brand of distributive justice. Again, our moral sympathies lie with the nonprofit Robin Hood because we like his altruistic motives better, but his actions are ethically in the same "ends justify the means" camp as those of the prince. After all, Machiavelli tells us, the prince is after power and control, but when he gets it, he can bring about order and stability, which benefits the people under his protection.

The ethics of the means and the ethics of the ends have a somewhat different focus in nonprofits than in business. Businesses face the challenge of how to make money ethically. Nonprofits face the challenge of how to raise money ethically. The economist Georg Simmel (1978) pointed out that the beauty of money is that it hides all sorts of things about its origin. The Wal-Mart clerk doesn't know if the $20 bill in her cash register came from a homemaker, robber, a rapist, or a terrorist. She just knows that it paid for goods in the store. In nonprofits, money often has names attached to it. On the one hand, it should not matter who gives money to a cause that helps children or alleviates pain and suffering. On the other hand, it does matter, because people expect a high level of moral consistency from nonprofits. For example, consider the following questions: Should an organization like Teach America accept a large donation from a tobacco company? Should a business school accept a donation from someone convicted of insider trading?

Mother Teresa accepted money for her organization from Colombian drug lords and felon Charles Keating, who was convicted in the savings and loan scandal (Hitchens, 1997). This isn't stealing from the rich and giving to the poor; it's accepting money from the corrupt to give to the poor. Here the public makes a number of distinctions based on the kind of corruption and its relationship to the goals and values of the organization. If tobacco companies are aiming advertising at teenagers, you may not want their name as supporters of educational programs. If the Colombian drug lords are giving money to an organization that helps drug addicts, there is a moral inconsistency in accepting the money. So some would find Keating's donation to Mother Teresa's organization less offensive than a donation from a Colombian drug lord. This matter is made even more complicated by the values of some religious organizations. Some religious groups believe that charitable donations are a way for people to ask for forgiveness for their sins—a kind of modern-day version of the medieval indulgence. After all, if charity is a means for making us better people, why deny this opportunity to criminals? The answer here lies in the moral due diligence of forgiveness. Forgiveness requires more than giving to charity. It requires that a person change. If the drug lord admits he is wrong, asks for forgiveness, and goes out of the drug business, his donation to a drug rehabilitation program may be acceptable, although the charity might still face public relations problems.

The Road to Hell: Still Paved with Good Intentions

There are moral issues associated not only with how nonprofits raise money but also with how they reach their goals. The drive in the nonprofit sector to alleviate the suffering of disadvantaged people can be just as strong as the drive in business to earn profits and beat the competition. Just as businesses can be blinded by their desire for profit, nonprofits can be blinded by their desire to aid others. In both cases, the end results can be disastrous. Take, for instance, the unfortunate case of the Swiss charity Christian Solidarity International. Its goal was to free an estimated two hundred thousand Dinka children who were enslaved in Sudan. The charity paid between $35 and $75 a head to free enslaved children. The unintended consequence of their actions was that they encouraged slaving by creating a market for it. Also, some clever Sudanese found that it paid to pretend that they were slaves so that they could make money getting freed. This deception made it difficult to identify the people who really needed help from those who were faking. The charity's intent and the means were not unethical in relation to what it could do to alleviate suffering in the short run, however, in the long run, the charity was inadvertently creating more suffering. All leaders, including those in nonprofits, operate in the context of long-term and short-term effects. The morality of their actions often looks different in the short run than in the long run. So if a nonprofit's goal is to care for the homeless or free slaves, the nonprofit must ensure that it pursues these goals in ways that do not increase homelessness and slavery. Here again the issue is the consistency of means and ends. While some nonprofits concern themselves with caring for immediate needs, others are concerned with eradicating those needs. For example, a soup kitchen feeds the homeless but does not work to get rid of homelessness. There is nothing wrong with this as long as meeting immediate need does not exacerbate the problem, as was the case of the Swiss charity.

Blinding Self-Righteousness

One of the reasons that there has been a push to make nonprofits more like for-profits is so that they will be run more efficiently. Sometimes when a group is "doing God's work," the prevailing belief is that it does not need to have the same control systems, transparency, and checks and balances that other organizations have. Religious groups are often prone to this mind-set. Consider the initial response of the Catholic Church hierarchy to accusations of sexual abuse of parishioners by priests. Church leaders still held the medieval view that they could play by different rules than the rest of society, in part because they were "doing God's work."

Leaders sometimes become so impassioned about their cause that they forget what they have learned in other areas of life or fail to learn or get the expertise they need to do their job. This is as true today as it was in the past. The story of Magellan is one such case. Magellan convinced King Carlos of Spain that he knew of a passage across South America that would provide a shorter route to the Spice Islands. Magellan thought there was a strait across South America through the Río de la Plata. When he arrived there, however, he discovered that there was no water route across South America. Magellan then led his three ships down the coast to the treacherous Tierra del Fuego and then on the 12,600-mile journey across the Pacific Ocean to the Philippines. There, having become the first navigator to circumvent the globe, he took up the Spanish cause of spreading Christianity. He began baptizing native leaders and gaining their allegiance to Spain. This meant that the enemies of a baptized leader were also the enemies of Spain. Magellan's religious fervor became so great that he began to think that he could perform miracles. His men tried to set him straight, but he would not listen.

Magellan took up the cause of a baptized chief in an unnecessary battle against an unbaptized chief on the island of Mactan. He invited other chieftains to watch the battle from a distance so that he could prove the superiority of Christians. The historian William Manchester (1993) describes the event this way: "Now in late April of 1521, on the eve of this wholly unnecessary battle, Magellan was everything he had never been. He had never before been reckless, impudent, careless, or forgetful of the tactical lessons he had learned during Portuguese operations in East Africa, India, Morocco, and Malaya. But he had not been a soldier of Christ then" (p. 276). Believing that he was protected by divine intervention, Magellan failed to get information about the tides prior to attacking the island. He did not know that Mactan had a reef around it that at low tide would not allow his ships to get close enough to provide covering fire. He also took with him not his seasoned marines but rather a ragtag group of cooks and other apprentices who were willing to follow him into this pointless encounter. The battle was a disaster. Magellan, one of the greatest navigators in the world, met his demise waist deep in water, burdened by heavy armor, and unprotected by his ships, which were helplessly anchored outside of the reef, too far from shore to provide him with cover. All because he thought human planning was not necessary when God is on your side.

The story of Magellan shows us how brilliant leaders can believe so much in themselves and the moral rightness of their goals that they begin to think that they don't need to take all the mundane precautions other people take to achieve their goals. This case is a dramatic way to think about the mistakes nonprofit leaders have made in the past, such as having earnest but unqualified volunteers keep the books or assuming that while providing meals for the homeless, it was not necessary to follow standard health procedures in the kitchen. Not only are nonprofit leaders subject to the same moral rules as everyone else, but they are also subject to the same standards of transparency, diligence, and care. Leaders have a moral obligation to consult with experts, get their facts straight, and do careful planning. The line between being stupid or incompetent and being unethical is sometimes very thin (Ciulla, 2001).

The Moral Challenge of Success

The cleavage between the personal morality of leaders and the morality of what leaders do on the job becomes all the more intense when one throws power into the equation. Power poses one of the distinctive ethical challenges to leadership. It does not always corrupt, but it creates temptations that leaders must understand and overcome. From the biblical story of King David and Bathsheba to the sex scandal of President Bill Clinton, we know that leaders face temptations that lead them astray (Ludwig and Longenecker, 1993). Often it is the successful leaders who fall the hardest. In the case of Magellan, King David, and President Clinton, the very qualities that made them exceptional, such as self-confidence and charisma, are the ones that led to their ultimate failure. Successful leaders have control over people and resources, and on a day-to-day basis, they usually work without supervision. Sometimes leaders become isolated from colleagues, spouses, and friends because of their position or because they put in long hours. Without contact with a variety of people, leaders may lose perspective on their work and themselves. Power and success cause some otherwise good people to lose their focus as leaders. They then abuse their power and influence by using these advantages to pursue things that are unrelated to their work. King David, for example pursues and seduces Bathsheba rather than paying attention to the war he is fighting; President

Clinton dallies with an intern when he should be attending to the affairs of state; and Magellan drowns because he has failed to check the tides.

In almost every famous scandal involving leaders, the cover-up is worse than the crime. It is in the cover-up that we usually see the most egregious abuse of a leader's power. King David tried to cover up his adultery by having Bathsheba's husband killed; Clinton lied to the nation about his affair. In both cases, their adulteries were moral failures as humans, but the cover-ups—murder and lying to the public on TV—were moral failures as leaders. Some people find it easier to forgive moral weaknesses in ordinary humans than to forgive such weaknesses in leaders. The distinction between the person and the leader is fuzzy, and it disappears quickly when we consider the issue of trust. Trust is the glue that unites the public and private morality of a leader. Although leaders' private behavior may be unrelated to their public behavior, once personal ethical lapses become public knowledge, they sow doubt in people's minds. Doubt erodes the delicate fabric of trust. When the trust of followers and colleagues wears thin, leaders find it more and more difficult to be effective. We entrust leaders with power, and most of us get nervous when we discover that they have not used it in the right way for the right things.

The Dangers of Acting Like For-Profit Leaders

One of the biggest scandals in the nonprofit world was the case of United Way of America (UWA) President William Aramony. Aramony was convicted of defrauding the UWA out of more than $1 million to support his lavish lifestyle and was consequently sentenced to seven years in prison. He was a very successful leader who in twenty-two years as head of the UWA not only transformed the national-level organization and led the transformation of local United Ways but also transformed the way Americans gave to charity through payroll deductions. In 1990 alone, the nationwide United Way system (of which the United Way of America is the national organization) raised $3.1 billion, a far cry from the $700,000 it brought in when he became head of the UWA. Friends and coworkers described Aramony as "a brilliant and creative man with boundless energy." Colleagues also said he exercised power capriciously and was "domineering and unorthodox" (Shepherd, 1992). Newspaper accounts focused on his $369,000 salary, his apartment in New York, his fondness for limos, his trips on the Concord, and his young girlfriends.

On the surface, this scandal looks like a case of arrogance, abuse of power, greed, and excess. However, the case also offers insight into the difference between what the public expects from nonprofit leaders versus business leaders. It highlights the potential dangers of treating the two the same. Some of the things Aramony did were egregiously wrong and illegal, such as using United Way of America funds to pay for girlfriends to travel with him. Other things that the press seized on were not illegal but tell us something about our expectations of nonprofit leaders.

In a 1992 article defending Aramony, Joseph Finder argues that if Aramony had been the CEO of a corporation, the press would not have crucified him for his "lavish" lifestyle. Finder notes that Aramony brought in huge sums of money for the organization and deserved and received a pay raise every year for his success. He points out that the New York condo was used by United Way officials and was cost effective, given the price of hotels in New York. According to Finder, the same was true for his limousine, which in Aramony's case was not a stretch limo, but a Ford sedan. Finder asserts that anyone with a number of back-to-back appointments in New York knows that it's cheaper and more efficient to have a car and driver at one's disposal. (Some observers might argue that it is not cheaper and that if the driver has to circle the block, it's not as easy to find a hired car as it is to find a cab.) Finder goes on to say that given Aramony's frantic travel schedule, flying first class helped conserve his energy so that he could be alert at meetings.

So what is wrong with this picture? Finder thinks the press treated Aramony unfairly. He states that Aramony's lavish lifestyle was simply "overhead" and that the problem was not that it was wrong but that it "looked bad." It looked bad because, as mentioned earlier, no one wants the money one gives to the needy to pay for Aramony's hired car in New York. Nonprofits struggle with the problem of overhead all the time. Donors want to give to the cause, but they don't want to pay the charity's electric bill. Then again, an electric bill is necessary in a way that a limo is not.

One might wonder why the board didn't notice that the condo, limos, and first-class plane tickets "looked bad" even if they were "overhead." The answer becomes pretty clear when you look at who was on the board. The United Way of America had many powerful board members from the business community, individuals like John Akers, who was then CEO of IBM. The UWA's board treated Aramony like the CEO of a business. Board members weren't about to quibble about perks that they themselves had, especially when Aramony was bringing in money for the organization. An *Economist* article about the overcompensation of executives offers an interesting insight ("Is Greed Good?" 2002). In it, a top American CEO says, "The chairman of your board's compensation committee should always be richer and older than you. That way, he won't get jealous when you make your fortune." Another CEO cited in the article provoked groans at a meeting when he confessed that he once made the mistake of putting an underpaid college professor on his board. Nonprofit boards and leaders need to understand when the standards of the business world apply to a nonprofit and its leader and when they do not.

Aramony's board and his salary were not out of line with those of other large foundations. Most observers would agree that there is something unfair about not rewarding someone who works hard and raises huge sums of money for the needy. So is this, as Finder says, simply a matter of taste and not ethics? Are we being unfair when we think that nonprofit leaders should not be paid well? If you look at it from a business standpoint, the answer is yes to both. However, as mentioned earlier, there is something else going on in a charity. Giving consists of a complex set of moral and social assumptions. People who lead nonprofits not only represent the values of the organization but also must model those values in their behavior. Hence it is not that nonprofit leaders have to starve, but they have to show that they believe so much in what they are doing that others should too. In other words, if you are Ongka asking others for their pigs, you have to be willing give up some of your own pigs too.

Conclusion

Most nonprofit leaders are dedicated to their cause and are not in their line of work for money. Like all leaders, they are subject to the pitfalls of power and influence mentioned earlier, and once in a while, someone like William Aramony comes along. Perhaps some of the greatest ethical challenges of nonprofit leaders arise from their commitment to their cause. They may forget to align personal behavior with the values of the organization. They face the danger of being blinded by the rightness of their cause to the point of either having the ends justify the means or forgetting that they too are subject to certain standards of quality and obligations of careful planning in pursuing their goals. We ask a lot of nonprofit leaders. We want them to be as productive and competent as corporate CEOs, but we also want them to be people who are strongly motivated by the intrinsic rewards of the job and not by money. This does not mean that they should be overworked and underpaid, but it does mean that the minute they lose sight of why they chose their work, they stand to lose their ability to influence the organization. All leaders are required to make sacrifices, but the sacrifices of leaders of nonprofit organizations are somewhat different from those in the for-profit sector. That is why we are all inspired and encouraged by those who are not only willing to lead nonprofits but do it well.

References

Ammons, D. "Eyman: I Took Money, Lied About It." *Seattle Times,* February 5, 2002, p. 1.

Ciulla, J. "The Importance of Leadership in Shaping Business Values." *Long Range Planning,* 1999, *32,* 166–172.

Ciulla, J. "Carving Leaders from the Warped Wood of Humanity." *Canadian Journal of Administrative Science,* 2001, *18,* 313–319.

Finder, J. "Charity Case: Why the United Way Lost Its Head." *New Republic,* May 4, 1992, p. 11.

Hitchens, C. *Missionary Position: Mother Teresa in Theory and Practice.* London: Verso, 1997.

"Is Greed Good?" *Economist,* May 18, 2002, p. 21.

Kant, I. *Grounding for the Metaphysics of Morals* (J. W. Ellington, trans.). (3rd ed.) Indianapolis, Ind.: Hackett, 1993.

Kanungo, R., and Mendonca, M. *The Ethical Dimensions of Leadership.* Thousand Oaks, Calif.: Sage, 1996.

Ludwig, D., and Longenecker, C. "The Bathsheba Syndrome: The Ethical Failure of Successful Leaders." *Journal of Business Ethics,* 1993, *12,* 265–273.

Manchester, W. *A World Lit Only by Fire.* New York: Little, Brown, 1993.

Nagel, T. *The Possibility of Altruism.* Oxford: Clarendon Press, 1970.

Nairn, C. (director/producer). *The Kawelka: Ongka's Big Moka.* Film featuring anthropologist Andrew Strathern. London: Granada Production, 1989.

Ozinga, J. R. *Altruism.* Westport, Conn.: Praeger, 1999.

Shepherd, C. E. "Perks, Privileges, and Power in a Nonprofit World." *Washington Post,* February 16, 1992, p. 1.

Simmel, G. *The Philosophy of Money* (T. Bottomore and D. Frisby, trans.). Boston: Routledge, 1978.

Strom, S. "Red Cross to Open Its Books on Aid." *New York Times,* June 5, 2002, p.1.

Yukl, G. *Leadership in Organizations.* (3rd ed.) Upper Saddle River, N.J.: Prentice Hall, 1994.

CHAPTER SEVEN

MANAGERIAL PAY IN NONPROFIT
AND FOR-PROFIT ORGANIZATIONS

Kevin F. Hallock

Managerial pay is a controversial and often studied subject in economics, sociology, accounting, finance, and human resource management. In fact, relative to the number of people who are actually top managers, this subject garners an incredible amount of attention. One of the reasons may be simply that the data are available. This has been true for managers in for-profit firms for decades, but only recently have data become available to permit the study of managerial compensation in the nonprofit sector. In this chapter, I compare how top managers in the for-profit and nonprofit sectors are paid using two unique panel data sets covering the years 1992 through 1998.

First I provide some simple background on the literature on managerial pay in for-profit firms. I then explore some of the institutional differences between the nonprofit and for-profit sectors and consider whether these differences should lead us to expect that managers in the two sectors might be paid differently. Next, I examine pay gaps between the for-profit and nonprofit sectors more generally and detail several hypotheses that have been widely discussed for differences in pay and describe how they can be applied to top managers as well.

In the main part of the chapter, I describe the data sources and explain how managers are actually paid in the two sectors. For the nonprofit sector, I use data from the Internal Revenue Service Form 990, which reports details of the compensation of top managers and a host of financial and accounting characteristics for each organization with at least $25,000 in net revenue. For the for-profit sector, I use a sample of over fifteen hundred firms from Standard & Poor's EXECUCOMP database. This set of data uses filings to the Securities and Exchange Commission to report on the compensation of top managers as well as accounting and financial information for publicly traded firms.

I note, first, that the relationship between firm size and managerial pay is strong in data from both sectors. Second, in both sectors, there is substantial diversity across industries on average pay rates for top managers. Third, I suggest some simple theoretical reasons for differences in pay across the sectors. Fourth, I provide a brief overview of differences in managerial pay by gender in both sectors. Finally, I document that although managers in nonprofits are paid substantially less than managers in for-profit organizations (especially when stock options are taken into account), this is largely due to organization size. When for-profits and nonprofits of similar asset size are compared, the average salary and bonus differences across sectors are not large for the samples investigated here. On the other hand, stock options (which are not available to leaders of nonprofits) nearly double the compensation of the leaders of for-profit firms. I end the chapter with a summary, some concluding comments, some lessons learned, and possible avenues for future research.

Overview of Managerial Pay

The study of managerial pay has focused almost exclusively on the for-profit sector. Only recently has there been interest in managerial compensation in nonprofit organizations. This, like many issues in labor economics, may be driven by the fact that data on managerial pay in the for-profit sector have been available for some time, whereas comparable data for nonprofits have only recently become available. There are at least three main reasons why top-managerial pay has received so much attention in the past few decades. First, the agency theory literature, beginning in the 1970s and early 1980s (for example, Jensen and Meckling, 1976; Holmstrom, 1979; Grossman and Hart, 1983; Fama, 1980; Lazear and Rosen, 1981) set a theoretical foundation for the work. Second, the data on for-profit firms have been publicly available for some time and since 1992 have been organized in a standardized format. Third, since CEO pay in for-profit firms has increased so dramatically, it has garnered a great deal of public attention.

The theoretical work in the 1970s and increased data availability in the 1980s and 1990s cleared the way for a great deal of empirical work on the compensation of top managers of firms. The areas of empirical work could be categorized into several areas (see Hallock and Murphy, 1999, for a more detailed summary). I will only very briefly describe a few of these. Each of these areas has received substantial attention using data from for-profit organizations and almost none using data from nonprofits (with the exceptions of Oster, 1998, and Hallock, 2002a, 2002b). Perhaps each of the areas described here will gain further attention from the nonprofit sector in the coming years.

The relationship between executive pay and company performance has been widely studied for decades. Rosen (1992) provides an outstanding overview of the empirical and theoretical literature. I will highlight several other publications in this literature. Murphy (1985) examines the relationship between executive compensation and firm financial performance (stock returns) using a longitudinal sample of CEOs from 1964 to 1981. Although most previous cross-sectional studies showed a weak relationship between managerial pay and company performance, Murphy carefully exploited the panel nature of the data to show that there was a substantial link.

In another important contribution to this literature, Jensen and Murphy (1990) consider whether the relation between CEO pay and stock price performance is strong enough to provide important incentives to managers. After a lengthy empirical analysis, they conclude that the pay-to-performance sensitivity is too low to provide important incentives. Hall and Liebman (1998) collect details on stock options and document an enormous increase in the receipt of options by executives in the 1980s and 1990s but also show that when options are valued as compensation at the time they are granted, there is a strong relationship between managerial pay and firm financial performance.

Antle and Smith (1986) and Gibbons and Murphy (1990) study relative performance evaluation for CEOs. They are interested in whether managers are paid for absolute performance (for example, how well their firm alone performs) or for how well their firm performs relative to a set of peer firms, which could be defined as those in the same industry or as the market as a whole. There seems to be some evidence (Gibbons and Murphy, 1990) that managers are paid for relative performance.

Another area in executive pay that has received some attention in recent decades is CEO turnover. Among the findings (Warner, Watts, and Wruck, 1988; Weisbach, 1988) is that top managers of firms are much more likely to turn over when their firms perform relatively poorly. There is also substantial new work in the area of international CEO compensation (for example, Conyon and Murphy, 2000).

Institutional Differences Between the For-Profit and Nonprofit Sectors That May Matter for Compensation

Obviously, nonprofit organizations do not have returns to shareholders or some other obvious "bottom line" by which to judge their managers (Hallock, 2002b). However, that does not mean that they should necessarily be paid a salary that is not in any way based on performance. In the literature on CEO pay and firm performance, most analysts use relatively few performance measures to test how well the top manager is doing. Among these measures are stock return and the change in market value of the firm (Murphy, 1985; Jensen and Murphy, 1990). Since nonprofits are not owned by shareholders, there is no stock price or "value" of the charities in this sense. Also, obviously the objectives of nonprofits are remarkably diverse. They may include such missions as serving a particular group or discovering the cure for a disease. It is therefore quite difficult to focus on a single particular objective of nonprofits generally. Consequently, the outcome of interest in nonprofits is likely to be much more diverse than for commercial firms. In a series of publications (for example, Steinberg, 1990a, 1990b; Weisbrod, 1989), incentive compensation for employees in nonprofits is examined mostly from a theoretical point of view. We know that designing incentive compensation plans in for-profit firms is difficult (Lazear, 1995). However, it may be more difficult to measure the performance of managers in nonprofits because these organizations are likely to be striving to create something much different from returns to shareholders. One feature that makes nonprofits distinct from for-profit organizations is that "a nonprofit organization is, in essence, an organization that is barred from distributing its net earnings, if any, to individuals who exercise control over it, such as members, officers, directors, or trustees" (Hansmann, 1980, p. 838). However, this does not mean that nonprofit organizations cannot make profits in a technical sense but rather that "it is only the distribution of profits that is prohibited" (p. 838). This "nondistribution constraint" does not imply, however, that employee pay cannot be based on incentives (Steinberg, 1990b).

A classic example of how difficult it is to measure output for managers in the nonprofit world is that of a manager of a nursing home (Weisbrod and Schlesinger, 1986). A nursing home manager's pay could be based on the profits he or she accrues, but this gives incentives to provide lower-quality care to the patients. The output that the board of the nursing home seeks (say, "trustworthiness") is difficult to observe. If we tried to measure trustworthiness, we could do it using an easy-to-observe measure such as the mortality rate. However, this might induce management to select patients who are mostly healthy, which is, no doubt, at odds with the mission of the board.

Clearly, studying incentive compensation in for-profit firms is extremely difficult. It may be even more difficult in nonprofits. Nevertheless, the attention paid to managerial pay in nonprofits is increasing, and as mentioned previously, nonprofit boards must now document how pay is determined ("Taxpayer Bill of Rights 2," 1996). Given the vast array of information available for each nonprofit and the fact that more nonprofits seem to be basing pay on incentives, there are potential ways to measure how well the charity is performing. Two will be examined in this chapter. One is the size of the organization. It may be that managers are given extra compensation for "growing the organization." Since the single largest predictor of CEO pay in the for-profit sector is the size of the organization, this may make sense in the nonprofit sector as well. The other issue investigated here is the fraction of total expenses that is spent on program services (Hallock, 2002b).

Conceptual Explanations for Differences in Pay Between Nonprofit and For-Profit Organizations

There are several conceptual explanations for differences in compensation between the for-profit and nonprofit sectors. They were first elaborated to apply to all nonprofit and for-profit workers but have been found to work equally well with top managers. The first is the so-called labor donations hypothesis, first introduced by Preston (1989); the second, what I will refer to as "screening," was first discussed in terms of nonprofits by Hansmann (1980); the third is the well-known labor economic idea of compensating differentials; and the final one is what I will refer to as differences in returns to characteristics, or ability bias (Hallock, 2000).

The idea of labor donations is made clear by Preston (1989). The basic idea is that workers may be willing to trade lower wages for higher social benefits. Since workers value both wages and the social benefits they provide to the world, an organization that provides lots of social benefits can pay its workers, on average, less. The most extreme case of this is volunteering where "workers" are effectively donating back all of their wages to the organization to which they provide volunteer work. So one obvious reason why workers with similar characteristics are paid less in the nonprofit sector is that they are essentially giving back some of their wages to the cause for which they work.

Another potential reason for differences in compensation between the for-profit and nonprofit sectors has to do with Hansmann's application of "screening" (1980, 1996). In this simple model, Hansmann assumes that there are two types of workers. Some are simply greedy, and others are interested in both the quality of service they provide and money. He also assumes that both groups are of equal ability and have similar alternative work opportunities. For nonprofit organizations to be able to survive and provide the requisite levels of service, they must pay people less to work in the nonprofits. One way for consumers to be assured that they are receiving the quality of service they want is for the organizations to organize as nonprofits. If they do so, only people who value both money and service quality will volunteer to work for them. Therefore, by virtue of being set up the way they are, nonprofits may be able to attract precisely the kinds of employees they want to attract.

Another possible explanation for differences in compensation between the nonprofit and for-profit sectors may be compensating wage differentials (Rosen, 1974, 1986). Several authors (for example, Burbridge, 1994, and James and Rose-Ackerman, 1986) have suggested that one reason to expect lower wages in nonprofits stems from the amenities associated with nonprofit jobs that are not present in for-profit jobs. Some employees will prefer the combination of attractive amenities and lower pay in nonprofits to higher pay in for-profit firms. The classic example of compensating differentials is the risk of death: workers prefer safe (and lower-paying) jobs to risky (and higher-paying) jobs. Perhaps nonprofits provide amenities for their workers such as more pleasant work environments, greater job flexibility, more stable positions, and more control over the job.

Several of these explanations are interesting and potentially important conceptual reasons for differences in pay between the for-profit and nonprofit sectors. However, they are sometimes referred to as "residual arguments"—they make sense after careful attempts have been made to control for "other factors," but they are very difficult to prove. Omitted-variables bias is another possibility. Perhaps there is some third variable that is correlated with both nonprofit status and compensation. Labor economists sometimes call this "ability," but it is often intended to refer to organization, motivation, cognitive ability, or some other set of unmeasured characteristics. If this unmeasured effect is not taken into account when estimating the relationship between wages and nonprofit status, we may attribute too much of the wage gap to the nonprofit status and not to these unmeasured effects. Gooddeeris (1988), in a follow-up to Weisbrod (1983), considers selection issues in the nonprofit sector and finds them to be of some importance.

Evidence on Top Managerial Pay from Two Sectors

One of the main purposes of this chapter is to compare levels, types of pay, and compensation styles for top managers across the nonprofit and for-profit sectors (Hallock, 2002b). Therefore, the data I have used are carefully described here.

Data Description and Sample Characteristics

The data on the nonprofit sector are collected from Form 990 from the Internal Revenue Service (IRS). The data from the for-profit sector are collected from Standard & Poor's EXECUCOMP database. Both nonprofit organizations above a certain size and all publicly traded for-profit organizations must disclose financial information about themselves. The nonprofits must release information to the IRS and the for-profits to the Securities and Exchange Commission (SEC). In both cases, in addition to basic financial information, details of the compensation of the five highest-paid employees must also be disclosed.

The data for the nonprofit organizations come from the Internal Revenue Service Form 990 for the years 1992–1998. The IRS data contain useful information on all officers and directors of the nonprofits as well as the five highest-paid nonofficer, director, or trustee employees (I will refer to these as "employees" throughout). The IRS data contain three pieces of information on each officer, director, or other "key" employee. A key employee is defined by the IRS as "any person having responsibilities or power similar to officers, directors, or trustees. The term includes the chief management and administrative officials of an organization (such as an executive director or chancellor) but does not include the heads of separate departments or smaller units within an organization" (Internal Revenue Service, 2002, p. 26). For each of these officers, I have information on the three components of their compensation summarized in Table 7.1. I know the base compensation including "salary, fees, bonuses, and severance payments paid" (p. 26). The mean for this variable over all years in the sample (in real 2002 dollars) is $146,587. The median is lower ($114,722), since some organizations pay their top people quite a bit more, which draws up the mean but not the median. I also have information on contributions to employee benefit plans and deferred compensation including medical and life insurance. The average value of this over all years of the sample is $15,747 (median, $7,034). Finally, I have information on "expense allowances or reimbursements that the recipients must report as income on their own separate income tax returns. These include the value of housing or cars provided by the organization" (p. 26). The mean for this category is $3,142. The average of the sum of all three categories is $165,476 (median, $127,239) over the sample period. The total compensation numbers for the top officer remained relatively constant from 1992 to 1998, as can be seen in the table.

The bottom panel of Table 7.1 reports some of the financial and potential "performance" measures for these nonprofit organizations. For example, the average net ending assets is $64.3 million, and the median is $17.8 million. This number increased over the sample period, except for a curious large drop in 1997. The sum of government grants, direct public support, and indirect public support is also displayed in the table. The average is just under $7.9 million, with a median of almost $1.1 million.

Table 7.1 also shows the percentage of total expenses that are spent on program services. This can be considered a measure of what fraction of spending is put toward programs for those in need. In fact, the Council of Better Business Bureaus' *Wise Giving Alliance Standards for Charitable Accountability* state (in Standard 8) that a charity must "spend at least 65 percent of its total expenses on program activities" (Council of Better Business Bureaus, 2003). For the sample of nonprofits

TABLE 7.1. SUMMARY STATISTICS FOR TOP MANAGERS OF NONPROFITS.

	All Years	1992	1993	1994	1995	1996	1997	1998
Compensation ($)								
Salary + bonus	146,587 (1,117) [114,722]	143,221 (2,024) [116,521]	151,822 (6,528) [117,295]	150,249 (2,023) [121,146]	148,072 (1,851) [118,451]	144,871 (1,601) [114,516]	143,940 (2,960) [106,636]	144,973 (1,681) [108,260]
Benefits	15,747 (245) [7,034]	13,247 (365) [5,234]	14,790 (523) [6,712]	15,235 (419) [7,375]	16,754 (556) [7,545]	16,643 (737) [7,701]	16,491 (1,018) [6,474]	16,216 (448) [7,166]
Expenses	3,142 (92) [0]	3,095 (195) [0]	3,150 (302) [0]	3,679 (315) [0]	3,169 (214) [0]	3,137 (213) [0]	2,964 (229) [0]	2,905 (223) [0]
Total compensation	165,476 (1,194) [127,239]	159,563 (2,232) [129,442]	169,762 (6,622) [129,716]	169,163 (2,260) [135,908]	167,995 (2,107) [131,609]	164,652 (1,951) [128,081]	163,395 (3,295) [117,738]	164,094 (1,944) [120,082]
Organization Characteristics								
Annual assets ($ thousands)	64,301 (1,511) [17,830]	59,507 (3,282) [18,435]	59,015 (3,104) [17,684]	61,255 (3,285) [18,598]	68,538 (4,825) [18,318]	71,078 (4,899) [18,038]	50,804 (1,152) [16,460]	76,517 (4,914) [16,526]
Program expenses (% of total expenses)	81.5 (0.1) [84.6]	81.6 (0.2) [85.0]	81.9 (0.2) [85.1]	81.9 (0.2) [85.2]	81.6 (0.2) [84.8]	81.3 (0.2) [84.3]	81.2 (0.2) [84.0]	81.3 (0.2) [84.1]
Grants + direct and indirect public support ($ thousands)	7,874 (161) [1,059]	7,926 (500) [959]	7,891 (468) [992]	8,291 (478) [1,089]	8,015 (443) [1,095]	8,103 (411) [1,173]	6,404 (257) [976]	8,535 (425) [1,078]
N	47,699	5,582	6,084	6,150	6,817	7,516	7,471	8,079

Source: Internal Revenue Service, Form 990 for individual organizations, 1992–1998.

Notes: Standard errors are in parentheses. Medians are in brackets. All financial numbers are in 1998 dollars.

for which I have data, the average share of expenses spent on program services is 81.5 percent. This number has declined slightly over time.

For the for-profit firms, I used data from Standard & Poor's EXECUCOMP database (see Table 7.2). The data contain specific financial and compensation information for all firms in the Standard & Poor's 500, the Standard & Poor's Midcap 400, and the Standard & Poor's Smallcap 600. Like the data for nonprofit organizations, these data are for the seven-year period 1992–1998. All financial and compensation data are adjusted to real 1998 dollars. There are 9,599 firm-year observations in the data.

EXECUCOMP is the standard in executive compensation research. Prior to the construction of EXECUCOMP, researchers who wished to study executive compensation had to compile their own data sets. EXECUCOMP is now used by most researchers in the field.

A problem for some of the research on executive compensation is the question of what to do about stock options. Options are often given to executives in blocks every few years, and previous research often focused on the value of options when they were exercised, not when they were granted. However, the total compensation figures I use in this chapter include not only salaries, bonuses, and "other" compensation but also the value of stock options granted in a particular year as valued by the Black and Scholes (1973) option-pricing formula. This measure of total compensation gives a much more accurate view of the actual compensation managers receive in a particular year.

Comparing Tables 7.1 and 7.2, it is immediately clear that managers in this sample of for-profit firms earn considerably more than managers in the sample of nonprofits. The average real (1998) salary over all years in the sample is $584,754 (median, $528,100). The average bonus is very similar, with a mean of $566,574 and a median of $304,769. The median is higher than the mean in this case, no doubt, because of the large number of managers with a zero bonus in a given year. The average "total compensation" for this group of CEOs is $3,189,836, with a median of $1,634,071. The mean is higher here since some managers have extremely large values of option grants in a given year, and this increases the mean substantially relative to the median.

It is also clear from Table 7.2 that while average (and even median) salaries declined somewhat during the 1990s, the total compensation packages for CEOs of these firms increased dramatically from $2.7 million in 1992 to more than $4.5 million in 1998. This is, in large part, due to the dramatic increase in the value of stock options granted to CEOs and other top managers over this period (see Hall and Liebman, 1998).

The bottom part of Table 7.2 presents some information on some simple financial characteristics of firms over the sample period. The average market value (total number of shares outstanding times the year-end price of a share) over the

TABLE 7.2. SUMMARY STATISTICS FOR TOP MANAGERS OF FOR-PROFIT FIRMS.

	All Years	1992	1993	1994	1995	1996	1997	1998
Compensation ($)								
Salary	584,754 (3,210) [528,100]	745,532 (17,728) [720,715]	613,200 (9,313) [564,014]	566,852 (7,918) [499,169]	570,010 (81,00) [505,097]	573,455 (7,830) [519,439]	575,211 (7,620) [527,305]	581,249 (7,408) [525,000]
Bonus	566,574 (16,579) [304,769]	579,126 (40,284) [435,044]	485,931 (27,235) [279,998]	482,703 (27,528) [274,966]	528,420 (48,433) [271,445]	623,019 (69,039) [311,664]	635,640 (28,931) [352,173]	608,155 (25,570) [321,600]
Salary + bonus	1,151,328 (17,555) [846,021]	1,324,658 (47,923) [1,158,076]	1,099,131 (30,956) [838,385]	1,049,555 (30,813) [776,505]	1,098,430 (50,399) [802,165]	1,196,473 (70,448) [836,783]	1,210,851 (32,556) [893,136]	1,189,404 (29,611) [856,250]
Total compensation	3,189,836 (93,737) [1,634,071]	2,703,545 (136,425) [2,008,583]	2,312,937 (90,924) [1,420,458]	2,369,908 (82,331) [1,380,489]	2,448,707 (99,847) [1,406,411]	3,280,915 (193,251) [1,661,505]	3,908,518 (189,806) [1,951,982]	4,520,212 (435,413) [1,971,105]
Firm Characteristics ($ thousands)								
Market value	4,642,320 (133,708) [1,158,297]	7,485,443 (604,427) [4,093,207]	3,897,954 (235,094) [1,400,229]	2,886,696 (177,913) [806,638]	3,692,669 (238,454) [946,913]	4,246,478 (273,213) [1,058,674]	5,514,892 (364,351) [1,322,248]	6,523,104 (500,725) [1,186,692]
Annual assets	8,370,944 (295,995) [1,276,819]	17,200,000 (1,723,930) [5,684,088]	8,787,973 (744,728) [1,654,892]	7,051,129 (587,814) [1,015,548]	8,370,944 (646,792) [1,049,545]	7,712,205 (670,613) [1,142,722]	8,468,711 (763,167) [1,217,625]	8,983,476 (897,435) [1,283,376]
Annual sales	3,775,554 (99,791) [1,103,049]	7,637,572 (704,288) [3,820,364]	4,026,606 (286,545) [1,358,708]	3,282,321 (231,529) [891,643]	7,234,817 (240,590) [947,577]	3,557,213 (233,792) [1,010,621]	3,763,705 (239,698) [1,075,780]	3,755,383 (231,401) [1,101,309]
N	9,599	362	1,145	1,531	1,581	1,621	1,650	1,709

Source: Standard & Poor's EXECUCOMP database.

Notes: Standard errors are in parentheses. Medians are in brackets. All financial figures are in 1998 dollars.

sample period is $4.64 billion. The median is obviously much smaller since some firms are extremely large and make the mean higher than the median. Assets for these firms are, on average, $8.37 billion (median, $1.28 billion), and average annual sales are $3.78 billion (median, $1.10 billion). So these are quite large firms in the United States. However, given the difference between the means and the medians and the size of the standard errors, there is quite a bit of variability in the size of these firms.

Differences by Industry in the Two Sectors

There are quite substantial differences in how managers are paid and in the makeup of the organizations across industries in both the nonprofit sample and the for-profit sample. In fact, in some industries, the average compensation is more than three times that in other industries.

Separating organizations into "industries" is rather clear-cut and straightforward in the for-profit sector but is more controversial in the nonprofit sector. I will use the National Taxonomy of Exempt Entities (NTEE) to classify the nonprofit organizations into separate groups (Stevenson, Pollack, and Lampkin, 1997; Hodgkinson, 1990; Hodgkinson and Toppe, 1991; Grønbjerg, 1994; Turner, Nygren, and Bowen, 1992). The NTEE classifies organizations into a variety of subgroups. For the purposes of this chapter, I have used the twenty-six "major NTEE groups" listed in Table 7.3. It is clear that the nonprofit organizations studied here are diverse. The organizations in the "medical research" group are without a doubt performing quite different tasks than those in the "religion-related, spiritual development" group. Although each organization represented in Table 7.3 is a nonprofit, there may be for-profit organizations that compete for employees and other staff with organizations in this group of nonprofits. Using these data from 1992–1998, the lowest industry median top officer compensation is $66,385, in the category "housing, shelter," and the highest is in "science and technology research institutions, services."

Table 7.3 also lists a set of medians of other important characteristics for each industry. The median assets vary from $2.2 million to $46.7 million. The variation in the percentage of total expenses spent on program services varies, but all industries are in the range of 75–95 percent. Obviously, some industries have a lot more organizations in them than others; the largest is "health—general and rehabilitative." This may suggest that many nonprofit hospitals are in the sample, and the data indicate that these are highly paid managers. One potential reason for this could be that the nonprofit organizations in this industry are competing with (potentially higher-paying) for-profit hospitals. (See Bertrand, Hallock, and Arnould, 2003, and Brickley and Van Horn, 2002, for more details on compensation for managers in nonprofit hospitals.)

TABLE 7.3. MEDIAN COMPENSATION AND ORGANIZATIONAL STATISTICS BY NONPROFIT "INDUSTRY."

NTEE "Industry" Classification	Top Officer or Director Total Compensation ($)	Top Other Employee Total Compensation ($)	Assets ($ thousands)	Program Expenses (% of total expenses)	Grants + Direct and Indirect Public Support ($)	Number of Organizations
1. Arts, culture, and humanities	113,511	66,014	15,724	75	2,402	3,092
2. Educational institutions and related activities	134,308	84,200	24,482	83	3,432	10,754
3. Environmental quality, protection, and beautification	93,277	61,366	14,713	76	1,842	658
4. Animal-related	112,325	69,976	15,043	77	2,885	418
5. Health—general and rehabilitative	176,548	139,148	29,242	87	264	16,165
6. Mental health, crisis prevention	105,566	86,968	46,700	85	993	923
7. Disease, disorders, medical disciplines	140,244	99,904	11,872	80	1,786	588
8. Medical research	146,858	110,009	15,949	84	3,644	559
9. Crime, legal-related	94,867	24,017	3,455	85	1,580	235
10. Employment, job-related	103,377	57,638	3,523	87	424	455
11. Food, agriculture, and nutrition	71,257	46,874	3,977	89	2,943	130
12. Housing, shelter	66,385	32,012	2,606	87	348	859
13. Public safety, disaster preparedness, and relief	106,860	56,631	2,227	75	218	65
14. Recreation, sports, leisure, athletics	99,373	58,280	7,680	83	575	436
15. Youth development	87,057	32,412	4,780	83	904	641
16. Human services: Multipurpose and other	93,041	61,184	6,686	86	917	5,444

TABLE 7.3. continued.

NTEE "Industry" Classification	Top Officer or Director Total Compensation ($)	Top Other Employee Total Compensation ($)	Assets ($ thousands)	Program Expenses (% of total expenses)	Grants + Direct and Indirect Public Support ($)	Number of Organizations
17. International, foreign affairs, and national security	141,450	91,255	14,159	82	11,708	584
18. Civil rights, social action, advocacy	111,622	94,730	9,685	76	6,656	85
19. Community improvement, capacity building	90,947	59,681	6,433	86	1,094	631
20. Philanthropy, volunteerism, and grantmaking foundations	92,244	40,068	19,624	87	3,012	2,794
21. Science and technology research institutes, services	192,680	129,828	19,868	84	1,407	570
22. Social science research institutes, services	184,336	103,277	16,708	81	2,524	129
23. Public, society benefit: Multipurpose and other	136,200	98,325	17,389	82	1,450	287
24. Religion-related, spiritual development	57,776	34,778	5,649	82	421	665
25. Mutual membership benefit organizations	44,012	42,895	15,649	95	0	362
26. Other	94,754	59,785	13,525	89	139	169

Source: Internal Revenue Service, Form 990 for individual organizations, 1992–1998.

Table 7.4 repeats this analysis for the set of for-profit firms by organizing the firms into twelve broad industry categories according to the Standard Industrial Classification (SIC). No firms in the EXECUCOMP sample were assigned to the category "public administration" or "environmental quality and housing." Even among the for-profit firms, there is substantial variation in mean compensation from one industry to another.

It is no particular surprise that finance, insurance, and real estate has the highest median total compensation ($2,277,112). Agricultural production has the lowest at $1,256,575. Comparing the total compensation column with the salary and bonus column, it is easy to see that although salaries and bonuses don't vary much across industries, total compensation does. Market value, sales, and assets all vary similarly across these industries.

Relationship Between Organization Size and Managerial Pay

One of the most important predictors of managerial pay in the for-profit sector is the size of the organization (Rosen, 1992), and this has been documented extensively (see, for example, Murphy, 1985, 1999; Kostiuk, 1990). The same also holds true in nonprofit organizations. Oster (1998) documents a relationship between managerial pay and assets in five samples of between thirty-one and ninety-five observations. I also document this relationship using roughly thirty-two thousand observations of data from 1992–1996 (Hallock, 2002b). Here I will extend this work and show that there is a substantial relationship between the compensation of the top manager of an organization and the size of the organization, using data for both the nonprofit and for-profit sectors between 1992 and 1998.

Figure 7.1 is a plot for the nonprofit data of median compensation versus median assets by industry (this is done by industry because if it were done by organization, there would be 47,699 points in the figure). A strong positive correlation between the two is apparent. The numbers in the figure correspond to the twenty-six NTEE "industries" identified in Table 7.3. A similar plot for median compensation versus median assets by industries for the for-profit sample in presented in Figure 7.2. The numbers on this plot correspond to the SIC industry classification used in Table 7.4. Industries in categories 8 (finance, insurance, and real estate) and 12 (unclassified establishments) are *much* larger, in terms of median assets, than any of the other industries. It is clear from this figure that the strong relationship between firm size and managerial pay described by Rosen (1992) holds up in these data.

This same relationship between managerial pay and organization size can been seen in a simple regression framework. The virtues of using a regression framework to summarize this relationship are many. First, we can give a description of the idea with one simple number. Second, we can control for the effects of

TABLE 7.4. MEDIAN COMPENSATION AND FIRM STATISTICS BY INDUSTRY.

SIC Industry Category	CEO Total Compensation ($)	CEO Salary + Bonus ($)	Market Value ($)	Assets ($)	Sales ($)	Number of Organizations
1. Agricultural production	1,256,575	523,886	909,383	1,380,763	1,632,458	34
2. Mining	1,397,642	702,323	994,880	1,026,742	458,961	383
3. Construction	1,609,412	1,016,572	506,103	984,245	1,289,252	95
4. Manufacturing	1,682,713	860,894	1,040,102	900,814	1,011,925	4,347
5. Transportation and public utilities	1,164,683	743,319	1,789,681	3,263,305	1,632,270	1,274
6. Wholesale trade	1,394,246	850,297	613,669	918,978	2,387,519	321
7. Retail trade	1,429,881	779,159	781,374	724,199	1,367,933	830
8. Finance, insurance, and real estate	2,277,112	1,178,862	2,635,297	10,500,000	1,654,735	1,231
9. Services	1,692,720	681,447	908,703	612,915	576,578	1,030
10. Public administration[a]	—	—	—	—	—	—
11. Environmental quality and housing[a]	—	—	—	—	—	—
12. Unclassified establishments	3,467,830	1,661,451	4,481,481	6,302,650	82,723,284	54

Source: Standard & Poor's EXECUCOMP database, 1992–1998.

[a]No firms are assigned to this category.

FIGURE 7.1. MEDIAN TOTAL TOP-MANAGER COMPENSATION AND MEDIAN ASSETS BY INDUSTRY FOR NONPROFIT ORGANIZATIONS.

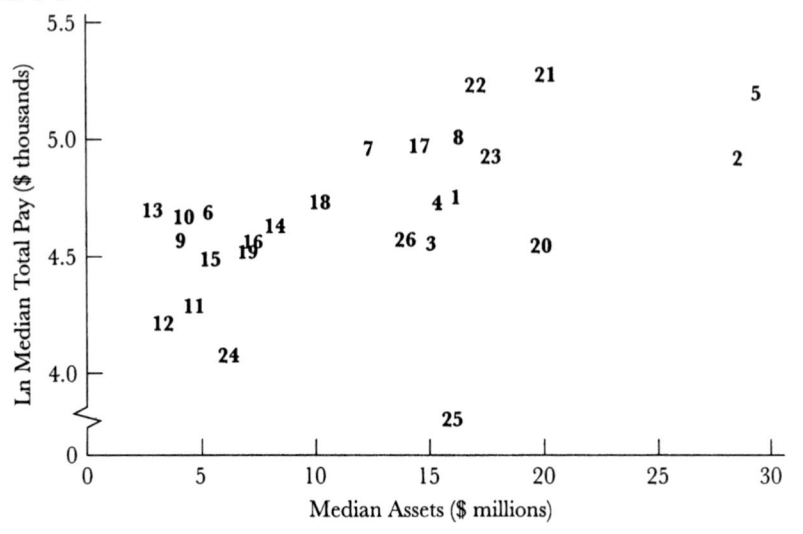

Source: Internal Revenue Service, Form 990 for individual organizations, 1992–1998.

Note: The numbers in the figure correspond to the "industry" numbers in Table 7.3.

time by using time indicators. Third, we can control for other characteristics of the organizations, such as their "industries" or even other unmeasured characteristics. The most basic of these specifications is at the top of Table 7.5. In column 1, the ln(total compensation of the top officer) is regressed on the ln(net ending assets) of the organization plus yearly time indicators to control for differences over time. The coefficient 0.229 suggests that as the assets increase by 10 percent, the average pay of the top manager increases by 2.29 percent.

Perhaps this relationship between the pay of the top manager and the size of the organization is due to unmeasured organization characteristics that are driving both the compensation and the size of the organization. One such possibility is the NTEE "industry" of the organization. Therefore, in column 2, the same analysis is repeated while controlling for the twenty-six NTEE indicator variables. The effect of ln(assets) is now smaller, 0.217, but is still significantly different from zero. Therefore, even when looking within industries, the organization size–managerial pay relationship holds up. Finally, we may imagine that different firms have unmeasured characteristics that we may want to consider. Column 3 then adds in 12,324 individual indicator variables, one for each distinct organization. The result, 0.059, indicates that when a firm gets larger (when its assets grow), the pay of the top manager also grows. However, the effect is

FIGURE 7.2. MEDIAN TOTAL TOP-MANAGER COMPENSATION AND MEDIAN ASSETS BY INDUSTRY FOR FOR-PROFIT FIRMS.

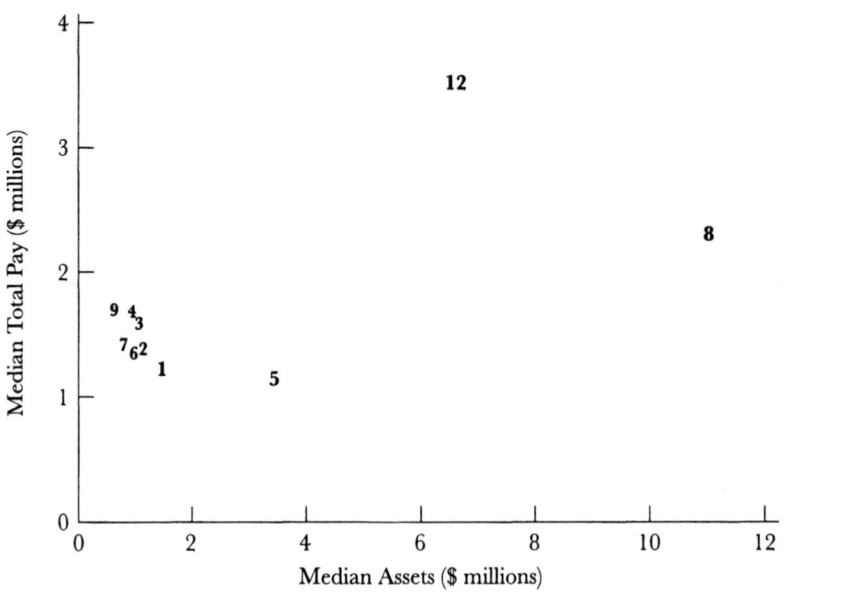

Source: Standard & Poor's EXECUCOMP database, 1992–1998.

Note: The numbers in the figure correspond to the industry numbers in Table 7.4.

much smaller than the cross-section estimate in column 1. Here, if the organization is 10 percent larger, the manager's pay increases by only 0.59 percent.

Columns 4 through 6 repeat this analysis for the highest-paid employee who is not an officer or a director. The results are somewhat similar in that the "return to firm size" decreases as we add control variables. Each coefficient is somewhat smaller than in the case where the dependent variable is ln(compensation of the top officer). This is consistent with my calculations using data from 1992–1996 (Hallock, 2002b).

The Council of Better Business Bureaus recommends that donors consider what percentage of resources is used directly for the purposes for which the organization was formed. Therefore, it is at least reasonable to think about "incentive compensation" for managers of nonprofits. The bottom portion of Table 7.5 evaluates whether there is a link between the percentage of total expenses spent on program services, conditional on the size of the organization (measured as a function of assets) and other organization characteristics. It appears that in the cross section (column 1), there is a relationship between the percentage of expenses spent on program services and top officer pay. This completely disappears when

TABLE 7.5. RELATIONSHIP OF ORGANIZATION SIZE TO MANAGERIAL PAY IN NONPROFITS.

	Dependent Variable: ln (Total Compensation Top Officer)			Dependent Variable: ln (Total Compensation Top Employee)		
	(1) Standard Regression	(2) Controlling for 26 NTEE Indicators	(3) Controlling for 12,324 Individual Indicators	(4) Standard Regression	(5) Controlling for 26 NTEE Indicators	(6) Controlling for 12,324 Individual Indicators
Firm Size Only						
ln(Assets)	0.229*** (0.002)	0.217*** (0.003)	0.059*** (0.007)	0.169*** (0.002)	0.156*** (0.002)	0.022*** (0.005)
26 NTEE indicators	no	yes	no	no	yes	no
12324 indicators	no	no	yes	no	no	yes
R^2	0.168	0.205	0.790	0.182	0.322	0.820
N	47,699	47,699	47,699	35,789	35,789	35,789
Firm Size and Program Service Expenses as a Percentage of Total Expenses						
ln(Assets)	0.228*** (0.002)	0.217*** (0.003)	0.058*** (0.007)	0.168*** (0.002)	0.155*** (0.002)	0.021*** (0.005)
ln(Program Expenses as a Percentage of Total Expenses)	0.113*** (0.030)	0.038 (0.030)	0.018 (0.037)	0.563*** (0.023)	0.355*** (0.022)	0.065** (0.028)
26 NTEE indicators	no	yes	no	no	yes	no
12324 indicators	no	no	yes	no	no	yes
R^2	0.168	0.205	0.790	0.196	0.327	0.820
N	47,699	47,699	47,699	35,789	35,789	35,789

Source: Internal Revenue Service, Form 990 for individual organizations, 1992–1998.

Notes: Standard errors are in parentheses. All specifications also include yearly indicator variables.

**$p > .05$; ***$p > .01$.

we consider the NTEE indicators or firm indicators. However, there does seem to be some relationship between this expense ratio and the pay of the top nonofficer, even conditional on organizational characteristics (columns 4–6).

A similar analysis is repeated for managers of for-profit organizations in Table 7.6. It is clear that whether we use ln(salary plus bonus) or ln(total compensation), the results are all strong and positive. They are somewhat higher for the ln(total compensation) dependent variable. It is also the case that the strength of the relationship holds up when we control for SIC industry indicators and even firm indicator variables. All of the "returns to assets" in the top portion of Table 7.6 and the "returns to market value" (another reasonable measure of size for firms) are higher than the corresponding numbers reported for nonprofit organizations in Table 7.5.

Why Are There Differences in Compensation?

There are many possible reasons for differences in compensation. Most are extremely difficult to identify, especially with the kinds of data being explored here. One possibility is the obvious issue of firm size. As documented in this chapter and elsewhere, there is an extremely strong correlation between the size of an organization and the pay of its top managers. Perhaps one reason that managers of for-profit firms are paid so much more than managers of nonprofit organizations is simply that the nonprofit organizations are so much smaller.

Table 7.7 reflects one attempt to investigate this empirically. The table sorts both the nonprofit and for-profit organizations by their assets and breaks them into ten groups containing equal numbers of organizations. The smallest 10 percent of nonprofit organizations are summarized in the first row ("Decile 1"), the next 10 percent are in the second row ("Decile 2"), on up to the largest 10 percent of the organizations in the bottom row ("Decile 10"). Column 2 shows that the median assets range from just under $360,000 for the smallest 10 percent of nonprofits all the way up to $252 million for the largest 10 percent. The median managerial total compensation for the bottom size group is $48,441 and for the top size group, $254,068.

A similar descriptive analysis is provided in columns 3–5 for for-profit firms using the EXECUCOMP data. It is clear from column 5 that the median assets of the for-profit firms are much higher than those of the nonprofits, and the median salary and bonus and total compensation are as well. However, it may be reasonable to compare nonprofit organizations with for-profit organizations of the same size. The closest comparison comes in decile 10 for the nonprofits, which has median assets of $252 million, and decile 2 for the for-profit organizations, which has median assets of $246 million. These represent a group of organizations of similar size in terms of assets. The median total compensation for the decile 10 nonprofits is

TABLE 7.6. RELATIONSHIP OF ORGANIZATION SIZE TO MANAGERIAL PAY IN FIRMS.

	Dependent Variable: ln (Salary + Bonus)			Dependent Variable: ln (Total Compensation)		
	(1) Standard Regression	(2) Controlling for 10 SIC Indicators	(3) Controlling for 2,125 Firm Indicators	(4) Standard Regression	(5) Controlling for 10 SIC Indicators	(6) Controlling for 2,125 Firm Indicators
Organization Size Measured as ln(Assets)						
Ln(Assets)	0.268*** (0.004)	0.301*** (0.005)	0.171*** (0.019)	0.313*** (0.005)	0.369*** (0.006)	0.331*** (0.025)
10 SIC indicators	no	yes	no	no	yes	no
2125 firm indicators	no	no	yes	no	no	yes
R^2	0.279	0.307	0.729	0.291	0.343	0.662
N	9,577	9,577	9,577	9,599	9,599	9,599
Organization Size Measured as ln (Market Value)						
ln(Market Value)	0.305*** (0.005)	0.304*** (0.005)	0.225*** (0.012)	0.396*** (0.006)	0.401*** (0.006)	0.352*** (0.025)
10 SIC indicators	no	yes	no	no	yes	no
2125 firm indicators	no	no	yes	no	no	yes
R^2	0.275	0.270	0.739	0.352	0.376	0.677
N	9,577	9,577	9,577	9,599	9,599	9,599

Source: Standard & Poor's EXECUCOMP database, 1992–1998.

Notes: Standard errors are in parentheses. All specifications also include yearly indicator variables.

***$p > .01$.

TABLE 7.7. MEDIAN MANAGERIAL COMPENSATION LEVELS BY ORGANIZATION SIZE IN NONPROFITS AND FOR-PROFIT FIRMS.

Asset Size Category (by decile, low to high)	Nonprofit Organizations		For-Profit Firms		
	(1) Median Total Compensation ($)	(2) Median Assets ($)	(3) Median Salary + Bonus ($)	(4) Median Total Compensation ($)	(5) Median Assets ($)
Decile 1	48,441	359,534	233,522	435,026	106,681,000
Decile 2	68,800	1,651,418	270,125	514,382	246,224,000
Decile 3	855,77	3,893,857	312,220	551,528	391,770,000
Decile 4	100,646	7,243,834	336,600	652,012	629,311,000
Decile 5	115,476	12,527,743	417,510	901,360	949,798,000
Decile 6	141,702	22,084,129	475,361	979,679	1,520,855,000
Decile 7	155,777	34,414,417	506,400	1,151,489	2,377,306,000
Decile 8	172,502	53,535,922	562,131	1,258,096	4,392,898,000
Decile 9	204,680	96,164,510	699,010	1,592,408	8,916,705,000
Decile 10	254,068	252,107,380	1,040,000	2,693,501	30,024,000,000

Sources: Internal Revenue Service, Form 990 for individual organizations, 1998; Standard & Poor's EXECUCOMP database, 1998.

$254,068, and the median salary and bonus and total compensation for the decile 2 for-profits are $270,125 and $514,382, respectively. So when comparing for-profits and nonprofits of similar size, the salary and bonus numbers are relatively similar. However, the nonsalary compensation (mostly the value of new stock option grants) nearly doubles the pay for the for-profit group.

Gender Differences in Managerial Pay

One other issue of note is the gender wage gap for managers in nonprofit and for-profit organizations. I will summarize two recent examinations of the issue. In one, my colleague Marianne Bertrand and I analyzed the gender pay and employment gap for managers of for-profit firms using data from EXECUCOMP from 1992–1997 (Bertrand and Hallock, 2001). In the other, I performed a similar analysis using a unique sample of nonprofit heads whose gender was identified (Hallock, 2002a).

In the latter, I studied the gender wage gap among managers of nonprofits using data from the *Annual Charity Index* published by the Philanthropic Advisory Service (PAS) of the Council of Better Business Bureaus from 1993 through 1996. The data collected from PAS are similar to those collected from the Forms 990 reported to the Internal Revenue Service, but in this case the gender of the top manager is identified and the number of cases is much smaller. But even though the PAS sample is much smaller than that of the IRS (only 606 observations), comparisons of means for several of the financial characteristics show that the organizations are quite similar in size.

About 19 percent of the organizations in the sample are run by women (Hallock, 2002a), and this ratio is fairly constant over the period of the sample. And although women are fairly well represented among the top managerial positions, these women earn roughly 20 percent less than their male counterparts who run other nonprofits. However, as we have noted with both the IRS nonprofit sample and the EXECUCOMP sample, managerial pay, even in nonprofits, is strongly related to the size of the organizations. Furthermore, there is a generally negative relationship between the size of a nonprofit and the probability that a woman runs it. When even very simple characteristics of the organizations are controlled for (such as industry or assets), the gender pay gap for nonprofit managers disappears.

The Bertrand and Hallock (2001) study of gender pay and employment gaps for managers of for-profit firms used Standard & Poor's EXECUCOMP data for the years 1992–1997. EXECUCOMP not only carefully details financial and accounting characteristics of the firms and the compensation of the top manager but also examines specifics of the compensation plans for each of the five highest-paid employees for each year. The gender of the managers is also identified.

Women are much more likely to lead large nonprofit organizations than they are to lead for-profit firms. The fraction of women leading for-profits in the EXECUCOMP sample rose from about 1.3 percent in 1992 to 3.4 percent in 1997. This is a dramatic increase, but the total number of women leading for-profits remains quite small. Furthermore, the women leading these for-profit organizations earn about 45 percent less than their male counterparts. Again, much of this gap can be explained by the fact that men and women are leading different kinds of organizations. Once firm size and the specific occupation of the manager are taken into account, the pay gap is reduced by about three-fourths. When firm size, occupation, age, and experience are all controlled for at once, the gender wage gap is only about 5 percent and is not statistically different from zero.

A great deal more attention needs to be devoted to determining why women are more likely than men to work for nonprofits (Odendahl and O'Neill, 1994) and to lead them (Hallock, 2002a). In addition, pay differences by gender within and across sectors should be further investigated.

Conclusion

Surprisingly little is known about compensation in the nonprofit sector, and data are hard to come by. Even though some large data sources (such as the U.S. Bureau of the Census) identify the sector in which workers are employed, because these data are cross-sectional, only so much can be done with them. New panel data sources such as those from the IRS will help us learn more about the nonprofit sector, how it is run, and how its managers are compensated. Many of the areas that have been explored in the literature on managerial compensation in the for-profit sector (relative performance, compensation differences internationally, gender gaps) need to be studied in the nonprofit sector.

It would also be useful to have access to research on specific "industries" in the nonprofit world. The comparisons in this chapter have assumed that within sectors (nonprofit and for-profit), all firms are interested in the same outcome (shareholder returns) and that all nonprofits are interested in some relatively common outcome. That assumption for the latter group may not be true. Therefore, studies of individual industries (like that of Ehrenberg, Cheslock, and Epifantseva, 2000, on university presidents) may be enlightening.

References

Antle, R., and Smith, A. "An Empirical Investigation of the Relative Performance Evaluation of Chief Executive Officers." *Journal of Accounting Research*, 1986, *24*, 1–39.

Bertrand, M., and Hallock, K. F. "The Gender Gap in Top Corporate Jobs." *Industrial and Labor Relations Review,* 2001, *55*(1), 3–21.

Bertrand, M., Hallock, K. F., and Arnould, R. "Does Managed Care Change the Mission of Nonprofit Hospitals? Evidence from the Managerial Labor Market." Unpublished manuscript, University of Chicago and University of Illinois, 2003.

Black, F., and Scholes, M. "The Pricing of Options and Corporate Liabilities." *Journal of Political Economy,* 1973, *81,* 637–654.

Brickley, J. A., and Van Horn, L. "Managerial Incentives in Nonprofit Organizations: Evidence from Hospitals." *Journal of Law and Economics,* 2002, *XLV,* 227–249.

Burbridge, L. C. "The Occupational Structure of Nonprofit Industries: Implications for Women." In T. Odendahl and M. O'Neil (eds.), *Women and Power in the Nonprofit Sector.* San Francisco: Jossey-Bass, 1994.

Conyon, M., and Murphy, K. J. "The Prince and the Pauper: CEO Pay in the U.S. and U.K." *Economic Journal,* 2000, *110,* 640–671.

Council of Better Business Bureaus. *BBB Wise Giving Alliance Standards for Charitable Accountability.* [http://www.give.org/standards/newcbbbstds.asp]. 2003.

Ehrenberg, R. G., Cheslock, J. J., and Epifantseva, J. "Paying Our Presidents: What Do Trustees Value?" Working paper no. 7886. Cambridge, Mass.: National Bureau of Economic Research, 2000.

Fama, E. "Agency Problems and the Theory of the Firm." *Journal of Political Economy,* 1980, *88,* 288–307.

Gibbons, R., and Murphy, K. J. "Relative Performance Evaluation for Chief Executive Officers." *Industrial and Labor Relations Review,* 1990, *43*(3), 30s–51s.

Gooddeeris, J. "Compensating Differentials and Self-Selection: An Application to Lawyers." *Journal of Political Economy,* 1988, *96,* 411–428.

Grønbjerg, K. "Using NTEE to Classify Nonprofit Organizations: An Assessment of Human Service and Regional Applications." *Voluntas,* 1994, *5,* 301–328.

Grossman, S., and Hart, O. "An Analysis of the Principal-Agent Problem." *Econometrica,* 1983, *51*(1), 7–45.

Hall, B., and Liebman, J. "Are CEOs Really Paid Like Bureaucrats?" *Quarterly Journal of Economics,* 1998, *113,* 653–691.

Hallock, K. F. "Compensation in Nonprofit Organizations." In G. R. Ferris (ed.), *Research in Personnel and Human Resources Management.* Vol. 19. New York: Elsevier Science, 2000.

Hallock, K. F. "The Gender and Employment Gaps for Top Managers in Nonprofits." Working paper, University of Illinois, 2002a.

Hallock, K. F. "Managerial Pay and Governance in American Nonprofits." *Industrial Relations,* 2002b, *41,* 377–406.

Hallock, K. F., and Murphy, K. J. "Introduction." In K. F. Hallock and K. J. Murphy (eds.), *Executive Compensation.* Northampton, Mass.: Elgar, 1999.

Hansmann, H. B. "The Role of Nonprofit Enterprise." *Yale Law Journal,* 1980, *89,* 835–901.

Hansmann, H. B. *The Ownership of Enterprise.* Cambridge, Mass.: Belknap Press, 1996.

Hodgkinson, V. A. "Mapping the Nonprofit Sector in the United States: Implications for Research." *Voluntas,* 1990, *1*(2), 6–32.

Hodgkinson, V. A., and Toppe, C. "A New Research and Planning Tool for Managers: The National Taxonomy of Exempt Entities." *Nonprofit Management and Leadership,* 1991, *1,* 403–414.

Holmstrom, B. "Moral Hazard and Observability." *Bell Journal of Economics,* 1979, *10*(1), 74–91.

Internal Revenue Service. *Instructions to Form 990.* Washington, D.C.: Government Printing Office, 2002.

James, E., and Rose-Ackerman, S. *The Nonprofit Enterprise in Market Economies.* New York: Harwood Academic Press, 1986.

Jensen, M., and Meckling, W. "Theory of the Firm: Managerial Behavior, Agency Costs, and Capital Structure." *Journal of Financial Economics,* 1976, *3,* 305–360.

Jensen, M., and Murphy, K. J. "Performance Pay and Top Management Incentives." *Journal of Political Economy,* 1990, *98,* 225–264.

Kostiuk, P. F. "Firm Size and Executive Compensation." *Journal of Human Resources,* 1990, *25,* 90–105.

Lazear, E. P. *Personnel Economics.* Cambridge, Mass.: MIT Press, 1995.

Lazear E. P., and Rosen, S. "Rank-Order Tournaments as Optimum Labor Contracts." *Journal of Political Economy,* 1981, *89,* 841–864.

Murphy, K. J. "Corporate Performance and Managerial Remuneration: An Empirical Analysis." *Journal of Accounting and Economics,* 1985, *7,* 11–42.

Murphy, K. J. "Executive Compensation." In O. Ashenfelter and D. Card (eds.), *Handbook of Labor Economics.* Vol. 3B. New York: Elsevier North-Holland, 1999.

Odendahl, T., and O'Neill, M. *Women and Power in the Nonprofit Sector.* San Francisco: Jossey-Bass, 1994.

Oster, S. "Executive Compensation in the Nonprofit Sector." *Nonprofit and Management Leadership,* 1998, *8,* 201–221.

Preston, A. "The Nonprofit Worker in a For-Profit World." *Journal of Labor Economics,* 1989, *7,* 438–463.

Rosen, S. "Hedonic Prices and Implicit Markets: Product Differentiation in Pure Competition." *Journal of Political Economy,* 1974, *82,* 34–55.

Rosen, S. "The Theory of Equalizing Differences." In O. Ashenfelter and R. Layard (eds.), *The Handbook of Labor Economics.* Elsevier Science: New York, 1986.

Rosen, S. "Contracts and the Market for Executives." In L. Werin and H. Wijkander (eds.), *Main Currents in Contract Economics.* Oxford: Blackwell, 1992.

Steinberg, R. "Labor Economics and the Nonprofit Sector: A Literature Review." *Nonprofit and Voluntary Sector Quarterly,* 1990a, *19,* 151–70.

Steinberg, R. "Profits and Incentive Compensation in Nonprofit Firms." *Nonprofit and Management Leadership,* 1990b, *1,* 137–152.

Stevensen, D. R., Pollack, T. H, and Lampkin, L. M. *The State Nonprofit Almanac, 1997: Profiles of Charitable Organizations.* Washington, D.C.: Urban Institute, 1997.

"Taxpayer Bill of Rights 2." *Public Law,* 104-168, July 30, 1996.

Turner, S. E., Nygren, T. I., and Bowen, W. G. "The NTEE Classification System: Tests of Reliability/Validity in the Field of Higher Education." *Voluntas,* 1992, *4*(1), 73–94.

Warner, J. B., Watts, R. L., and Wruck, K. H. "Stock Prices and Top Management Changes." *Journal of Financial Economics,* 1988, *20,* 461–492.

Weisbach, M. "Outside Directors and CEO Turnover." *Journal of Financial Economics,* 1988, *20,* 431–460.

Weisbrod, B. A. "Nonprofit and Proprietary Sector Behavior: Wage Differentials Among Lawyers." *Journal of Labor Economics,* 1983, *1,* 246–263.

Weisbrod, B. A. "Rewarding Performance That Is Hard to Measure: The Private Nonprofit Sector." *Science,* May 5, 1989, pp. 541–546.

Weisbrod, B. A., and Schlesinger, M. "Public, Private, Nonprofit Ownership and the Response to Asymmetric Information: The Case of Nursing Homes." In S. R. Ackerman (ed.), *The Economics of Nonprofit Institutions: Studies in Structure and Policy.* New York: Oxford University Press, 1986.

CHAPTER EIGHT

SUCCESSION AND ITS DISCONTENTS

The Perils and Promise of Change

Georgia Sorenson

The Japanese term *hanamichi* means "flower walk" or "flower path." In the ancient art of Kabuki theater, the *hanamichi* is the runway off stage right to the rear of the theater (Michener, 1983). After delivering their final lines, actors gracefully exit via the *hanamichi* through the audience and out the door. Likewise, retiring or transitioning Japanese business titans follow the well-mannered tradition of *hanamichi* when leaving their companies, and companies throw traditional flower walk parties, with much fanfare, in their honor.

In America, leadership succession is seldom so prosaic. As I have noted before, American leadership scholars are strangely silent on the issue of leadership succession (Sorenson, 2000). Research and scholarly wisdom abound on topics such as becoming a leader, being a leader, being a woman leader, being an ethical leader, transforming followers to leaders, and leading change, but very little attention has been focused on leadership succession.

Based on a study of the available literature on leadership succession in America, it appears that most leaders are coerced into retirement, are fired, are rotated into different positions, are recruited away, or die in office. Almost no research exists on leaders who voluntarily choose to relinquish their leadership positions to

The author thanks Cassie King for editing this chapter and Sarah Smith Orr, Bob Gerber, Lynn Kahn, and Gill Hickman for their useful comments on an earlier draft.

others (Schall, 1997). Such a scenario occurs very infrequently in the case of founders of organizations, for example, and when it does occur, the leadership transition is successful only about half the time. Apparently, most leaders do not give up power easily, and few actively seek to give it up (Fiegener, Brown, Prince, and File, 1996). When I chose to step down from my own organization recently, Shakespeare scholar Sandy Mack remarked to me, "Nowhere in Shakespeare's writing do you find kings or queens or anyone else willingly giving up power; what you find is power wrested from their cold, dead hands." In Shakespearean terms, then, succession is the natural consequence of murder coupled with ambition.

Business literature focuses on the succession process primarily from the standpoint of shareholder value, earnings, stock prices, and organizational fluidity. Given the inevitable changes in leadership in organizations, one might expect business gurus to devote considerable attention to the leadership issues inherent in the succession process, but this is not the case (Kets de Vries, 1988). In 1998, *Business Horizons* highlighted a crisis in CEO succession planning and executive development (Beeson, 1998). Another study found that less than 25 percent of companies address the need for a top leadership succession plan (Cutting Edge, 2002). According to a survey by the National Association of Corporate Directors (1998), 45 percent of companies with sales in excess of $500 million have no meaningful process for grooming potential CEOs. In fact, the American Society of Training and Development (1998) found that of all the organizational issues confronting CEOs today, the leadership succession process is the least understood and most in need of further study.

The succession process is problematic for nonprofit organizations as well. While there is little empirical information about the long-term impact of founding executive directors and founding board chairs in nonprofit organizations, the issue frequently plagues the healthy evolution of nonprofit organizations. One of the few analysts who has addressed the issue head on is John Carver, who describes the intricate transfer of power and suggests ways to handle the power invested in the founder in an article titled "The Founding Parent Syndrome" (1992).

Why don't more organizations (for-profit and nonprofit) invest in succession planning? Because succession planning is a bit like estate planning—often neglected in the face of taboos surrounding death. CEOs and executive directors put off succession planning for the same reasons most people avoid writing a will. Founders of private businesses and nonprofit organizations identify feelings of immortality, lack of a suitable successor, a surfeit of successors, and fear of retirement as some of the many factors that inhibit their own succession planning (Brown and Coverley, 1999). Yet succession planning is more crucial now than ever before, given that America will be facing a leadership exodus in the next ten years as baby boomers begin to retire.

Departure of the Boomers

The baby boomers, born between the years 1946 and 1964, came of age during the Vietnam War and inspired an era of movements and reforms. In the face of war and injustice, boomers created and led a myriad of institutions, most of them nongovernmental. These institutions—Common Cause, the Children's Defense Fund, Physicians for Social Responsibility, and People for the Ethical Treatment of Animals, to name just a few—are now so much a part of everyday life that we take them for granted. In addition to founding these various organizations, many boomers still hold leadership positions in them.

Today, boomers comprise almost 77 million of the country's total population of approximately 282 million. Eighty-four percent of boomers are in the labor force, but as boomers begin to reach retirement age in the next ten years, that will change. Although eight in ten boomers "plan to work at least part-time during their retirement," and the downturn in the economy will keep some from retiring as early as planned, in the end, demographics will prevail (AARP, 1999). In the next few years, the vast majority of boomers who founded organizations will leave the leadership positions they held in those organizations for reasons ranging from retirement to corporate reorganization to death. And as boomers withdraw, the workplace will change dramatically, with people of color eventually becoming the dominant workforce (Fullerton, 1999). How leaders and organizations negotiate this inevitable transition—a transition that will alter both the generational and racial composition of the workforce—will be of paramount importance.

Private and Public Exits

The departure of boomer generation leaders will have an enormous impact on the private and nonprofit sectors. In the private sector, for example, 20 percent of the largest U.S. companies will lose 40 percent or more of their top executives by 2005 (Schafer, 2000). In the past five years alone, almost two-thirds of all major companies replaced their CEOs (Cambron, 2002).

Although Fortune 100 companies grab the headlines, small family businesses have always been the backbone of the American private sector. Indeed, small businesses represent almost half of the total business wealth in this country, and they employ approximately half of the private sector workforce (CyberAtlas, 2002; Ward, 1987). These businesses account for 65 percent of all wages paid (Handler, 1991) and generate more than 50 percent of the nation's gross domestic product (Popkin, 1997). Clearly, healthy leadership in the small business arena is vital to a vigorous national economy. It is therefore worth noting that the looming boomer leadership exodus will have a disproportionate impact on small businesses. At the beginning of 2003, more than 33 percent of family business owners were sixty-one years of age or older and were facing a crucial succession. Even in the best of times, family-owned businesses survive a generational transition only 30 percent of the time, and only 10 percent endure to the third generation (Dingle, 1997). The success or failure of leadership transfers in small family-owned businesses in the next ten years will almost certainly have a profound effect on the economic well-being of the nation.

The boomer era witnessed a rapid expansion in the number of nonprofits in the United States, with a net increase of more than 78 percent (Central Intelligence Agency, 2001). This is not surprising considering that so many boomers wanted to effect radical change and frequently chose to work through nonprofits to accomplish their ends. The IRS has granted formal tax-exempt status to more than 1.25 million organizations,[1] which employ 7 percent of the nation's workforce (National Center for Charitable Statistics, 2003). These nonprofits mobilize volunteers who donate approximately twenty billion hours of service annually, with an estimated value of a quarter of a trillion dollars, to address a multitude of needs (INDEPENDENT SECTOR, 2003).

Nonprofits are dispersed among many fields and activities, and many have an educational focus. On this track, succession issues in community colleges are often the most dramatic. Community colleges are the quintessential boomer nonprofits, having been founded to meet the needs of returning World War II soldiers and the burgeoning boomer population. According to research conducted in 2001 and subsequently published by the American Association of Community Colleges, more than 79 percent of community college presidents plan to retire between 2001 and 2011 (Weisman and Vaughan, 2002). A report published in the [The] *Chronicle of Higher Education* notes that many experts worry that the sector faces "a crisis of leadership" (Evelyn, 2001).

Americans may soon find themselves facing a leadership crisis in many other sectors as well. Whether considering the public sector or the private sector, small businesses or international nonprofits, the boomer exodus worldwide and the subsequent transitions will affect each one of us in both direct and indirect ways.

The Syndromes

We are facing a great ebb and flow of founders and successors. Both founders and successors describe the succession process as turbulent and fraught with complicated issues. Although those dynamics are personal, institutional, and historical, a basic grasp of the projections, introjections, and psychological dimensions of the transition experience can provide leaders with an understanding of some of the issues they will face. *Founder's syndrome* and *successor's syndrome* are often deployed to explain problems in transitions.

Founder's Syndrome

Recent attention has focused on the so-called founder's syndrome (McNamara, 2001), a subject introduced during a group online discussion by Carter McNamara in September 2000. This syndrome arises when an individual refuses to step down from the formal leadership of an organization he or she founded, presumably assuming that doing so would be to the detriment of the organization. The concept has gained a certain currency, at least among ambitious underlings. It is rare for a founder to choose to step away from the forefront of a robust organization. In fact, many boomer founders, such as Marian Wright Edelman (founder of the Children's Defense Fund) and Brian Lamb (founder of CSPAN), continue to enhance the institutions they founded. "I have more work to do, and this is the place to do it," Lamb told me recently when I asked about his succession plans for CSPAN. Certainly, more research is needed on the relationship between the longevity of the founder as CEO and the long-term health of an institution.

Successor's Syndrome

A successor is always a Janus-like figure, looking forward and backward simultaneously. Smart successors look not only to the future but also to the past to glean insights from history, wisdom, and experience. "I hear your voice whenever I have to make a decision," one successor told the founder. "I plan to carry your work forward." "Good," responded the predecessor. "But you must find your own voice as well." Consider Krishna's advice to Arjuna in the Hindu Bhagavad Gita: "Better to do one's own duty imperfectly than to do another person's well." The parallel work of integrating the past and the future—tradition and innovation—is only for the truly adept.

In the final analysis, a successor is the new leader of an organization, but like it or not, he or she is also following in the founder's footsteps. A successor is, by definition, both a leader *and* a follower and must come to terms with the founder's ghost. Too often, however, the ghost of the founder-past threatens the successor, and the successor's own envy, jealousy, fear, and paranoia hinder his or her best efforts. Successor's syndrome can become utterly disabling for the individual and for the institution. According to one founder of a nonprofit, his successor told him that she could not lead while the founder was still alive. "Well, I'm not going to die for you, if that's what you're asking—so get over it," the founder shot back.

Neither founder's syndrome nor successor's syndrome adequately describes the multitude of nuances inherent in the succession process. The use of archetypes juxtaposed against organizational conditions and founder exit conditions provides a more subtle understanding of the complexity of the interactions.

The Use of Archetypes in Succession Scenarios

Psychologist Carl Jung first introduced archetypes as "forms or images of a collective nature which occur practically all over the earth as constituents of myths and at the same time as autochthonous, individual products of unconscious origin" (Jung, 1958, p. 50). In an early work, Jung writes:

> The concept of the archetype, which is an indispensable correlate of the idea of the collective unconscious, indicates the existence of definite forms in the psyche which seem to be present always and everywhere. Mythological research calls them "motifs"; in the psychology of primitives they correspond to Lévy-Bruhl's concept of "représentations collectives," and in the field of comparative religion they have been defined by Hubert and Mauss as "categories of the imagination." Adolf Bastian long ago called them "elementary" or "primordial" thoughts. From these references it should be clear enough that my idea of the archetype—literally a pre-existent form—does not stand alone but is something that is recognized and named in other fields of knowledge [Jung, 1969, pp. 42-43]

In his later work, Jung saw archetypes as shaping matter as well as mind, as universal and yet having individual variation. The *Gale Encyclopedia of Psychology* (2001) describes them as follows:

> Jungian archetypes are like prototypes or molds that each person fills in differently depending on his or her individual experience. For example, although the term "mother" has certain universal connotations that come to mind for most people, the details of this archetype will be different for everyone. For Jung, archetypes . . . are as varied as human experience itself. Many take the form of persons, such as the hero, the child, the trickster, the demon, and the earth mother. Others are expressed as forces of nature (sun, moon, wind, fire) or animals. They may also occur as situations, events (birth, rebirth, death), or places.

These archetypes are remarkably universal over time and can be deployed when looking at business, nonprofits, corporate brands, or even individual brands.

Research Methods

The archetypes presented in Table 8.1 were identified through a review of business journals and news and nonprofit literature, as well as through interviews with nonprofit founders and successors. Many of the archetypes are in the developmental stages and are part of my ongoing research. Some are offered as preliminary hypotheses. Some, such as the savior archetype, appear to be quite stable over time, as borne out in both the literature and the interviews.

The identified archetypes were placed in a matrix that incorporates the following: (1) exit conditions of the founder, (2) types of successors, (3) and a descriptive rating of the overall health of the organization at the time of transition, subjectively derived from media reports. Future research could include obtaining financial statements and conducting employee surveys for framing this third variable.

Founder Exit Conditions

I have identified nine exit conditions that affect the organizational environment a successor enters when a founder leaves his or her organization: illness, death, voluntary retirement, coerced retirement, coerced departure, firing, term limitation, acceptance of another role in the organization, and voluntary departure to take a new job. I will not address a tenth possibility, that of merger or acquisition—certainly one of the most common scenarios in the private sector—because merged organizations become, in effect, new organizations, and the resulting analysis takes on greater complexity.[2]

Types of Successors

The nine exit conditions interact with the two types of successors, what I call the inside successor and the outside successor. Inside successors are most often selected when the organization is in good health and someone is needed to continue the work of the founder. In a healthy organization, the inside successor will typically continue to champion the founder's vision, in addition to honing his or her own vision for the organization. Outside successors are brought in during times of crisis or decline—driven by the organization's leadership to forge a new direction or to save the organization from possible demise. In the private sector, Wall Street often drives the push for outside successors.

TABLE 8.1. EXITING FOUNDER ARCHETYPES, REFLECTING SUCCESSOR TYPE, ORGANIZATIONAL HEALTH, AND FOUNDER EXIT CONDITIONS.

Successor Type and Organizational Health[a]	Founder Exit Conditions								
	Illness	Death	Voluntary Retirement	Coerced Retirement	Coerced Departure	Firing	Term Limitation	Acceptance of Another Role in Organization	Voluntary Departure for New Job
Inside successor, good health	Virus or Clone	Holy Ghost	Inheritor or Favorite Child	Disloyal Lieutenant	Assassin	Traitor	Pretender or Functionary	Eunuch or Puppet	Inheritor or Abandoned Child
Inside successor, poor health	Martyr	Murderer or Phoenix	"Neutron" or Dreamer	Flawed or Disloyal Hero	Samurai	Flawed Hero	Innocent	Diplomat or Disloyal Lieutenant	"Iron Man" Rebuilder or Abandoned Child
Outside successor, good health	Doctor or Healer	Interloper	Pretender to the Throne	Intruder	Terrorist or Innocent	Saint	Usurper	Innocent or Pretender or Collaborator	Good Step-parent
Outside successor, poor health	Caretaker	Undertaker	Rebuilder or Fool	Fool	Accomplice	Savior	Fool or Dreamer	Prisoner or Diplomat	Fixer or Slash and Burn Vandal

[a]"Good health" reflects a general perception, inside and outside, of financial solvency and vitality and good employee morale; "poor health" indicates financial problems and employee dissatisfaction.

Organizational Health

The fate of an inside or outside successor can vary with the health of the organization—the state of financial health and employee morale—at the time the founder exits and the successor enters. So, for example, an outside successor following a term-limited founder in a financially healthy organization with high employee morale will face a very different scenario than an outside successor following a term-limited founder in an organization experiencing financial difficulties and employee dissatisfaction.

If we view an organization's transition period through the lens of founder exit conditions, types of successors, and organizational health, a matrix of archetypes emerges, as depicted in Table 8.1.

Archetype Scenarios

To demonstrate the utility of this archetype matrix, I outline two brief scenarios and describe several dominant founder-successor archetypes in the literature.

Scenario 1

If a founder dies (death) during a time of organizational prosperity (good health), organization members perceive the inside successor as the resurrection or reincarnation of the founder. Indeed, the successor often takes on the projections of others, and some organization members report that they feel like the founder has risen from the dead. The environment may become oppressive, imbued with the sense that an omnipresent holy ghost is always looking over things. Conversely, a holy ghost may confer a sense of comfort, reassurance, and organizational stability by upholding the founder's values and enduring legacy. More than three decades after Walt Disney's death, employees (or rather, "associates") of the Disney Company are still known to say in staff meetings, "That's not the way Walt would have done it" (McDonnell, 1999). Companies or organizations named after their founders, such as the Walt Disney Company or the W. K. Kellogg Company, have a tendency toward the holy ghost archetype.

Though most nonprofits are not named for their founder, some that are strongly identified with their founder, such as the Children's Defense Fund or MADD, may carry vestiges of the holy ghost. An organizational consultant, brought in to exorcize a holy ghost and deal with her "eunuch" in a nonprofit, provides this fascinating account:

A nonprofit was created nearly fifty years ago to support children with developmental disabilities. The founder and early supporters were parents of children with these disorders. At the time, there was little or no governmental legislation supporting the rights of these children to an education or support services. The founder was a passionate advocate and quickly engaged others who shared her passion. A politically astute parent was one of the individuals responsible for forging state legislation mandating educational programs and social services for this population of children. Over the years, the agency grew, developing residential programs along with educational programs as the response to the need generated resources. After nearly thirty years, the founder decided to retire. The board, with her support and involvement, hired her replacement from within (eunuch or puppet). The board, in appreciation of the retiring founder's tireless effort and deep commitment, created a "director emeritus" role for her, giving her a voting position on the board. The agency, after being cited for numerous issues, including alleged client neglect and staff management irregularities, called me in as a consultant. The regulatory agency that had cited the agency was prepared to suspend the agency's license. My role, initially, was to either refute or affirm the regulatory agency's allegations.

There were clearly management issues, but the eunuch was consistently undermined—by staff that still informally and "off the record" reported to the retired founder (who had every right to go into the agency under her mantle of executive director emeritus). The client neglect issues were due to staff incompetence, primarily on the part of employees hired by the founder, employees who were "protected" and beyond the reach of the successor to direct or even replace. In addition, the board, as is often the case in organizations with strong and very persuasive founders, was made up of "friends" and "family" who had been handpicked by the founder, and nearly every one of them was the parent of a child in the care of the agency. They were consumed with fear that something would happen to the agency which might adversely affect the placement of their disabled children. They understandably sought stability—albeit a flawed stability—in the form of an internal eunuch who cohabited with the founder and her ghost.

In time, the eunuch was asked to leave, an interim was hired, and a search for the next successor was launched. The first pick by the board didn't work out and was asked to leave within the one-year probationary period. The third person who assumed leadership of the agency after the founder has been able to move the organization forward. The third pick had both the necessary skill set to focus on the program and the experience in fundraising and financial management the agency needed. From the first sign of trouble (the citing of the organization by the regulatory agency), it took the agency nearly three years to reach a level of stability and over eight years (including lawsuits) to clear the way for the agency's transformation—through its programs, staff, and board (now representative of the community with a small representation of parents).

Scenario 2

The pretender archetype arises when an inside successor assumes the leadership role after a successful founder in a healthy organization steps down due to term limitation. I interviewed a pretender successor of a small professional association who followed on the heels of a term-limited president. He had some difficult hurdles early in his tenure. For example, the organization continued to meet in the offices of his predecessor. Clearly, organization members still felt a strong emotional attachment to his predecessor, in part because the predecessor had imbued members with a sense of healing during a tough time in the organization's history. Initially, the pretender had a hard time dealing with his predecessor's legacy and moving the organization forward. Describing his presidency in its early days, he said, "I was talking to a colleague in our organization, and she suggested that I conduct an upcoming conference as well as serve as the organization's president. She said to me, 'Pierre [the previous president] used to conduct conferences and run the organization just fine.' 'I am *not* Pierre,' I shouted at her. God, it felt so good to be clear about it: I am not Pierre."

Pretenders need to confront the issue of founder transference—the tendency of employees to transfer the founder's attributes and leadership style to the successor—directly. Second, pretenders should define a new agenda that communicates successes in new arenas. The pretender in this organization had done an outstanding job of reducing the deficits, responding to organizational demands inside and outside, and developing new markets of profitability for the organization. Still, he was stuck in "not-Pierre" mode for longer than he might have been, as he failed to communicate his successes in meeting those goals.

Finally, if the pretender can convey, to some degree, the persona associated with the favorite child or inheritor archetype, he can deploy the memory of the founder in a way that serves everyone. Some pretenders and favorite children or inheritors have successfully used founders as sounding boards, fundraisers, pubic relations promoters, and advocates for the organization and its new leadership. A well-known example is founder John Gardner, who continued to play a strong and important role in promoting the work of Common Cause long after he had left the organization.

The Usefulness of Archetypes

Viewing succession as a product of three conditions—founder exit, organizational health, and successor type—allows a myriad of archetypes to emerge, as Table 8.1 clearly shows. These images abound in the media and in the research about transitions. I'll briefly define some of the more common succession archetypes.[3]

Innocent: An inside successor who assumes leadership of a sick organization when a founder steps down because of term limits is portrayed as an innocent with the power and burden of purity.

Savior: An outside successor who assumes leadership of a sick organization when a founder is fired is seen as a savior or messiah.

Assassin: An inside successor who takes the reins of a healthy organization after a founder is thrown out can be perceived as a terrorist.

Disloyal lieutenant: An inside successor succeeding a founder who has been coerced into retirement from a healthy organization is viewed as the architect of a coup.

Succession Archetypes in a Historical Context

I have found that studying the successions of great leaders can also contribute to a better overall understanding of the leadership succession process and the complicated terrain of archetypes. James MacGregor Burns and I have written about presidential successions in modern times (Burns and Sorenson, 1999), but now I would like to consider an earlier period in our nation's history. Of all the presidents, I look to Jefferson as perhaps the most astute student of succession and the most graceful of successors.

In 1785, Jefferson succeeded Benjamin Franklin as minister to France. Franklin, beloved both at home and in France, was a hard act to follow. Historian Joseph Ellis described Franklin's reputation in France as "reaching epic proportions" and noted that when Franklin and Voltaire embraced publicly, the French press heralded "the union of the two greatest champions of human enlightenment in history's most enlightened century" (Ellis, 1997, p. 77). The ever-astute Jefferson knew that following in Franklin's footsteps would be risky. At his introduction to the French court, the French foreign minister, Charles Vergennes, asked him if he would be serving as Franklin's replacement, to which Jefferson famously replied, "No one can replace him, Sir. I am only his successor" (Ellis, 1997, p. 77).

Later, as Washington's presidency was drawing to a close, Jefferson wrote to James Madison about his wish to warn John Adams about the perils of following in the footsteps of the "founder of our country." Understanding the loaded archetype, Jefferson wrote, "The President [Washington] is fortunate to get off just as the bubble is bursting, leaving others to hold the bag. Yet, as his departure will mark the moment when the difficulties begin to work, you will see, that they will be ascribed to the new administration, and that he will have his usual good fortune of reaping credit from the good acts of others, and leaving to them that of his errors" (Ellis, 1997, pp. 165-166). In short, succeeding Washington would be fraught with difficulties, and as Jefferson predicted of Washington's successor, "no man will bring out of that office the reputation which carries him into it" (Ellis, 1997, p. 166). At least for the Federalist Adams, his archetypal projections were pretender, functionary, and innocent. It would have been far worse for an outside successor like the Republican Jefferson to succeed Washington—he would have carried the usurper, fool, or dreamer archetype.

Perhaps most notable in Jefferson's succession planning was the fact that he devoted so much time and attention to grooming his younger colleagues for leadership. He carefully mentored Virginians James Madison and James Monroe for more than fifty years, and as Madison succeeded Jefferson and Monroe succeeded Madison, he achieved what Ellis (1997) claims no other American president has accomplished: he ensured that the first quarter of the nineteenth century was guided by Jeffersonian presidents.

Jefferson understood well the delicacy and the dangers of succession. He was a true master of succession, having achieved the enduring actualization of his values and vision through his successors. Certainly, he picked his successors well.

Few of us have Jefferson's wisdom, foresight, and shrewdness in terms of our ability to assess human nature. Succession is a tricky business, no more so for founders than for successors. The passing of the torch brings with it both promise and peril, much of the latter hidden. Nevertheless, perhaps through careful study of archetypes, it will be possible to glean valuable insights into the succession process, insights that Jefferson sensed intuitively but that most of us have to work harder to grasp.

Notes

1. This figure does not include 501(c)3 organizations with annual incomes under $5,000 that are not required to register with the IRS or file an annual income report.
2. Many strong companies or organizations (such as Starbucks and Nike) also have their own brand identity, as described in Mark and Pearson's brilliant book, *The Hero and the Outlaw: Building Extraordinary Brands Through the Power of Archetypes* (2001). Brand identities contribute to the complexity of the interaction of the other variables. I will investigate the interaction of the brand archetype in future research.
3. Readers interested in a fuller description of the archetypes may contact the author at georgiasorenson@aol.com.

References

AARP. "Baby Boomers Envision Their Retirement: An AARP Segmentation Analysis." 1999. [http://www.research.aarp.org/econ/boomer_seg_1.html#Key].

American Society of Training and Development. *ASTD Reports.* Fall 1998.

Beeson, J. "Succession Planning: Building the Management Corps." *Business Horizons*, 1998, *41,* 61–66.

Brown, R. B., and Coverley, R. "Succession Planning in Family Businesses: A Study from East Anglia, U.K." *Journal of Small Business Management*, 1999, *37,* 93–97.

Burns, J. M., and Sorenson, G. *Dead Center: Clinton-Gore Leadership and the Perils of Moderation.* New York: Scribner, 1999.

Cambron, L. "Who Moves to the Top When a CEO Exits?" [http://www.expressitpeople.com/ 20020311/management2.shtml]. 2002.

Carver, J. "The Founding Parent Syndrome: Governing in the CEO's Shadow." *Nonprofit World*, 1992, *10,*5, pp. 14–16.

Central Intelligence Agency. "Global Trends 2015." 2001. [http://www.cia.gov/cia/ publications/globaltrends2015].

Cutting Edge Information. "Succession Planning for Results." 2002. [http:// www.cuttingedgeinfo.com/reports/FL52_Succession_Planning.htm].

CyberAtlas. "Small Biz, Small Growth." CyberAtlas, October 9, 2002. [www.isp-planet.com/research/2002/smallbiz_021009.html].

Dingle, D. T. "The Next Generation of CEOs: Many of the B.E. 100s Must Prepare Now to Enter the New Millennium with New Leadership." *Black Enterprise*, 1997, *27,* pp. 159–160, 164, 166–167.

Ellis, J. J. *American Sphinx: The Character of Thomas Jefferson.* New York: Knopf, 1997.

Evelyn, J. "Community Colleges Face a Crisis of Leadership: Most Presidents Will Retire in the Next Decade, and the Pool of Replacements Is Shallow." *The Chronicle of Higher Education*, April 6, 2001, *47,* A36–A37.

Fiegener, M. K., Brown, B. M., Prince, R. A., and File, K. M. "Passing on Strategic Vision: Favored Modes of Successor Preparation by CEOs of Family and Nonfamily Firms." *Journal of Small Business Management*, 1996, *34,* 15–26.

Fullerton, H. N., Jr. "Labor Force Projections to 2008: Steady Growth and Changing Composition." *Monthly Labor Review*, 1999, *122,* 19–32.

Gale Encyclopedia of Psychology. (2nd ed.). [http://www.findarticles.com/cf_dls/g2699/0000/ 2699000022/p1/article.jhtml?term=archetypes+and+strickland]. 2001.

Handler, W. C. "Key Interpersonal Relationships of Next-Generation Family Members in Family Firms." *Journal of Small Business Management*, 1991, *29*(3), 21–32.

INDEPENDENT SECTOR. "Value of Volunteer Time." 2003. [http://www.independentsector.org/ programs/research/volunteer_time.html].

Jung, C. G. *Collected Works of C. G. Jung.* Vol. 11, *Psychology and Religion: West and East* (trans. R.F.C. Hull). New York: Pantheon Books, 1958. (Originally published 1938.)

Jung, C. G. *Collected Works of C. G. Jung.* Vol. 9, Pt. 1, *The Archetypes and the Collective Unconscious* (trans. R.F.C. Hull). (2nd ed.) Princeton, N.J.: Princeton University Press, 1969. (Originally published 1934.)

Kets de Vries, M.F.R. "The Dark Side of CEO Succession." *Harvard Business Review*, January-February 1988, *66,* 56–60.

Mark, M., and Pearson, C. S. *The Hero and the Outlaw: Building Extraordinary Brands Through the Power of Archetypes.* New York: McGraw-Hill, 2001.

McDonnell, K. Personal Communication with author, 1999.

McNamara, C. "Founder's Syndrome: How Corporations Suffer—and Can Recover." *The Difference*, May 2001, *1,* 2 [http://www.e-thedifference.com/Issue_2/ founders_syndrome.html].

Michener, J. *The Floating World*. Honolulu: University of Hawaii Press, 1983.

National Association of Corporate Directors. *Report of the NACD Blue Ribbon Commission on CEO Succession*. Washington, D.C.: National Association of Corporate Directors, 1998.

National Center for Charitable Statistics. "NCCS Frequently Asked Questions." [http://nccs.urban.org/faqs.htm#general]. 2003.

Popkin, J. "Small Business Share of Private, Nonfarm Gross Domestic Product," in *Small Business Research Summary*. October 1997.

Schafer, M. "Developing Leaders." *Software Magazine*, December 2000. [http://www.softwaremag.com/L.cfm?Doc=archive/2000dec/Leaders.html].

Schall, E. "Public Sector Succession: A Strategic Approach to Sustaining Innovation." *Public Administration Review*, January-February 1997, *57*(1), 4–10.

Sorenson, G. "Taking Robes Off: When Leaders Step Down." In B. Kellerman and L. Matusak (eds.), *Cutting Edge: Leadership 2000*. College Park, Md.: Center for the Advanced Study of Leadership, James MacGregor Burns Academy of Leadership, 2000.

Ward, J. L. *Keeping the Family Business Healthy: How to Plan for Continuing Growth, Profitability, and Family Leadership*. San Francisco: Jossey-Bass, 1987.

Weisman, I. M., and Vaughan, G. B. "The Community College Presidency, 2001." American Association of Community Colleges, 2002. [http://www.aacc.nche.edu/Content/ContentGroups/Research_Briefs2/Presidency_Briefv1.pdf].

PART THREE

BOARD LEADERSHIP

Over the door to the nonprofit's boardroom there should be an inscription in big letters that says: Membership on this board is not power, it is responsibility. Board membership means responsibility not just to the organization but to the board itself, to the staff, and to the institution's mission.

PETER F. DRUCKER, *MANAGING THE NONPROFIT ORGANIZATION* (P. 158)

Nonprofit boards and for-profit boards have similar obligations under law. Because their accounting systems and legal descriptions differ, they have a different bottom line. Nevertheless, there is value to making comparisons as to effectiveness and accountability.

The authors in Part Three approach the topic from the two different perspectives. However, just as Drucker admonishes, it is responsibility and the ways in which board members (and their chief executive officers or executive directors) interact and fulfill their responsibilities that determine the success or failure of the nonprofit organization.

CHAPTER NINE

TRANSFORMING NONPROFIT BOARDS

Lessons from the World of Corporate Governance

Jay A. Conger

When I was asked to write this chapter, with its focus on whether the governance practices of corporate boards might hold lessons for nonprofit boards, I was at first quite skeptical about the assignment. After all, they represent two distinct worlds. Their missions are different. Their metrics of performance are different. Their workforces are different. Their constituents are different. Even their board structures are different. For example, a corporate board generally has a small number of directors—typically eleven to fifteen. In contrast, nonprofit boards might have as many as fifty or sixty or even one hundred directors. Corporate directors play a largely advisory role. In contrast, nonprofits expect their board members not only to advise but also to provide funding. Leadership on a corporate board is essentially in the hands of the CEO. This individual typically holds the position of boardroom chair. In contrast, leadership on nonprofit boards is more diffuse. There is usually a separate board chair who shares leadership with the CEO. Corporate directors see themselves as largely accountable to shareholders. A company's financial performance is the primary concern of directors. In contrast, most directors of nonprofits would define their constituents and the determinants of "successful performance" more broadly. Nonprofit boards rarely rely on clear-cut financial metrics to gauge their overall performance.

So would it be meaningful to explore what the world of nonprofit boards might learn from corporate governance? As I reflected on the issue, I began to realize that nonprofit boards might indeed find some corporate board practices to be of value. This premise rests on important similarities that boardrooms in both cases share. For example, both for-profit and nonprofit boards have a mandate to provide oversight of the organization, its activities, and its management team. Both are concerned with enhancing the overall performance of the organization and the CEO. Both boards depend on their directors as a source of advice, strategic guidance, and influence. Both rely on directors who are successful and influential individuals in their own right. Both boards need to operate as a team rather than simply a collection of individuals gathering for a meeting. Both boards need to be deeply concerned about their own effectiveness. It is in these similarities that certain lessons from the world of corporate governance may be applicable to nonprofit boardrooms.

The premise behind this chapter is that the governance practices of corporate boards have undergone far more scrutiny and research than those of nonprofits. As a result, in the corporate world, we have a wealth of knowledge about what makes for effective governance practices. Boardroom failures at companies like Enron and WorldCom have only heightened the intensity of this scrutiny. Their boards completely stumbled in their ability to provide genuine oversight and leadership. In the Enron case, directors knowingly waived their own code of ethical conduct to permit the off-balance-sheet partnerships that led to the company's financial collapse. Scandals such as these have put corporate boards and their governance practices into an intense spotlight. In an attempt to preempt further governance crises, a growing body of research on corporate governance has appeared. From these studies, we now have substantial insights into what makes for a well-functioning corporate board (Conger, Lawler, and Finegold, 2001; Daily and Dalton, 1997; Firstenberg and Malkiel, 1994; Lorsch and McIver, 1989; National Association of Corporate Directors, 2000). The intense scrutiny to which corporate boards have been subjected has also encouraged a remarkable amount of experimentation with boardroom governance practices since the late 1980s. Many corporate boards have become hotbeds of innovation. Their experiments have been extensively researched to determine whether these innovative practices positively influenced both boardroom and organizational performance. In summary, we have learned a great deal about corporate governance. In sharp contrast, nonprofit boards have received little attention despite the crucial role that their boards play. Yet quite a number of the governance practices of corporate boards may be transferable to the world of nonprofits.

With two colleagues, I have been studying corporate boards for a number of years (see Conger, Lawler, and Finegold, 2001). In our research, we have examined a wide range of governance practices to determine which enhance the leadership effectiveness of a board of directors. In this chapter, I will share the findings that I feel have the greatest relevance for nonprofit boards. Having served on several nonprofit boards and as the director of a nonprofit institute with a governing board, I am reasonably well positioned to see where potential lessons might lie from the perspective of a nonprofit organization. That said, "best practices" of any sort need to be carefully adapted to the unique requirements of each organization. What follows are therefore not the "surefire" answers to the many challenges facing nonprofit boards but rather a set of suggestions that are worthy of consideration and experimentation.

There are four corporate governance areas that I believe hold lessons for nonprofit boards: board size, boardroom evaluations, assessments of directors' capabilities, and efficient formats for board meetings.

Board Size: Smaller Is Better

Several decades ago, it was not uncommon for corporate boards to have a large number of directors. Today, the reverse is true. Corporate boards are nowadays quite lean—the average number of directors for a Fortune 500 company is eleven. Many corporate CEOs report that their ideal board size is eight to twelve members (National Association of Corporate Directors, 2000). In general, the trend toward smaller boards has been pronounced. Large boards have proved too difficult to effectively engage in useful decision making. They end up operating as legislative bodies rather than as working groups. When boards are too large, it is difficult for individual directors to get sufficient time and attention. It is hard to engage in fruitful discussions and to build consensus around issues. Some researchers even suggest that larger boards are less likely to be involved when it comes to critical responsibilities like strategic decision making (Dalton, Daily, Johnson, and Ellstrand, 1999; Judge and Zeithan, 1992).

In contrast, many nonprofits have large boards. It has been a long-standing belief among many nonprofits that board membership is the pathway to philanthropy. Directorships in these organizations often come with financial strings attached. In return for a directorship, an individual is often expected to make a sizable donation to the organization. It is a "give or get off" mind-set. More and more nonprofits now make this an explicit expectation with the appointment. The larger boardrooms of nonprofits are therefore based on a very simple logic: the more directors on the board, the more donations for the organization. Surprisingly few boards have challenged this assumption. Yet in discussions with consultants to nonprofit boards, I have discovered that this belief may largely be a myth—especially in cases where there is no explicit quid pro quo of a donation in return for a seat on the board. Indeed, these nonprofit consultants point out that many individuals are willing to make sizable donations without the added responsibility of a board seat. In addition, directors on a smaller board who are highly committed may prove to be more motivated to engage in fundraising among their network of relationships outside the board. Their commitment may produce more funding for the organization than relying on a large but disengaged group of board members. In essence, a significant trade-off is made with a large board. It is a commonly held belief that groups are most effective when they have seven members, plus or minus two. As a board grows in size, the quality of dialogue begins to diminish. In addition, consensus becomes extremely difficult to achieve. And members' commitment to their board responsibilities may also diminish, each knowing that he or she is but one of many. A perennial problem for nonprofit boards is the "no show" factor—absenteeism at board meetings. A smaller board may promote more frequent attendance on the assumption that board members feel more engaged when their numbers are fewer and more self-conscious about failing to show up. In conclusion, it is fair to say that many nonprofit boards are too large to be truly effective.

To compensate for this shortcoming, more and more nonprofits are relying on a smaller executive committee. While this approach restores the advantages of a small group, it creates the dilemma of an "in-group" and an "out-group." The executive or "upstairs" board, as it is often called, becomes the real board. The larger or "downstairs" board is essentially an honorary board. As Warren McFarlan (1999) has argued, this dynamic often alienates the downstairs board and leaves its members' talents poorly leveraged. For example, board members are often left out of critical decisions, which are instead made by the executive committee. So it is not clear that an executive committee actually resolves the dilemmas of a large board. For nonprofits wishing to experiment with smaller boards, a first step would be to shrink the number of directors to, say, twenty to thirty, relying primarily on attrition to achieve this outcome. It is not reasonable to expect nonprofit boards to be as small as corporate boards. I say this because I believe that nonprofits must rely on their directors for a greater number of responsibilities than they would in a corporate setting. Beyond philanthropy, nonprofit directors also can play important influence roles in the larger community. Corporations can afford internal specialists to perform certain of the roles that nonprofit boards must play without outside assistance. So the average of eleven on a Fortune 500 board is on the small side for nonprofits. That said, nonprofit boards of more than thirty directors are not likely to be effective. Smaller is indeed better. As with a corporate board, committees are still likely to be the real place where board members are best engaged and deployed in activities essential to the nonprofit. Ideally, committee membership would be limited to five to seven members—an appropriate size for effective teamwork. Activities over which board members have genuine influence should be the organizing principle for the formation of committees—

fundraising, director nominations, mission oversight of the organization, and so forth. Members of these committees should be carefully selected so that they bring a genuine expertise needed by that committee or have access to such expertise.

Accountability for Performance: Formally Evaluating the Board

An increasingly common practice for corporate boards today is an evaluation of their own performance as operating bodies. My own research shows that feedback about performance can help directors enhance their skills as board directors and motivate the board to focus on its performance (Conger, Lawler, and Finegold, 2001). Formal evaluations can also provide an ongoing discipline for directors to reflect on and assess their individual and collective contributions. Nonprofit boards may find them to be of similar value.

An effective board evaluation requires the right combination of timing, content, process, and individuals. In terms of timing, board evaluations should occur on an annual basis, although in a few organizations they are performed every other year. The board's performance, however, is so important and potentially so dynamic that it makes sense to have the evaluation process occur annually—especially if there is director turnover.

Board evaluations, which are almost always self-appraisals, start at the beginning of the organization's fiscal year. Directors typically agree to a set of objectives for the board and then assess performance against these targets at year end.

In terms of determining the right content and process for an evaluation, it is best to engage the entire board. Typically, a board committee designs an initial set of objectives that it feels covers the essential responsibilities of an effective board. These are presented to the full board, the CEO, and the chair for discussion and debate. A final list is produced, setting forth the evaluation criteria. Ideally, an effective evaluation would cover both the overall contribution of the board and the adequacy of support provided to the board. Typical questions in a board evaluation could include the following:

- Is the information the board receives of sufficient quality and quantity?
- How well are new directors brought up to speed on the organization and its critical issues?
- Are board members well prepared for meetings?
- What is the overall attendance record of the directors?
- Is sufficient time spent discussing the long-range future of the organization?
- Does the board effectively assist the CEO in his or her leadership role?

- Is the organization's mission well understood by all board members?
- Are appropriate processes in place to assess the CEO's performance effectively?
- What is the board's actual contribution to fundraising for the organization?

In setting objectives and measures, it is important that the board focus on the right number of key areas. Select too few, and certain essential responsibilities may be overlooked. Select too many, and there will be little sense of the board's priorities. For development, it is generally best to pick four to seven areas that the board needs to improve over the coming year. At the end-of-year review, it is a good idea to add to these developmental objectives a checklist of process-related measures. For example, a set of questions might assess the quality and quantity of information that the board receives on issues or whether this information is received in a timely manner or whether new directors are effectively brought up to speed on organizational issues or whether committees are being used efficiently.

Following identification of the key performance dimensions, board evaluations need to include a number of specific steps. First, board members should be provided with existing information about the board's activities and performance for the year under consideration. A committee chairperson, highly regarded director, or respected counselor to the board then distributes to every board member a questionnaire that uses both numerical rankings for boardroom activities and open-ended questions. Following the survey, this individual has a confidential one-on-one, more in-depth interview with each director. The results of both approaches are presented to the board in summary form and without attribution to individual directors unless an individual specifically requests that his or her name be used. A full board discussion follows, focusing on the areas identified for improvement.

This combination of appraisal steps provides several advantages. First, the scores on the questionnaires help board members numerically benchmark how they rank themselves along a series of dimensions. They can also see where they have differing viewpoints on the same activity. The interviews allow for greater detail and for topics to surface that are not covered by the questionnaire measuring formal objectives.

The evaluation report itself must be presented in a balanced way, highlighting the areas where there are divergent ratings or viewpoints. The selection of the presenter of the evaluation results is critical. Whether this person is a respected outsider, the chair of a committee, or a counselor to the board, his or her personal characteristics are just as important as the role he or she is asked to perform. Effective individuals are good listeners and communicators and are trusted by board members.

In summary, nonprofit boards may find formal evaluations valuable for reflectzing on their performance as governing bodies. Such evaluations can highlight both the strengths and limitations of the board and guide actions that enhance the overall leadership of the board. One important caveat applies to both the world of nonprofit and corporate boards. Once an effective board appraisal is up and running, there is a strong argument for regularly reexamining the process and the objectives to see how they can be improved or varied to avoid their becoming stale and bureaucratic.

Directors' Capabilities: Leveraging the Resources Around the Table

Highly effective corporate boards spend a great deal of time ensuring that their directors' talents and time are well leveraged. The first step begins with the selection process. When it comes to director selection, a number of criteria must be weighed if the right mix of directors is to be chosen. A seemingly obvious but often overlooked principle is that board members must be individuals who have time to invest in their board duties. All too often, board members serve on multiple boards and as a result simply cannot find the time to devote to their regular duties as a board member, much less to respond when extra time may need to be spent on committee work. Nonprofit boards are especially prone to this dilemma. One straightforward way to assess this issue is to inquire how many board memberships a prospective director currently holds. A person who serves on multiple boards and has a demanding full-time professional career is unlikely to contribute much to the board. Renewing directorships once every two or three years can allow boards to gracefully eliminate members who are not active contributors or repeatedly fail to attend meetings.

Even more important, the selection of board members needs to consider the expertise and knowledge of members so that the board as a whole has the ability to grasp the organization's central challenges, to assess and develop the management of the organization, and to address organizational and strategic issues the organization faces. Issues can range from financial to legal to technical to human resources to development. For example, experience on other nonprofits that have been highly successful with fundraising would be a desirable background characteristic of a prospective board member. They could share the "lessons learned." Familiarity with leading volunteer organizations is another important experience set. Ideally, boards would identify the knowledge bases that correspond to their current and emerging needs and attempt to find directors with expertise in those areas. It is important that boards have the knowledge to discuss all these issues intelligently and offer guidance. This argument suggests that boards must build their membership on the basis of the competencies and knowledge that individual directors bring so that the board as an entity constitutes an expertise base that covers all the key organizational and strategic issues they will face. In reality, too many nonprofits select their directors solely on the basis of their potential for philanthropy, their status in the community, or their interest in the nonprofit's mission. While these are important criteria, they should not be the only ones guiding director selection.

This understanding of the right knowledge bases for a board starts by identifying the key areas where the board needs to be knowledgeable. Each organization, of course, must develop its own list of key competencies that are needed and then staff the board accordingly. An important staffing criterion for a board is to ensure that each individual director brings at least one key competency (beyond philanthropy) so as to create a board that has both knowledge of the key issues and complementarity among the members' expertise. A number of highly effective corporate boards draw up a board member expertise matrix or chart for use in selecting board members. This matrix shows board members along one axis and key knowledge areas along the other. This allows the board to quickly assess where it has knowledge gaps and to take that into consideration when making appointments to the board. A critical first step in developing an effective matrix is the identification of the knowledge areas that should be represented on the board (see Exhibit 9.1 for a list of possible knowledge areas).

Beyond knowledge or expertise, it is a useful practice to have existing board members interview prospective new members to determine if there is a good fit. Boards need more than just the right mixture of technical and business expertise; they need to be able to make effective use of their members' knowledge and operate as a team. Selecting individuals who can work well with the existing board members can help create an effective team dynamic. At the same time, it is critical that boards have a diversity of perspectives to ensure fresh thinking about issues and alternative views on issues. It is important to select directors who have differing backgrounds and who bring experiences and worldviews that are distinct from one another. Otherwise, too much similarity in board members can foster a lack of innovative problem solving and a failure to explore issues from multiple angles.

It is not reasonable to expect all board members to come to any board with all the knowledge that they need to operate effectively as members of a group. The board therefore needs to take steps to build the knowledge base of its members and of the board as a functioning team. The most effective corporate boards provide ongoing learning opportunities that focus on the internal and external challenges that the organization faces. They create educational forums for their directors. They set up conversations with important constituents and presentations by internal managers to enhance the directors' knowledge about the organization. They also set up special "on-boarding" days for new members to educate them about the organization and the board.

EXHIBIT 9.1. POSSIBLE KEY KNOWLEDGE AREAS FOR DIRECTORS.

Organizational Mission and Strategy

Organizational mission: Knowledge of the nonprofit's primary mission and the constituents it serves.

Strategy formulation: Knowledge of the strengths and weaknesses of alternative models for the nonprofit's services.

Leadership

Senior executive development: Skills in coaching senior leaders and helping them set goals for self-development. Ability to provide meaningful and constructive feedback to the CEO.

Organizational Issues

Implementation: Understanding of how plans can be most successfully implemented through the organization's systems, core competencies, and human resources.

Change management: Knowledge of basic change processes.

Organizational design: Understanding of alternative organizational structures, their strengths and weaknesses, and how they affect the nonprofit's mission.

Relationships

Community: Knowledge of key communities that the nonprofit serves and draws on for resources.

Government: Understanding of how to deal with government agencies and the network of relationships in those agencies.

Volunteers: Knowledge of volunteer resources and how to recruit and retain talented volunteers.

Functional Knowledge

Development: Knowledge of strategies for fundraising and the organizational competencies required for successful developmental activities.

Finance and accounting: Understanding of financial and accounting issues relevant to the nonprofit.

Legal: Understanding of the legal issues the nonprofit faces.

Human resources: Knowledge of the critical talent issues the organization faces and effective approaches for talent development.

Marketing: Understanding of the nonprofit's constituents and effective approaches for marketing to them.

MEETING FORMATS: LEVERAGING THE TIME SPENT TOGETHER

A board needs to have sufficient time and opportunity to make effective decisions. The dilemma is that most meeting formats get in the way of this outcome. In place of useful discussions, board meetings in both the corporate and nonprofit worlds tend to be short on time for dialogue and long on formal one-way presentations to the board. As a result, they often feel more like a ritual or ceremony than like a constructive use of the time and talent of the board.

What the more effective corporate boards have done in recent years is to move away from highly regimented meetings with tight schedules and an array of formal presentations. They focus each meeting on only a few of the priority issues before the organization. Meeting time is scheduled to ensure that individual issues can be discussed thoroughly. Although there may be presentations about a specific issue, sufficient time is set aside for discussion and debate following each presentation. In poorly governed corporate boardrooms, not only is meeting time consumed by presentations, but the presentations often contain a great deal of background information on issues. For example, they might review the organization's mission and strategy—information that is already widely known. Or presentations might explore in depth an issue of relatively low priority. Well-led boards provide their directors with this information in advance of the board meeting so that meeting time can be used to make decisions rather than simply to educate directors. Achieving the proper balance isn't easy; I have seen boards err on both the side of too little information and the side of too much. It is crucial that the CEO, the board chair, and perhaps certain committee members ascertain the right type and amount of information for directors to receive. This information must be received by directors sufficiently in advance of meetings that they will be prepared to discuss critical issues when the meeting begins. In addition, directors must be informed that they are expected to arrive at meetings having read the advance materials. If the information is complex and difficult to understand, it may be advisable to schedule phone conferences before the regular board meeting in order to be sure that individuals come with an understanding of the issues.

One issue related to time is the frequency of meetings. I am often asked, "What is the correct number of meetings an effective board should hold each year?" There is of course no magic number of meetings, but logic suggests that a minimum of eight or ten full-day meetings a year would seem to be necessary. In addition, committee meetings need to be scheduled to complement full board meetings, and these may be held anywhere from four to ten times a year, depending on the issue before the committee. At least once every year or two, a board retreat should be scheduled to focus tightly on key strategic issues and the overall mission of the organization. These meetings would open with the CEO presenting the current and future state of the organization and then raise the major strategic challenges with which he or she would like to engage the board during the retreat. Individual committees could be assigned issues relevant to their particular committee. After discussions within the committee groups, the entire board would convene and discuss the conclusions or perspectives of the committee discussions. In addition, committee members could receive in advance detailed descriptions of the challenges that will be discussed so that individual members could ponder the issues before the retreat. These retreats are about educating board members in the opportunities and dilemmas facing the nonprofit and at the same time enlisting the board's help in addressing them successfully.

CONCLUSION

Beyond the four practices that I have identified in this chapter, there may be additional practices in the world of corporate governance that are transferable to nonprofit boards. Readers should therefore not regard this list as exhaustive but rather as a starting point for experimentation. Boards might wish to review the literature on corporate governance practices and debate those that have the greatest relevance and application to their particular organization and situation. Careful experimentation with individual practices can determine what is transferable and what is not. That said, not all of the practices of the corporate boardroom can or should be transferred. Consequently, nonprofits boards must also take the lead in devising boardroom governance practices that uniquely fit their special needs and requirements.

REFERENCES

Conger, J. A., Lawler, E. E., and Finegold, D. L. *Corporate Boards: New Strategies for Adding Value at the Top.* Jossey-Bass: San Francisco, 2001.

Daily, C. M., and Dalton, D. R. "CEO and Board Chair Roles Held Jointly or Separately: Much Ado About Nothing?" *Academy of Management Executive,* 1997, *11*(3), 11–20.

Dalton, D. R., Daily, C. M., Johnson, J. L., and Ellstrand, A. E. "Number of Directors and Financial Performance: A Meta-Analysis." *Academy of Management Journal,* 1999, *42*(6), 674–686.

Firstenberg, P., and Malkiel, B. "The Twenty-First-Century Boardroom: Who Will Be in Charge?" *Sloan Management Review,* 1994, *36*(1), 27–37.

Judge, W., and Zeithan, C. "Institutional and Strategic Choice Perspectives on Board Involvement in the Strategic Decision Process." *Academy of Management Journal,* 1992, *35*(4), 766–794.

Lorsch, J. W., and MacIver, E. A. *Pawns or Potentates: The Reality of America's Corporate Boards.* Boston: Harvard Business School Press, 1989.

McFarlan, F. W. "Working on Nonprofit Boards: Don't Assume the Shoe Fits." *Harvard Business Review,* November-December 1999, pp. 65–80.

National Association of Corporate Directors/Center for Board Leadership. *1999–2000 Public Company Governance Survey.* Washington, D.C.: National Association of Corporate Directors, 2000.

CHAPTER TEN

LAST THINGS FIRST— THEORIES AND REALITIES

A Perspective on Nonprofit Leadership

Susan M. Scribner

Studies. Surveys. Questionnaires. We know more than ever about why people volunteer, effective "buzzwords" to attract them to our agencies, and innovative ways to keep them happy and, most important, active. A wagonload of valuable information is available to help us strengthen our boards and volunteers in new ways. Implementing those bright ideas is the challenge!

Many nonprofit organizations tend to operate backward: focusing on solutions instead of problems, chasing funds to create programs, seeking people of wealth and power to (it is hoped) infuse their agencies with support. For what? Rather than focusing on clients, the agency's survival often becomes the organization's mission. Yet I don't recall seeing that in a single one of the thousands of mission statements I have read over the years.

Structure is a solution. Fundraising is a solution. Staff and volunteers are solutions. The agency itself is a solution. The only problems worth solving are those facing the clients served. When that perspective reverses, panicked agencies seek to build their resources of funds, volunteers, and connections in order to keep the agency viable. That's nice, but who cares? A panicked "grabbing at straws" attitude can create an agency that operates partly, if not totally, outside its intended mission or can create a leadership without a commitment to the clients served. Both those outcomes are dead ends.

Rather than jumping into the middle of a funeral procession, it can be much more effective to start at the beginning of the parade. Organizations concerned about attracting diverse leadership and funding need to take the time to ensure that all involved are heading in the same direction (which often is not the case). Without a consensus of understanding, staff and volunteer leadership skills and talents can get diffused in a wide variety of well-meaning but often frustrating and ineffective directions, with some people focusing on one program while others are interested in a different issue and on and on. Strength comes from subscribing to a common vision achieved through a partnership of volunteers and staff.

I have had the pleasure (and at times the extreme challenge!) of working with boards of directors throughout the United States and several foreign countries for more than twenty years. As the U.S. Representative of Nevsky Angel in Saint Petersburg, Russia, I work with hundreds of emerging nongovernment organizations (NGOs) representing thousands of people new to the concepts of volunteerism, fundraising, and board development. As is the case with their counterparts in the United States, I find volunteer and staff leadership roles crucial to the success of group consensus and action.

I have worked with strong and gifted staff leaders who are hesitant to use the expertise of their board members for fear of threatening their control. I have worked with talented board members who, due to their lack of understanding their own roles, micromanage staff issues.

Many of my weekends are spent conducting board-staff retreats. I am continually stunned by the boards' and staff's realizations of the talents, interests, passions, and skills each of them can provide. "I didn't know you can do that!" "You know him?" "I'd be willing to join that group." "I work with her too!" are phrases heard constantly throughout the process. Monthly meetings provide little opportunity for true communication. Meetings are held at night. Meetings are held offsite. Talk is about and over stacks of paper. There isn't time to work together; the focus is on pushing to get through agendas. Rarely do people get to know each other, let alone the wealth of talent that may be accessible in their midst.

I obtained a trademark recently for the phrase I've heard most often during the years: Fonly™. "Fonly we had more rich people on our board." "Fonly a corporation would adopt us." Fonly. Fonly. Fonly. A great deal of time is spent whining that "if only" this or that would happen, we would be fine rather than dealing the cards from the deck of strengths already in the room.

Each of us who work with nonprofit organizations has the responsibility of serving as champions on behalf of others, making educated, thoughtful, and prudent decisions and commitments for the people or issues we represent. Uniting the talents and strengths of board and staff is the most effective way to do so.

A strong and united partnership between board and staff leadership is critical to the success of any agency's efforts to create a positive, inclusive atmosphere of ownership in a unified vision and identify and to make best use of the talents and skills of all involved.

The following strategies are aimed at both identifying and applying often hidden talents and strengths of gifted people in organizations who simply need opportunities to engage and involve them. The first tackles our greatest enemy, assumptions.

Choices, Not Assumptions

Staff and volunteers often assume that they all want the same thing, but I usually find that this is not the case. One of the first issues I ask a group to consider is the important choices that they face at any given time as fiduciaries on behalf of those they serve and what is best for them. The discussions are difficult. The choices are simple: (1) stay the same, (2) grow, (3) shrink, or (4) dissolve. Many staff and volunteers disagree regarding these basic issues. At times, staff may want to move forward but board members may feel the need to stabilize or even cut back programs. The reverse can be true as well. Individuals within the staff and volunteer ranks are often not in agreement either. Without resolution of this basic foundation of intent, collective resources cannot be brought together in strength. Each option needs to be discussed in detail as to its impact on the agency's clients as well as the individuals responsible for implementing them, forcing staff and board to focus on the mission instead of the agency itself. Let us now examine each of the four choices and the implications for each.

Stay the Same

What would it mean to the people we serve if we stay the same—same programs, same funding, same policies, board, volunteers, and so on? For some, it may mean a slow death; for others, it may simply mean continuing to provide the same service! Some may consider this boring. Others might consider it safe. Many organizations have found that what they are doing is "just fine" and simply need to give themselves permission to stop growing! Individuals who disagree with such decisions tend to leave these agencies to start new ones; a strong indicator as to why we have so many nonprofit organizations.

Grow

Volunteer and staff leaders often do not discuss the issues of growth in detail. "Of course we want to grow" does not address what that actually means in terms of personal commitment, involvement, and the other ramifications of such a decision. What type of growth does the agency seek? Stabilization? More programs? Stronger programs? Bigger isn't necessarily better—better is better. As much as leadership may tend to jump on this seemingly "correct" focus, there is a need to discuss and consider what it means to them, personally, and to the organization as a whole. More work. More recruitment. More outreach for expertise. More effort. More funds. Change. If an organization is having difficulties maintaining its current services, choosing to grow may not be the answer—it can make things worse.

Shrink

One of my favorite analogies regards Christian the Plate Thrower, who used to appear regularly on the Ed Sullivan Show. Most people who had TV in the 1950s remember the scene of Christian's many plates spinning in the air, each supported by a long stick underneath. Christian would run back and forth down the rows of plates and sticks, having to spin a stick whenever the plate atop it started to wobble.

Our gifted nonprofit agencies, like Christian, tend to keep many plates spinning in the air—just because they can. With mission statements the size of elephants, they can almost instantly be perceived as offering something for everyone. They are gifted. They are diversely talented. They are wrong. Attracting donations (sticks) for new programs (plates) is fine, as long as the sticks remain strong and sustainable. However, what often happens is that as more and more plates are added, some of them start to wobble due to lack of support. And if you don't give the stick another whirl in time, wham! The plate hits the floor. And what was on that plate? People.

I would much prefer that an organization spin just three or four plates and have strong sticks to support them, rather than keep identifying new plates to twirl in the air without adequate support. Agencies should not start a program they can't sustain beyond the start-up stage, when funding is often more plentiful.

Shrinking doesn't necessarily mean "less." It can mean strengthening; for example, it can mean building reserves and community support to ensure that the agency "does not write checks it can't cash." It can mean collaboration, joint ventures, branding, undertaking for-profit business ventures—all utilizing the gifts and talents already accessible to the organization.

Dissolve

Most nonprofit agencies consider this a horrifying option. However, when an organization is client-focused rather than agency-focused, the dissolution option can be explored without panic. There are more than one million nonprofit agencies in the United States. The survival of any one of them is of absolutely no concern to me. Sorry. What is important is their effectiveness. Are they serving their clients in the best manner, or are they getting in the way, using up resources that could be put to better use? More than a few times, I have seen relief in the eyes of stressed volunteers and staff who have finally been "given permission" to do what is best for their clients—merge with another agency or "get out of the way." This is unthinkable if one is agency-focused but very thinkable if the focus is on the clients and what is best for them.

The bottom line is that if some of the leaders within an organization (staff, volunteer, or both) want to grow and some want to stay the same, there can be no "same page," only frustration and confusion and poor results. Assumptions are one of the worst (and most easily solved) problems facing volunteer-staff partnerships. Creating a shared vision with all the supporting components defined is the only way to eliminate assumptions. What's next? The important areas of focus deal with specifics for building your volunteer resources—the whys, hows, and what's in it for me's of developing your organization's volunteer capacity.

Ready, Set, Now What?

Once board and staff members are moving in the same general direction, the issues regarding appropriate "solutions" need to be addressed.

1. How many board members should we have? That depends on how many are needed to meet identified goals, objectives, and work plans. Board members are not like aspirin (if one is good, three are better). The types of skills and diversity needed on the board can be determined only once its tasks have been identified.

2. What type of staff and volunteer expertise do we need to implement our plans? That also depends on specific goals and the skills necessary and available to achieve them. Once objectives and work plans are completed, the "skills needed" and the "who should we recruit for what" list is not difficult to develop.

Realistic Roles and Rules

The days of full-time, in-your-face volunteers are virtually gone. People have jobs. People have interests. People have lives.

Trying to get people to join boards and even standing committees is almost impossible due to fears about time constraints. People have limited time, and nonprofit boards and committees have a (well-earned) reputation for conducting long and not always succinct meetings, which is why people are generally more eager to volunteer for special events—these have an end, which is usually in clear sight!

A valuable solution I have recommended and implemented for many years is "tiger teams"—focused, short-term task groups to address specific organizational issues or needs. Once priorities have been identified, tasks and goals can be divided into short-term projects for tiger teams, each with specific goals, objectives, and skill requirements related to the tasks to be completed, with generally no more than four meetings of two hours each, and accompanied by massive doses of sugary food.

Chaired by a member of the board and consisting of a minority of board members and a majority of carefully selected (and shamelessly flattered) community experts, tiger teams can attract and engage new and willing volunteers to provide critical expertise in the short term. In turn, volunteers are given the opportunity to learn more about the agency and will often seek ways to continue the relationship. In the end, everyone wins. The leadership gains the expertise it needs, a project is completed in a timely manner, new volunteers get involved with the organization, and its leadership is given the opportunity to work with prospective volunteer leaders before considering them for committee or even board positions.

Sticking Power

To attract and keep caring, committed people, agency leaders need to treat volunteers, prospects, donors, and staff with the same consideration and compassion as they treat their clients. The operative phrase is WIIFM ("What's in it for me?").

People give their time, skills, passion, and funds because of their own unique WIIFMs. Plaques are not for everyone. Some people want to learn new things; others want to use their skills in new ways; some want to meet new people or use their time to make a difference. The challenge for nonprofit leadership is to identify and meet the WIIFMs of all those involved, establishing an exchange—you have something we want, and we have something you want. When people's needs are met, they act. When their needs are not met, they don't act. Each person, now and tomorrow, needs to participate in a process that helps identify his or her WIIFMs and match them up with agency opportunities, followed by ongoing communication to ensure that the needs of both are being met.

Expertise assumptions tend to rear their heads regarding recruitment as well. Having been involved professionally in financial development for almost thirty years, I am constantly asked if I would like to serve on a nonprofit financial development committee. No, thank you; I do that all day long! Why not offer me an opportunity to do something that I would like to do?

We often assume that a CPA should be the treasurer for life, that someone who knows shorthand or how to write nice memos should be the secretary, and so on. We tend to attract people by what they do rather than who they are. That's the wrong approach. In addition to identifying WIIFMs, individuals need to be able to make choices: some may want to use their expertise in a new way; others may be seeking new and refreshing opportunities far removed from their normal routine.

Your Place—and Your Place in It

OK, we've got our volunteer development capacity figured out. We now need to consider some important descriptors and elements of the place that volunteers will become a part of—your nonprofit organization and the expectations for performance—on both sides, volunteer and staff.

The Place to Be

Nonprofit staff and volunteers have been apologizing (and, frankly, lying) for years about board positions. "I promise, all you have to do is attend a few meetings." "I swear you won't have to ask anyone for anything." "It's nothing—you can do it with your eyes closed." Baloney. The less value placed on the positions, the less they are worth having or keeping. Boards of directors I work with are encouraged to sign letters of agreements or contracts that simply state expectations between themselves and the agency: uphold the bylaws, attend meetings, serve on at least one committee, make a thoughtful donation, and so on. Fiduciaries are responsible champions on behalf of others. If individuals are treated as such and held accountable for what they do (or do not do), it is amazing how long waiting lists can become to join nonprofit boards that actually stand for something.

The Place to Stay

Orientations accompanied by fifty-pound notebooks are usually both boring and ineffective. Pass a budget around the boardroom once in a while and ask anyone except the treasurer to explain it. The silence will be frightening. But why would anyone know how to read a financial statement? How many volunteers go to board school? In lieu of an "orientation avalanche," regular brief "trainettes" during each board meeting can be extremely effective. Try ten minutes at one meeting on "what to look for in our financial statements," another at the next meeting on "what board insurance covers," and so on. All the important aspects of agency operation, policies, and procedures can be addressed throughout the year in smaller, easier-to-swallow doses. In addition to ongoing communication, board and staff members need to clarify their roles. A simple discussion between board and staff leaders can address a surprising number of current problems and assumptions and help eliminate most future problems and misunderstandings.

Let's look more closely at some possible trainette topics.

What Do Board Members Expect of Each Other? This discussion helps the board write its own job description, clarifying such items as "attend meetings," "make meaningful contributions," and "join at least one committee." Rather than hand a prewritten (and thereafter ignored) board job description sheet to members, having them create their own provides a much stronger sense of ownership (and reality). The group should avoid such generalizations as "I expect my fellow board members to be committed." What exactly does that mean? Specifics are extremely important and should be identified as much as possible.

In response to a need I perceived to state the roles of boards and staff in more human terms, I have written and published a number of books and guides referenced in this chapter. Much to my surprise, my own need to simplify IRS, attorney general, and bylaws issues seems to be shared by many, as the books are distributed throughout the world in three languages, reflecting, I must assume, a growing universal desire to simply understand the rules!

In *Boards from Hell* (1991), I help identify the rights and roles of board members, which often are misunderstood. For example, I point out that attend monthly meetings is not a job description and that to make sound, prudent decisions, each board member shares in all the responsibilities and powers of the directors. However, sharing in responsibilities and powers does not eliminate the need for every board member to exercise independent judgment. Directors should not be satisfied with things as they have always been. All board members should submit financial, conflict-of-interest, and conflict-of-commitment statements to ensure full disclosure; members who face potential conflict in specific agency activities should disclose them before the board takes action.

Although the board usually relies on information provided primarily by staff, board members have the responsibility, the obligation, and the right to inspect records and materials or to engage outside expertise to do so. Members should feel free to contact the executive director or CEO yet must restrain themselves from undermining staff leadership by working too closely with other agency staff or management.

It can also be extremely helpful for members of the board to write their own "contracts" or letters of agreement, which state the rules, expectations, and general policies. Signed by the board chair or president, these agreements clarify a great number of issues and provide accountability. A sample board contract or letter of agreement is presented in Exhibit 10.1.

EXHIBIT 10.1. SAMPLE BOARD "CONTRACT" OR LETTER OF AGREEMENT.

Ms. Sara Jones
1234 Second Street
Los Angeles, CA 90278

Dear Sara:

On behalf of the board and staff of _____ , I am delighted to invite you to become a member of the board of directors.

With the other members of the board, you will be responsible for determining agency policy, developing the annual budget, monitoring and evaluating the agency's goals, and authorizing and taking responsibility for funding.

As we discussed, the key responsibility areas for a board member are the following:

1. Policy Administration: Ensures that the agency operates within its bylaws. Acts on proposed revisions to bylaws. Recommends policies, which determine the purpose, governing principles, functions, and activities of the agency.

2. Evaluation: Regularly monitors the activities of the agency, including committee work, proposals, and agency operation.

3. Public and Community Relations: Understands the work of the agency and interprets it to the community.

4. Personnel: Annually evaluates the executive director or CEO. Approves all personnel policies. Participates in recruitment and development of board, advisory council, and committee members.

5. Finance: Approves and monitors the agency's finances. Maintains an appropriate financial climate for fulfilling the agency's purposes through personal contributions and fundraising activities. Authorizes and approves the annual audit. Makes recommendations and monitors all agency expenditures dealing with the facilities and their operation. Participates in agency fundraising activities.

6. Program: Maintains familiarity with agency programs and participates when appropriate. Participates in program planning, monitoring, and evaluation.

Your signature on this agreement indicates your willingness to adhere to board duties and responsibilities as outlined in the agency's board manual and bylaws, to serve for a two-year period, to attend all board meetings, to serve on at least one board committee, and to participate in public relations and fundraising activities.

You have been given a schedule of board meeting dates and times and a calendar of agency activities and have indicated a desire to serve on the _____ committee.

All of us at _____ appreciate your commitment to our clients in the community and look forward to working with you.

     Sincerely,

     Sandra Smith
     President, Board of Directors

Agreed to on _____ , 20____

_____
Sara Jones, Member, Board of Directors

What Should the Board Expect of the Staff? Hilarity usually greets any discussion of board expectations of often underpaid and overworked staff members. What does the board expect? "Everything!" tends to be the answer of choice. Of course, that response is not acceptable. Board and staff need to discuss realistic expectations. Having five staff and twenty-six board members can be difficult enough under the best of circumstances and intolerable when clarity is lacking. What type of information does the board need and when? How should the staff help the board avoid "surprises"? Board members must also realize that they have a number of roles to play in the organization and that they are not always wearing their board member hat. For example, board members who work as program volunteers report to and are supervised by staff. It is inappropriate for them to maintain a director leadership role while fulfilling the program volunteer responsibilities. Of course, the board member hat will be donned again at the next board meeting—staff are cautioned not to take advantage of this (temporary) change of status!

What Should the Staff Expect of the Board? This is usually the most critical and least discussed issue regarding the partnership of board and staff. Staff members rarely understand how to work with the board, how and when to communicate with members, and how to set limits, use expertise appropriately through committees, and avoid misunderstandings. Expectations of board members among the staff are usually minimal due to the fact that both board and staff frequently misunderstand the board's true role in the organization.

Meetings can be more effective if sample scenarios are developed and randomly discussed. For example, a board member enters the organization and is told by the receptionist that he or she cannot see the executive director because "all board members do is waste the director's time." The upset board member calls the executive director to complain and is told, "Don't worry about it; that's just my cousin." Now what?

The discussion that follows such extreme examples will often provide a safe climate in which to clarify the staff leadership's role with the board; the board members need to respect executive director–staff boundaries (as well as hold the executive director accountable for staff performance!) and personnel, grievance, and other policies. It is an effective approach to specifically discuss problems and solutions before they occur.

What Should the Organization Expect of Its Chair and Officers? Few people attend board leadership school. Gavels do not come with instructions. In *Are You Chairing a Board by the Seat of Your Pants?* (Scribner, 1999a), I have tried to find a number of ways for agencies to create rules and regulations that are tailored to their own unique situations. Exhibit 10.2 presents a list of things to include in a board chair kit. The text will focus on a number of specifics.

The chair is responsible to ensure that the board discusses and adopts rules and regulations. Policies are rules for organizational behavior: statements of authority, values, and procedures for how things will be done within the agency. Procedures give us consistency. The board should discuss and approve policies in the following areas:

- Program scope and objectives
- General organization and procedures of agency and board operation
- Defining the management areas of staff
- Personnel relations and procedures
- Public relations, information distribution
- Financial development

Thanks to an endless number of statutes and constitutional provisions, in most of the United States, the state attorney general has the authority to hold a director of a public benefit or religious corporation accountable. The main role of the attorney general's office is to ensure that funds are used properly and that the organization is operating within its original charitable purposes. Board chairs are encouraged to contact their state attorney general's office to obtain a copy of their responsibilities, as each state differs slightly.

Although nonprofit organizations have an "obligation" to ensure that donor funds are used appropriately (especially restricted donations), it truly is the role of the board, not donors, to determine how agency funds are to be spent.

All boards should reexamine their mission and responsibilities from time to time to ensure that they are flexible and responsive to changing community and economic issues. Remember, the mission of the organization is to do what is best for the clients, not what will ensure the preservation of the nonprofit agency itself!

Fruitful discussion can provide board officers with the tools and permission they need to do their jobs. Many people are reluctant to uphold agency bylaws or to take action if a board member does not come to meetings or complete an assignment as agreed. Board members can tell their leaders exactly how to do their jobs by clarifying expectations as to how to enforce bylaws, what to do when board members do not fulfill their responsibilities, how to delegate effectively, and so on.

Each organization that has both a board chair and an executive director operates uniquely, depending on the styles and personalities of the individuals involved. Ideally, chairs and executive directors work in an atmosphere of friendship, support, tolerance, honesty, and partnership; helping each other with the difficult tasks they face separately and together. Ideally.

EXHIBIT 10.2. WHAT TO INCLUDE IN A BOARD CHAIR KIT.

1. Aspirin
2. A sense of humor
3. Permission to have fun
4. Perspective—get away once in a while
5. Communication—individual and group
6. Limits and boundaries so you can have a life
7. A clear understanding of your role with others in the agency
8. Opportunities to attend training sessions and leadership development workshops
9. Willingness to change and grow
10. Ongoing connection with agency clients to keep them foremost in your mind
11. Permission to yourself to make mistakes, even big ones
12. Permission to forgive yourself
13. Permission not to know everything
14. Willingness to let others help and make mistakes, even big ones
15. The right to miss a meeting once in a while
16. Access to skills you need—whether in finance, funding, marketing, or programs—surround yourself with others who know more than you, and let them help; people *love* giving advice
17. The wisdom to listen to others' suggestions; there is a lot to learn
18. Enough kindness to ensure that everyone is appropriately included in activities ranging from planning to fundraising, to build ownership; remember, process often is more important than product
19. Respect for all volunteers, staff, and members of your agency's "family"
20. Respect for yourself: know when to stay and when to leave
21. Above all, respect for your clients and what is best for them

Some pairs of leaders have, shall we say, less than ideal relationships. Board chairs have been equally guilty of undermining executive director decisions as directors have been of working around the chair to get to the rest of the board.

Working together as staff and volunteer leaders is similar to getting married. In marriage, one notices irritating little habits like missing toothpaste caps or chronic channel surfing. Many of these new discoveries are overlooked or accepted as part of the whole of the partnership. The same can be true for volunteer and staff leaders: at first, a few new quirks are noticed—failure to return phone calls, missed deadlines, and so on. In time, however, just as in some marriages, these little annoyances can explode into major problems, creating barriers and "camps" of support and diverting organizational energy from its clients to itself and the behavior of its leaders. What a terrible waste of time, talent, and energy!

Nonprofit organizations face unique problems of staff-volunteer leadership sharing, though many for-profit agencies often have their own boards with which to deal. Nonprofits, however, often stand an easier chance of resolving problems, as they are, or should be, vision-driven rather than resource-driven.

The more realistic board leadership positions can be made through the clear definition and delegation of responsibility, the more attractive they will be for future volunteers.

What Should We All Expect of Ourselves? Not only do board and staff members need to clarify expectations of each other, but time should also be spent discussing individual (staff and board) and personal expectations and limitations. Most people tend to believe that the two roles on boards are "all" or "nothing," without much room in between. As a result, promises get broken due to unrealistic expectations, members start developing negative attitudes, and in time, these roles tend to become cemented and taken for granted—"our board of fifteen has four active members!"

Every group includes people with a variety of activity levels; some people will always do more than others. Effective leaders, however, can help individuals tailor their interests, passions, talents, and time to agency needs. People need to be given permission to say, "I'm sorry, I can't do that" or "I don't know how" or "I can't do ten of those, but I'll try for five"—permission to set limits and to speak the truth.

The Place to Thrive

"I'll do anything for this group except raise money." "I don't know anybody who has money to give." "I don't want to ask."

Board members have historically come up with creative excuses not to ask for funds. It is almost as if agreements have been signed stating that the volunteer leaders "promise never to meet anyone with funds and, if they do, not to tell the agency about it."

Nonprofit staff and board leaders have wondered since nonprofit agencies began why this problem has plagued the industry. It's our fault. It is common knowledge that the number one fear of people in the United States is public speaking. Second is asking for money; third is death. People would rather die than ask for anything! It's small wonder, therefore, why a volunteer heads for the door when well-meaning staff and a few brave board members seek their help in attracting funds to organizations.

The only solution to eliminate this time-honored problem is to eliminate it! If asked to seek funding from even the best-researched prospect, volunteers are likely to head for the hills. However, if simply asked to serve as ambassadors on behalf of the agency's clients and to go along, with a staff person or another volunteer in tow, to speak their own truth for a few minutes about why they care about the agency, most will be happy to do so. Words such as *solicitor, fundraiser,* and *asker* should be banned from boardrooms and replaced with *ambassador, champion,* and *voice on behalf of others.* (Additional fundraising recommendations and tools can be found in *How to Ask for Money Without Fainting;* Scribner, 1999b.)

Board members do not have to know every statistic about the agency and its clients or be able to explain each and every number on its financial statements. As fiduciaries, they are, of course, responsible for educating themselves about the business of the agency in order to fulfill their leadership responsibility; however, one of the most often stated concerns of volunteers regarding "asking" is that the volunteer may not be able to answer all the questions. They fear that they must know the same information that staff leaders and personnel work with in detail every day. This puts unreasonable (and unrealistic) pressure on the volunteers, who can indeed voice tremendous issues of truth and concern. Ensuring that experienced staff or volunteer leaders accompany agency volunteers when meeting with prospects can relieve a great deal of concern and pressure on the part of well-meaning but nervous volunteers, giving them the opportunity to talk about their favorite subject—why they are involved and their commitment to the organization's clients.

Sometimes the Place to Leave

Having been a floundering founder myself, it is always a tricky business to know when it's time to leave, how to leave, or when it's time for *others* to leave.

I stayed too long at "my" nonprofit. The warning signs (though in retrospect they seem the size of billboards) were not as visible to me as they were to everyone else. Too much control, too much worrying, too much expecting. Just too much! I was gently, and kindly, told by family and friends that I was making everybody (including myself) crazy and losing any semblance of objectivity—my mission had become MY MISSION. And gifted volunteers and staff around me were more than capable of doing the job, thank you very much. And they did the job even better. Wasn't that what I wanted in the first place?

But how can you fire a volunteer? How rude—after all, these people are *donating* their time (and sometimes their troubles) to the agency.

First of all, abandon that assumption. You may think it's easier to live with a difficult or invisible volunteer, but rest assured that the rest of the board is not thrilled about it, and it almost always is a terrible drain on the agency. What should you do? Consider the following eight points.

1. Put your clients in the front of your mind. What is best for them? A well-run organization with involved board membership. Empty seats do not help at all. Inactivity is not acceptable.

2. Banish the word *fire* from your thoughts. What you really want is this person to create a board vacancy, not necessarily go away. In some cases, going away is necessary, but usually it's a matter of finding a new and more suitable role for the person (and a new and more suitable person for the board).

3. Accept the fact that *you must do something.* It is a matter of what, not if.

4. Identify your options. You can deal with difficult or phantom board members in many ways:

- Ask them to separate from the agency (for example, with a testimonial dinner).
- Invite them to join endowment councils or special groups.
- Invite them to become advisory council members.
- Encourage them to participate in a special project.

Is there some issue of special interest to the person who is not performing up to expectations? Do you want the person to maintain a relationship with the organization? If so, be sure it is for the right reasons. Do not fear retaliation; often the person's reputation with other organizations is the same, so don't let that issue get in your way. If you are afraid that you may lose promised funds, forget it. More often than not, difficult or phantom people try to bribe agencies with "potential" gifts that never materialize. Even if you know the gift is legitimate, consider your options and what is best for your organization. It's better to put your energies into other, more promising gift opportunities.

5. If you have a signed board contract or job description, life will be much easier. Members can be approached to discuss their apparent inability to follow through with their initial commitments—the perfect time for suggesting, might it be better for *them* to look for a more appropriate role in the agency? In other words, tell them, "We love you still, but *over there.*"

6. Obviously, the easiest difficult members to remove are those who never show up at all. To confirm your responsibility and that of board members for attendance, consult your bylaws. Most organizations have a "three strikes and you're out" clause. Write a letter and be done with it. This is actually for the recipients' own good, as they bear the same legal responsibility as the rest of the board, even if they don't show up. In some cases, you may wish to invite them to join an advisory council or some other activity for which their expertise can be valuable.

7. Don't bother moving your board meetings or changing the time. Difficult people always find them.

8. Bite the bullet. If the member is active (and many difficult ones are), you must gather your courage, bring another board member with you, and just *do it.* You are doing no one any favors by prolonging the inevitable. As a matter of fact, you are probably losing good board members due to ongoing problems with difficult

or phantom board members that can be eliminated or avoided with appropriate and decisive action.

Try a nice approach first: appreciating their efforts and realizing that the position is more than they had probably understood to be the case; that they would be a great help on the advisory council or whatever. The firm approach is next. Clearly both sides aren't happy, and it seems that their needs aren't being met either, blah, blah, blah. Regardless of your approach, as in fundraising, you must be *specific*. You must say the words: "We believe it is in everyone's best interest, including yours, if you resign from the board of directors." *Say it*. If the situation is extreme (and it may well be), you may have to go back to your bylaws and vote the offender off the board. Be sure to contact legal counsel before making such a move. It must be orchestrated legally.

Is it ever easy? Never! Is it necessary? Absolutely. And it's the job as the chair to treat volunteers (and staff, donors, and others) with the same concern and compassion that all should hold for the people served by your agency. Sometimes that means undertaking difficult measures. It might mean that some board members will be angry. Some might even resign. It might also mean that your agency can get on with its real job.

Founding board members are particularly difficult to address. Many founders work with agencies forever without a problem; they are willing to permit others to assume leadership positions, enabling the agency to remain flexible to changing community need. Some founders, unfortunately, can turn parades into funerals—building bases of board loyalty to "secure" their positions; they are people often threatened by any suggestion, no matter how creative or helpful.

All board members, including founders, have the obligation to limit their service with boards—not because they run out of energy, input, or expertise but because "habitual membership" can create an atmosphere of sameness that is not always in the best interests of the clients served. An infusion of new people with fresh ideas and energy (who have earned their way onto the board through committees or tiger teams) can provide valuable perspectives. Members rotating away from board service (either permanently or for one-year periods) can still stay actively involved in the organization through service on committees and task forces. Such breaks are healthy for all concerned.

When to Start

Start now. If you are even a bit concerned, know that you are not the only one! Often it takes but a single voice to draw like-thinking people together. If you are the board chair, take the executive director out for a long lunch. If you are the executive director, meet with your board chair off-site (and let the chair buy the lunch). If you are a board member who wants to strengthen this important leadership partnership, talk about forming a tiger team to strengthen the board. If you are a staff person or volunteer, enlist the partnership of a member of the board to work with you on this issue; it is usually best for board and leadership changes to be initiated by board members. If you are the founder, consider taking a cruise. . . .

The bottom line is that change is an incredible strength. And it doesn't take great strength to start change. It takes a voice.

One of my favorite sayings remains taped to my mirror as a daily reminder of what I have observed throughout my life:

If you think your effectiveness is small,

You've never been in bed with a mosquito.

References

Scribner, S. M. *Boards from Hell.* Long Beach, Calif.: Scribner & Associates, 1991.

Scribner, S. M. *Are You Chairing a Board by the Seat of Your Pants?* Long Beach, Calif.: Scribner & Associates, 1999a.

Scribner, S. M. *How to Ask for Money Without Fainting.* Long Beach, Calif.: Scribner & Associates, 1999b.

PART FOUR

A FOCUS ON THE NONPROFIT ORGANIZATION

All signs indicate that global interdependence is accelerating at a furious pace.
Politically, economically, and environmentally, we are living in a world where leadership
decisions anywhere now affect everything and everyone everywhere.
JEAN LIPMAN-BLUMEN, CONNECTIVE LEADERSHIP (P. 4)

The new competencies for the world of today and tomorrow include thinking globally, appreciating and embracing diversity, building partnerships, and sharing leadership. The opportunity for nonprofits at the beginning of the twenty-first century is to improve the way public problems are addressed in the United States and around the world.

The authors of the chapters in Part Four share important research supporting the critical importance for nonprofit leaders and organizations to increase their capacity to engage people and organizations in other sectors in ways that integrate both the personal and organization missions.

New models of engagement are required to solve problems—to move beyond the traditional ways of engaging people and beyond the walls of the organization to involve others, and to develop a variety of collaborative relationships or strategic alliances where people and organizations share similar motivations and values. Through these relationships, each person is able to leverage his or her talents and resources for the benefit of society—a new reality designed to address the social challenges of the future.

CHAPTER ELEVEN

ORGANIZATIONS OF HOPE

Leading the Way to Transformation, Social Action, and Profitability

Gill Robinson Hickman

In today's environment, organizations are expected to demonstrate responsibility and contribute to the collective good of society beyond their traditional role of job creation. I submit that an important social imperative for organizations in this era is to understand the interdependent nature of the environment in which they operate and purposely link their survival efforts to the survival and well-being of society.

The Business-Nonprofit Connection

This chapter presents a framework for leadership of organizations that intentionally incorporate transformation, social action, and profitability into their regular business functions. The intent in presenting this research is to help organizations sustain themselves as dynamic, thriving entities while engaging in shared social sector work. Business and nonprofit collaboration efforts require a different kind of leadership and a new understanding of the dynamics that produce organizations of hope in both sectors.

Peter Drucker (1994) describes organizations of the twenty-first century as new integrating mechanisms. He indicates that together public, private and nonprofit organizations form the capacity that the community will need to determine how to balance two apparently contradictory requirements—the primary functions for which specific organizations exist and the social responsibility to work on the problems and challenges of the community. This, Drucker contends, is the joint work of both public and private organizations that are capable of social sector work.

There has been a significant expansion of social sector work, a trend that will accelerate in the new century. James Austin offers useful tools and insights for executives and directors of business and nonprofit organizations in *The Collaboration Challenge: How Nonprofits and Businesses Succeed Through Strategic Alliances* (2000). He states that "these alliances between nonprofits and corporations [businesses of any size] hold considerable potential for enhancing business and nonprofit performance and for generating social value. . . . The age of alliances is upon us. For those with vision and entrepreneurial spirit, the path of social purpose partnering will lead to mutual gains and produce significant benefits for society" (p. 185). How can such efforts be prudent in a time of fierce global competition, downsizing, layoffs, outsourcing, and "lean-and-mean" strategizing? Organizations with a social imperative that link their survival to the well-being of society may be better positioned in the long run to maintain their human and economic viability. Verification of this perspective will require longitudinal studies of companies that engage in social action.

Several organizational initiatives illustrate this strong commitment to organizational purpose *and* social change. For example, the Timberland Company, maker of rugged outdoor footwear and clothing, won the Corporate Conscience Award given each year by the Council on Economic Priorities. Timberland incorporates social commitment into its mission statement: "Each individual can, and must, make a difference in the way we experience life on this planet" (Will, 1995, p. 18). The company provides its employees with forty hours of paid time off and five company-sponsored events to allow them to volunteer their services to make a difference in society. The company made a five-year commitment of services and funding to the nonprofit organization City Year, which is considered a contemporary urban "peace corps." The youth corps members teach children to read, clean up trash-strewn lots, and interact with different segments of the community. Timberland shares its private sector expertise with City Year, and the youth corps gives its employees opportunities to do community service. Beyond its social commitment in the United States, the company sets forth international guidelines for choosing business partners based on its "Standards for Social Responsibility."

Organizational Gains

In a case study conducted with the Timberland Company, the researchers found that Timberland's intentional commitment to meeting its organizational purpose *and* engaging actively in social enterprise contributed strongly to capacity building and transformation at multiple levels (individual, organizational, and social) (Horan and Levin, 1998). Further, Timberland institutionalized its social commitment by establishing a social enterprise unit in the organization. Involvement in social enterprise by Timberland employees contributed greatly to the community and equally greatly to the capacity building of the employees and the company. Lessons learned by participants in community projects about leadership without positional roles, building trust, and effective teamwork were brought back into the organization.

Companies report numerous gains (*social investment*) from their nonprofit partnerships and volunteering activities, according to data provided by Business for Social Responsibility (2003). Benefits derived from participation in social action include the following:

- Increased employee capacity (employee skills and training)
- Increased employee teamwork
- Increased employee leadership skills (followers become leaders)
- More innovative work structures (organizational structures)
- Increased employee morale, retention, attendance, and performance
- New or improved relationships across the organization
- Enhanced moral expectations and standards for the organization
- New or improved relationships between the organization and the external community or society
- Sustained or improved financial performance
- Development of the local labor pool
- Recruitment and retention of employees
- Strengthened community relationships
- Enhanced company reputation
- Increased customer goodwill and loyalty
- Improved access to markets
- The attracting of investors
- Leveraged philanthropic resources

Gains by the Community and Nonprofit Organizations

Benefits for the community include enhancements such as these:

- Improved quality of life—better housing, facilities, neighborhoods, health
- Improved capacity of people and nonprofit organizations (social capital) in the community
- New or enhanced knowledge or skills

- New or improved educational opportunities
- Job or business creation
- Economic development and enhancement

Is There Reason to Be Hopeful?

It is Thursday afternoon at Micro-Tech Systems. Bright colors adorn the walls, matched by energetic people moving in and out of flexible spaces. Dressed in khakis, polo shirts, and the occasional baseball cap, they exchange ideas about how to solve customer problems while checking out the latest baby pictures and candid employee photos in a collage created by the company's vice president. Technology is everywhere and fits the culture as comfortably as each person's favorite chair. Today is the company meeting. I head to the conference room and find it filled with sandwiches, drinks, and sofas, only to discover that the meeting takes place in the hall. Adjusting to this change of venue, I think—a company meeting in the hall? I've heard of hallway conferencing, but I've never seen it adopted as an official company practice. As I take my seat on a cushy sofa and wait for the meeting to begin, I wonder—where is everyone? In a few minutes, the large open space in the hall begins to fill with people dragging their unique chairs from offices and meeting rooms. An employee advises me, "If you don't bring your own chair, you have to sit on the floor."

Soon PowerPoint presentations of the company's sales, financial status, and latest benefit plan flash on the wall. The company president sits along the wall and blends into the group. Micro-Tech Systems has made a strong profit after suffering setbacks and layoffs during a downturn in the economy. This news is greeted with rousing cheers from the group. Each speaker highlights the accomplishments of its team and superstars who put forth valiant efforts to make this success possible. Again, the news is greeted with rousing cheers, congratulations, and special company dollars to be traded for tangible rewards. A serious discussion ensues about the new benefit plan, complete with tough questions and responses. It is clear that suggestions and objections are welcome. The employees' questions receive responses and a plan of action that assures adaptability and a willingness to work out all of the kinks.

The company president saves the best for last. She introduces members of a local nonprofit organization, who show examples of their work. Their presentation entertains and elicits interest from the group. At the end, a member of the nonprofit agency and the president of Micro-Tech ask for volunteers to use their expertise to help this agency meet its mission. Several people respond to the volunteering request. In an anticlimactic moment, I step forward and make a plea for company members to complete a survey and participate in a study of organizations like theirs—nothing like a little academic research to spoil the fun. I leave the experience energized and thinking that I have just experienced an *organization of hope*. I can see Max Weber, Fredrick Taylor, and Adam Smith turning over in their graves. This is *not* your father's work environment.

This scenario, based on a composite of three existing organizations, represents the direction in which many of us hope organizations will move. As one company executive indicated, "Organizations like ours are still in an embryonic state."

This embryonic state serves to inspire hope for a new generation of people and organizations. Hope is more than a dream—it is the overall perception that one's goals can be met. According to Richard Snyder (2000), the necessary components of hope include three factors:

> *Goal-oriented thoughts:* Directed behavior to achieve outcomes that are valued by individuals
>
> *Pathways to achievement:* Plausible routes to achieve goals, including alternative or multiple pathways
>
> *Agency thoughts:* Motivating force of hope that comes from the belief that individuals can succeed by initiating and sustaining the pathway to achieving their goal

The motivation for hope in new-era organizations stems from goal-oriented leadership behavior, which creates a context where people develop and thrive, the organization profits, and its members contribute to social action in the community. Leaders and members develop alternative pathways to achieve company and social goals in an unpredictable environment. They develop resilience and flexibility in the face of continual change. Their hope is anchored in collective agency.

Evolution of a Research Study: Hope Floats

My hope for new era organizations began in the mid-1970s while studying the works of scholars such as Warren Bennis and Philip Slater (1968), Fred Emery and Eric Trist (1972), Donald Schön (1971), and Chris Argyris (1973). Their work focused on a new era in which organizations would function in a "highly turbulent" and "dynamic" environment. Change in such environments would be unpredictable and erratic. As Bennis would say, "The future has no shelf life" (Bennis, 2001, p. 14). Who among us could have foreseen such divergent occurrences as the tragedy of September 11, 2001, or the remarkable discoveries of the Human Genome Project? These dissimilar yet coexisting events illustrate the complexity of highly turbulent environments.

Scholars characterized the approaching future as transforming, technological, learning-focused, global, and interdependent. I raised the question in my own work: What kind of organization will be best suited for this context? This question began the genesis of my Organizations of Hope study and the development of a conceptual framework for how these organizations might function. I speculated that organizations, especially in the business sector, would need to become far more integrated in the social issues of an interdependent world.

The purpose of my current research is to identify and study organizations that incorporate transformation, social action, and profitability into their regular business functions and to determine how leadership serves to facilitate these organizations. Specifically, I ask:

- What do organizations gain as a result of combining transformation, social action, and profitability? What are the disadvantages of this approach?
- How does leadership function to create and sustain these kinds of organizations?
- Where does this leadership originate (does it permeate the organization at all levels, does it come from the top and filter down, and so on)?
- What does the community gain from working with such organizations? Are there disadvantages for the community?
- What does the nonprofit organization gain as a result of its collaboration with corporate volunteering programs? Are there disadvantages for the organization?

To examine these questions, I use an original framework with components that have been refined over the years. There are two phases of the research—a pilot study and larger national study. The pilot study has identified several companies that have joined together to form a community outreach and partnering effort between business and nonprofit sectors. Company members completed a survey instrument, participated in focus group sessions, and responded to qualitative interviews. Results from this study serve as the source for development of a national study.

Figure 11.1 illustrates the interdependent nature of the framework's components. Leadership and change are shown as embedded capabilities of the organization. The concept of embedded capabilities is supported in the findings of a study of leadership in large corporations. James O'Toole (2001) discovered a different pattern of leadership in companies where key leadership tasks and responsibilities are institutionalized in the systems, processes, and culture. Such organizations are not dependent on the presence of a "high-profile" leader. People at all levels engage in leadership practices throughout these companies. Their members

- Act more like owners and entrepreneurs than employees or hired hands (that is, they assume ownerlike responsibility for financial performance and managing risk)

FIGURE 11.1. COMPONENTS OF ORGANIZATIONS OF HOPE.

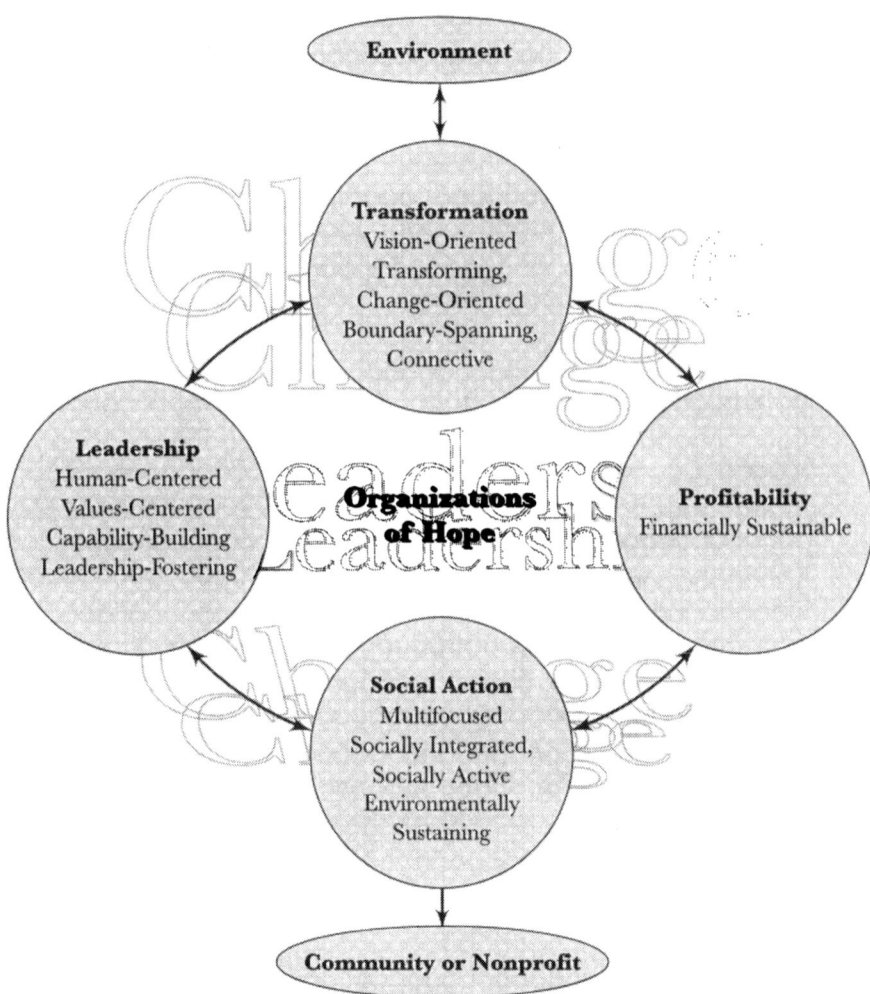

- Take the initiative to solve problems and to act, in general, with a sense of urgency
- Willingly accept accountability for meeting commitments and for living the values of the organization
- Share a common philosophy and language of leadership that paradoxically includes tolerance for contrary views and a willingness to experiment
- Create, maintain, and adhere to systems and procedures designed to measure and reward these distributed leadership behaviors.

O'Toole identified two factors that contributed to the long-term success of these companies: coherence and agility. *Coherence* refers to common behaviors found throughout an organization. *Agility* represents a company's institutional abilities to anticipate and respond to change (similar to embedded change in the framework).

Nonprofit organizations are major participants in this new environment. They, too, are organizations of hope. Since service to society is the primary function of nonprofit agencies, internal transformation and financial sustainability apply equally to nonprofits. Leadership and change need to become embedded capabilities of the agency. Key leadership tasks and responsibilities can be institutionalized in the systems, processes, and culture to allow maximum engagement of organizational capabilities.

Transforming Leadership and Organizations of Hope

James M. Burns (1978) explains that the ultimate goal of transforming leadership is to enhance the well-being of human existence. Though leadership scholars have adapted his concept of transforming leadership and incorporated it in the organizational context, they have not adopted his imperative to link leadership with "collective purpose and social change" (p. 20). Burns sees the nature of bureaucratic organizations as antithetical to the type of leadership that brings about real intended social change. I would agree that "bureaucratic" organizations are typically not compatible with the goals and purpose of transforming leadership. However, the emerging organizations of the present era offer a new promise of organizational flexibility and leadership involvement that differs significantly from the concepts of bureaucratic organizations.

Components of the Framework

The study examines the *ideal* components of the framework in relation to the actual experience of companies in the study. Exhibit 11.1 defines and delineates the components of the framework.

The "Potential" of This Study: Keeping Hope Alive

We are constantly inundated with stories of corporate greed, inequity, and callous disregard for the interest and security of employees. Skeptics maintain that profit-making organizations are too self-interested to have genuine concern about the

EXHIBIT 11.1. COMPONENTS OF THE FRAMEWORK DEFINED.

Components	Qualities
Leadership A *process* that facilitates the shared work of leaders and members to reach common goals. The term *leadership* is also used in this study to refer to the *people* (leaders and members) in the process. Accordingly, leadership encompasses both the process and the people.	*Human-Centered* • The philosophy and practices in the company communicate that its people are the organization's primary asset and concern. • Each person matters and is treated with respect and dignity. • The culture of the company fosters care and support for every member of the organization. *Values-Centered* • The company's direction, decisions, and practices are guided by core values held in common by its members. • Capability-Building • Company leaders see their jobs as people developers who help members unleash their capabilities. • The organizational culture promotes learning and innovation. • Company leaders provide resources for learning—funding, time, and opportunities. *Leadership-Fostering* • Company leaders share responsibility with members throughout the organization. • The company provides leadership experiences and learning opportunities to members throughout the organization. • The company makes use of its increased leadership talent.
Transformation The ability to change, innovate, or reconfigure employee capabilities and organizational structure (agility) to meet opportunities and challenges.	*Vision-Oriented* • Company leaders and members strive to anticipate and meet future opportunities and challenges. • Company leaders and members envision what the organization will become, not just what it is now. • Company leaders and members use such tools as environmental scanning, forecasting, and scenario building to anticipate future changes.

EXHIBIT 11.1. Continued.

Components	Qualities
	• Company leaders and members use or- ganizational planning to shape the com- pany for its future.
	Transforming, Change-Oriented • Company leaders and members embrace change. • The company is fluid and able to recon- figure its structure and human capacity to meet new opportunities or challenges. • Company members readily use or learn different abilities and expertise for inno- vation or problem solving. • The culture within the company encour- ages any member of the organization to present new ideas, innovations, and solutions. • The company takes action on good ideas, innovations, and solutions from any member of the organization. • The company recognizes and credits members who generate good ideas, in- novations, or solutions.
	Boundary-Spanning, Connective • Company leaders and members build re- lationships and eliminate boundaries in the organization to achieve shared goals. • Company leaders and members develop linkages with other organizations to pur- sue common aims (Luke, 1991, 1998; Lipman-Blumen, 1996).
Social Action Volunteering or community service by mem- bers of the organization. *Community* can be local, national, or international, depending on the company's locale or area of operation.	*Multifocused* • Company leaders and members focus on achieving the purpose of the organiza- tion (products and services) and meeting needs in the community through social action.
	Socially Integrated, Socially Active • Company leaders and members view the organization as an integral part of the community. • Company leaders and members see their future as connected to the community's future.

EXHIBIT 11.1. Continued.

Components	Qualities
	• Company leaders and members identify pressing social needs and problems by involving community stakeholders. • Company leaders and members are committed to helping the community meet social needs and resolve social problems. • The company shares the capabilities of its members through formal or informal interaction with the community. *Environmentally Sustaining* • The company's products and services are safe for society. • The company's practices and policies contribute to a sustainable environment and harmony with nature.
Profitability A financial measure of a company's earnings. (In nonprofit or public sector organizations, this is a measure of viability and service delivery.)	*Financially Sustainable* • The company is able to improve or sustain its profitability while engaging in social action. • Leaders and members of the company are shareholders with a stake in the company's future. • Financial gains become resources to improve the well-being of the company members, investors, and the community.

people in their companies and the conditions that plague our communities and environment. Everyone complains about these issues, but few people believe that things will change.

There is a promising group of organizations that view their institutions as "contexts" for capacity building and contributors to the common good. Such organizations focus on human purposes and values as the driving force of the institution so that gains in economic resources become instruments for concerted human activity in the organization and society. This focus does not mean that significant service and products do not result or that economic (bottom-line) considerations and productivity are minimized. It simply means that organizations become human entities with multiple bottom lines and economic interests.

Companies on the cutting edge of this change have encountered definite challenges. They face the difficulties inherent in building appropriate infrastructures, human capacity, and resilience to economic downturns while sustaining their engagement in cross-sector alliances and social change. Encountering challenges and even setbacks in these areas does not mean that this pursuit should be abandoned or that it is imprudent. It means that pioneering efforts in this new arena require organizational learning, concerted analysis, refinement, and corrections. It is my hope that the results of this work and future research will inspire, inform, and support leadership in organizations that strive for transformation, social action, and profitability.

REFERENCES

Argyris, C. *On Organizations of the Future.* Thousand Oaks, Calif.: Sage, 1973.

Austin, J. E. *The Collaboration Challenge: How Nonprofits and Businesses Succeed Through Strategic Alliances.* San Francisco: Jossey-Bass, 2000.

Bennis, W. "The Future Has No Shelf Life." In W. Bennis, G. M. Spreitzer, and T. G. Cummings (eds.), *The Future of Leadership: Today's Top Leadership Thinkers Speak to Tomorrow's Leaders.* San Francisco: Jossey-Bass, 2001.

Bennis, W., and Slater, P. *The Temporary Society.* New York: HarperCollins, 1968.

Burns, J. M. *Leadership.* New York: Harper Torchbooks, 1978.

Business for Social Responsibility. "Overview of Corporate Social Responsibility." [http://www.bsr.org/BSRResources/IssueBriefDetail.cfm?DocumentID=48809#business]. 2003.

Drucker, P. F. "The Age of Social Transformation." *Atlantic Monthly,* May 1994, pp. 53–56.

Emery, F. E. and Trist, E. L. *Towards a Social Ecology: Contextual Appreciation of the Future in the Present.* New York: Plenum, 1972.

Horan, J., and Levin., J. "Transforming Corporations to Transform Society: A Case Study of the Timberland Corporation." Unpublished senior project, University of Richmond, Jepson School of Leadership Studies, 1998.

Lipman-Blumen, J. *Connective Edge: Leading in an Interdependent World.* San Francisco: Jossey-Bass, 1996.

Luke, J. S. "Managing Interconnectedness: The Challenge of Shared Power." In J. M. Bryson and R. C. Einsweiler (eds.), *Shared Power: What Is It? How Does It Work? How Can We Make It Work Better?* Lanham, Md.: University Press of America. 1991.

Luke, J. S. *Catalytic Leadership: Strategies for an Interconnected World.* San Francisco: Jossey-Bass, 1998.

O'Toole, J. "When Leadership Is an Organizational Trait." In W. Bennis, G. M. Spreitzer, and T. G. Cummings (eds.), *The Future of Leadership: Today's Top Leadership Thinkers Speak to Tomorrow's Leaders.* San Francisco: Jossey-Bass, 2001.

Schön, D. A. *Beyond the Stable State.* New York: Norton, 1971.

Snyder, C. R. (ed.). *Handbook of Hope: Theory, Measures, and Applications.* Orlando, Fla.: Academic Press, 2000.

Will, R. "Corporations with a Conscience." *Business and Society Review,* 1995, *95,* 17–20.

CHAPTER TWELVE

VOLUNTEERS AND VOLUNTEER ORGANIZATIONS

Theoretical Perspectives and Practical Concerns

Mark Snyder, Allen M. Omoto

Every year, millions of people volunteer to devote substantial amounts of their time and energy to helping others—for example, by volunteering to provide companionship to the elderly, tutoring to the illiterate, counseling to the troubled, or health care to the sick. In fact, according to one recent survey, in 1998 alone, 109.4 million American adults engaged in some form of volunteerism, and doing so an average of 3.5 hours per week (INDEPENDENT SECTOR, 1999). Whereas the United States has long been known for relatively high rates of volunteerism, people engage in voluntary activities in many countries around the world (Curtis, Grabb, and Baer, 1992).

Volunteerism can be distinguished from philanthropy by the fact that instead of or in addition to donating money or goods, participants in volunteer efforts provide valuable time, resources, and energy to causes and recipients of service. Philanthropic efforts are of course crucial to the success of many organizations and service programs; our focus here is on volunteer behavior as a separate phenomenon. We also distinguish between "forced" and freely chosen volunteer efforts. Many schools, businesses, and other institutions provide volunteer opportunities that are mandatory for students or employees or perceived as

The research described in this chapter was supported by grants from the American Foundation for AIDS Research and the National Institute of Mental Health.

such (as may be true of service learning programs and some corporate-community partnerships). And although some of the outcomes of these programs may be similar (see Clary, Snyder, and Stukas, 1998; Stukas, Snyder, and Clary, 1999), our interest is in situations in which individuals provide assistance to causes and other people without receiving compensation or having been coerced. In short, for us, volunteerism is a form of helping in which people freely seek out opportunities to provide nonmonetary assistance to others in need.

Working with volunteers presents special challenges for leaders of volunteer-based organizations. For example, a workforce has to be identified and recruited for action, but without the usual work inducements of rates of pay, benefit packages, and other nonsalary forms of compensation. The first challenge that leaders face, then, is how best to recruit volunteers and sustain their motivation for service once they have become involved. Almost by their very nature, and especially for organizations working at the grassroots level, nonprofit and volunteer organizations often eschew complicated hierarchical structuring and "top-down" forms of leadership. Instead, voluntary and mutual participation in decision making, program design and implementation, and strategic planning is often highly prized in such organizations. In fact, the more that organizations drift away from fully participatory models and past operating procedures, the more that volunteers may become upset and feel that the organization has lost its direction and sense of purpose. Volunteers may opt out, leaving the organization high and dry in its attempts to meet program and client service demands. For leaders in such organizations, then, there are many challenges involved in working with a diverse volunteer workforce, being aware of and responsive to volunteer needs and opinions, and minimizing volunteer turnover. In preventing attrition, and in the absence of tangible monetary rewards, leaders must be especially concerned with the social and psychological benefits that volunteers receive as a result of their service work.

In addition to these practical considerations of volunteerism and the leading of volunteer organizations, studying volunteerism provides a distinct perspective on the nature of helping and prosocial action. In psychology, helping has long been studied in terms of brief, low-cost, generally spontaneous assistance provided by strangers (such as bystander intervention) or more recently in terms of care provided to chronically sick or severely debilitated members of one's own family (see Schroeder, Penner, Dovidio, and Piliavin, 1995; for reviews of the sociological literature, see Piliavin and Charng, 1990; Wilson, 2000). However, a careful consideration of features of volunteerism makes clear that it is a distinctive form of prosocial action that incorporates aspects of both of these forms of helping (see Omoto and Snyder, 1995; Snyder, Clary, and Stukas, 2000). Specifically, volunteerism typically involves people choosing to help others in need. Moreover, their acts of helping are often ones that have been actively sought out by the volunteers themselves and that may be sustained over extended periods of time and considerable expenditure of time and effort. And since volunteers typically help people with whom they have had no prior contact or association, it is a form of helping that occurs without any bonds of prior obligation or commitment to the recipients of volunteer services.

Guided by a functional approach to personality, motivation, and social behavior, we are engaged in a coordinated program of basic and applied investigations, conducted in the field and in the laboratory, to examine personal and social motivations that dispose people to volunteer and sustain their involvement in such ongoing helping relationships. After reviewing the central tenets of our theorizing about volunteerism and some of the major findings of empirical research on volunteerism guided by this theoretical approach, we will examine practical implications of our theorizing and research for optimizing the functioning of volunteer service organizations and effectively facing the leadership challenges that they pose.

Theory and Research on the Processes of Volunteerism

We have developed a conceptual model of what we refer to as the volunteer process that takes account of the defining and characteristic features of volunteerism as a form of sustained helping without obligation. The model conceptualizes volunteerism as a process that unfolds over time. It specifies psychological and behavioral features associated with each of three sequential and interactive stages. At the *antecedents* stage, it identifies personality, motivational, and circumstantial characteristics of individuals that predict who becomes involved as volunteers and, if they do, who will be most effective and satisfied in their volunteer service. At the *experiences* stage, the model explores psychological and behavioral aspects of the interpersonal relationships that develop between volunteers and recipients of their services, paying particular attention to the behavioral patterns and relationship dynamics that facilitate the continued service of volunteers and positive benefits to the recipients of their services. Finally, at the *consequences* stage, the volunteer process model focuses on the impact of volunteer service on the attitudes, knowledge, and behavior of volunteers, the recipients of their services, and the members of their social networks. Taken together, then, the stages of the volunteer process model address the initiation and maintenance of volunteer service and its effectiveness.

Moreover, the volunteer process model seeks to characterize volunteerism as a phenomenon that is situated at, and builds bridges between, many levels of analysis and that unfolds over time. At the level of the *individual*, the model calls attention to the activities and psychological processes of individual volunteers and recipients of volunteer services. For example, volunteers make decisions to get involved as volunteers, seek out service opportunities, engage in volunteer work for some period of time, and eventually cease their efforts. At the *interpersonal* level, the model expands this focus to incorporate the dynamics of the helping relationships between volunteers and recipients of service. At an *organizational* or *agency* level, the model focuses on the goals associated with recruiting, managing, and retaining an unpaid workforce as well as associated concerns about work performance, compensation, and evaluation. That is, many volunteer efforts take place through or in cooperation with community-based organizations or other institutions. Consequently, we have incorporated aspects of organizational structure, roles, and operations into the volunteer process model. Finally, at the broader *social* level, the model considers the linkages between individuals and the social structures of their societies as well as collective and cultural dynamics. The volunteer process model is summarized in Exhibit 12.1.

The model conceptualizes volunteerism as a process that unfolds over time and involves multiple levels of analysis. It specifies psychological and behavioral features associated with each of three broad sequential and interactive stages. In addition, the model addresses activity at different levels of analysis that can interact and influence one another. The model reflects not so much a theory of volunteerism as a broad framework for organizing research on volunteerism and identifying conceptual issues for future study. Although our model emphasizes the dynamic properties of volunteerism within and between stages and levels of analysis, for ease of explication, we discuss the stages of the volunteer process separately, focusing primarily on the level of the individual volunteer. (For further discussion of the volunteer process model, see Omoto, Snyder, and Berghuis, 1993; Omoto and Snyder, 1990, 2002; Snyder and Omoto, 1992a, 1992b.)

We believe that it is important for leaders in organizations to be able to recognize and appreciate these different levels of analysis, as well as the sometimes inconsistent or conflicting goals that crop up across levels. For example, conflict may arise between organizational concerns about the provision of services and volunteer concerns about time availability and competing responsibilities. Volunteers may not always have the amount of time available or may be available only during the specific time frame required for the service programs that the agency hopes to staff. Similarly, social system antecedents and consequences (such as social climates and public education efforts) may clash with individual volunteers' attitudes and expectations or those of the volunteers' social network members. To effectively manage and lead a nonprofit or volunteer organization, then, leaders may need to pinpoint the sources of interlevel conflict. Rather than chastise volunteers for their lack of commitment or revamp or reprioritize agency programs in re-

EXHIBIT 12.1. MODEL OF THE VOLUNTEER PROCESS.

Stages of the Volunteer Process

Level of Analysis	Antecedents	Experiences	Consequences
Agency	Identification of volunteers Recruitment of volunteers Training of volunteers	Assignment of volunteers Tracking of volunteers Delivery of services	Quantity and quality of services Retention and reenlistment Fulfillment of mission
Individual volunteer	Demographics Prior experiences Personality differences Resources and skills Motivations Identity concerns Expectations Existing social support	Volunteer's choice of role Volunteer's performance Relationship with client Support from agency staff and other volunteers Organizational integration Satisfaction Stigmatization	Changes in knowledge, attitude, behavior, motivation Identity development Commitment to volunteering Evaluation of volunteerism Commitment to organization Recruitment of other volunteers Length of service
Social system	Social climates Community resources Cultural context	Recipients of services Volunteers' social network Clients' social network	Social diffusion Public education Systems of service delivery

sponse to community or volunteer complaints, then, the effective leader may be able to isolate the source of the problem in terms of level and stage in this model (or between levels, as noted) and plan appropriate ameliorative action. Our point here is that a deeper analysis is sometimes required to solve problems in volunteer organizations, and our model of the volunteer process may be a useful heuristic for facilitating this analysis.

Although we believe that our conceptual model and the issues of interest are applicable to many, if not most, forms of volunteerism, much of our empirical research on the volunteer process has focused on volunteer service programs that have emerged in the United States in response to the epidemic of HIV and AIDS (Omoto and Snyder, 1990, 1995; Snyder and Omoto, 1992a, 1992b). HIV disease, including AIDS, has had and continues to have major medical, economic, and social impact throughout the world. A critical component of the social response to the HIV epidemic in the United States has been community-based organizations of volunteers involved in caring for people living with HIV or AIDS (PWAs) and in educating the public about HIV and PWAs (see Chambré, 1991). In the United States, AIDS service organizations have emerged in every state, in cities large and small, and in rural areas as well. Some volunteers provide emotional and social support as "buddies" to PWAs, others help PWAs with household chores or transportation, and still others staff information and referral hotlines, make educational presentations, or engage in advocacy (see Bebbington and Gatter, 1994; Chambré, 1991; Kayal, 1993; Omoto and Snyder, 1990, 1993). AIDS volunteers donate valuable services; in fact, it has been documented that the cost of caring for PWAs is greatly reduced in areas with active volunteer programs, and AIDS-related deaths have become less likely to take place in inpatient hospital settings and more likely to occur at home or in hospices, most likely because of support services provided by volunteers (Hellinger, 1993; Kelly, Chu, and Buehler, 1993; Turner, Catania, and Gagnon, 1994).

In our research, we have most often used the specific case of AIDS volunteerism to inform a more general understanding of the social and psychological aspects and processes of volunteerism. Like other volunteers, AIDS volunteers seek out opportunities to help, make substantial commitments to their work, and provide assistance to one or more persons who are initially strangers to them. Many AIDS volunteers also provide care and assistance in potentially trying and stressful situations (spending time with seriously ill PWAs) and at some personal cost. For these reasons, we see AIDS volunteerism as paradigmatic of volunteerism more generally speaking. In our research, we have examined the processes of volunteerism as they occur in the world, focusing on "real" individuals involved in "real" acts of volunteerism in "real" settings. We have in effect entered a naturally occurring laboratory to investigate a phenomenon of significance for individual and collective action. Moreover, we have supplemented our field-based data collections with focused laboratory studies that have permitted us to more carefully nail down causal mechanisms and processes of volunteerism. And finally, our research has employed both longitudinal and cross-sectional designs and has drawn data from diverse populations of volunteers and nonvolunteers.

Antecedents of AIDS Volunteerism

Among the questions at the antecedents stage of the volunteer process that we have sought to answer in our empirical work is, What motivates some people to become AIDS volunteers? We have attempted to identify personality, motivational, and circumstantial characteristics of AIDS volunteers that predict who becomes an effective and satisfied volunteer and hope ultimately to build on this knowledge to develop effective strategies for recruiting and retaining volunteers.

Of special concern in our research at this stage have been the motivations of AIDS volunteers. In this regard, our work has been informed by a functional approach to personality, motivation, and social behavior, one in which the purposive and agentic nature of human action is emphasized (see Snyder and Cantor, 1998). Consistent with functional theorizing (Clary and Snyder, 1991; Maio and Olson, 2000; Smith, Bruner, and White, 1956; Snyder and Omoto, 2000, 2001; Snyder, Clary, and Stukas, 2000), we have found that AIDS volunteerism is enacted by different people to serve different goals, psychological functions, or motivations. Specifically, we have employed exploratory and confirmatory factor analytic techniques in multiple samples to identify five primary motivations for AIDS volunteerism (Omoto and Snyder, 1995; see also Clary and others, 1994, 1998; Ferrari, McCown, and Pantano, 1994; Ouellette, Cassel, Maslanka, and Wong, 1995; Schondel, Shields, and Orel, 1992; Simon, Stürmer, and Steffens, 2000).

Our investigations of the motivations behind volunteerism indicate that some people volunteer to express their *personal values* or to satisfy felt humanitarian obligations to help others, whereas others volunteer out of *community concern.* In terms of AIDS volunteerism in the United States, this has meant volunteering out of concern for people affected by HIV disease or for the gay community (Omoto and Crain, 1995). The remaining motivations are more self-focused: some people volunteer in search of greater *understanding* of AIDS and how people live with HIV disease; some for reasons related to *personal development,* such as to challenge themselves or enlarge their social networks; and some to fulfill *esteem enhancement* needs (for example, to feel better about themselves or to escape other pressures).

Of the motivations that we have identified, values motivation tends to be endorsed most strongly and esteem enhancement least among the AIDS volunteers that we have studied, with the other three motivations falling in between (see Omoto and Snyder, 1993). In short, however, it is clear that the same act of AIDS volunteerism is initiated and maintained for different, and sometimes changing, reasons. Exploring the generality of these motivations, we have found the same five motivation categories in data from volunteers in hospice agencies who are *not* working with people with HIV disease (see Omoto and Snyder, 1995).

An appreciation of the strength and variety of different motivations that lead people to do volunteer work, we believe, is necessary as leaders, especially those in nonprofit and volunteer organizations, attempt to develop effective methods of attracting people who wish to involve themselves in volunteer activities and associations. Indeed, research on persuasive messages for recruiting volunteers has focused on appeals to prospective volunteers' motivations. A recurring theme in these investigations is the importance of the *matching* of messages to motivation. That is, building on research indicating a diversity of potential motivations for volunteering (for example, Clary, Snyder, and Stukas, 1998; Omoto and Snyder, 1995), these studies have demonstrated that the persuasive impact of a message is greater when it directly addresses the recipient's primary motivations than when it does not (see Clary and others, 1994, 1998; Omoto, Snyder, and Smith, 1999; Smith, Omoto, and Snyder, 2001). Potential volunteers evaluate more highly recruitment messages that are targeted at and directly address their motivations for service (as opposed to other motivations for service); moreover, they are more likely to be moved to action in response to these targeted advertisements.

The practical implications of these findings for the recruitment of volunteers are considerable. Rather than adopt a "one size fits all" approach to volunteer recruitment and training, leaders and organizations may be better served by creating advertisements and recruitment materials that address the various motivations for volunteerism differentially. Leaders in nonprofit organizations must remain sensitive to the fact that volunteers become involved for a variety of reasons and that they look to their volunteer work to meet different needs. This is but one example of how basic theory and research can not only be enhanced by but also contribute to practical issues in volunteerism.

Experiences of Volunteerism

The second stage of the volunteer process concerns the experiences of volunteers that may promote or deter continuing involvement. At this stage, we have explored the interpersonal relationships that develop between volunteers and recipients of their services (especially PWAs in buddy programs), the extent to which volunteers feel their service has met their expectations and fulfilled their needs, and volunteers' perceptions of their work, their service organization, and other people's reactions to their work. Illustrative of findings at this stage, we found that volunteers have relatively high expectations for the quality of the relationships they will develop with client PWAs and that actual volunteer-PWA relationships fall short of these expectations (Omoto, Gunn, & Crain, 1998). Volunteer satisfaction also falls short of expectations, and volunteers report some stress from these relationships in connection with relationship closeness and client health. Specifically, volunteer stress increases with relationship closeness early on, and working with a relatively healthy client engenders less stress.

Moreover, the more closely volunteers' experiences match the motivations that drew them into volunteer service and the expectations that they formed early on about volunteering, the more likely they are to be satisfied with their service as volunteers. As part of a longitudinal study of the volunteer process, Crain, Omoto, and Snyder (1998) examined the role that the matching between volunteers' motivations, expectations, and experiences plays in determining volunteers' satisfaction and burnout. In this study, AIDS volunteers completed four questionnaires in which they reported the importance of each of a set of functional motivations for volunteering (prior to their training to serve as volunteers), the extent to which they expected that volunteering would fulfill their motivations (following training), the extent to which their experiences met these expectations (after volunteering for three months), and their feelings of satisfaction and burnout (after having volunteered for six months). Overall matching between motivations, expectations, and experiences was predictive of greater satisfaction and less burnout, suggesting that a stronger match is associated with more positive consequences of volunteerism. Similar evidence of the importance of the matching of volunteers' experiences to their motivations in predicting their satisfaction is provided by research by Clary and colleagues (1998).

Moreover, the matching of volunteers' experiences to their motivations may have implications for their commitment to their volunteer service and their intentions to continue in service as volunteers. For example, in a longitudinal field study of AIDS volunteers, commitment to sustained service was greater among volunteers whose experiences were congruent with, or matched, their motivations for volunteering as espoused six months earlier (O'Brien, Crain, Omoto, and Snyder, 2000; see also Crain, Omoto, and Snyder, 1998). Moreover, in a pair of laboratory experiments in which college students were induced to participate in analogues of volunteer service, attitudes and intentions facilitative of continuing service were increased by interventions designed to encourage them to frame their volunteer service in ways that were congruent with their own motivations (O'Brien, Crain, Omoto, and Snyder, 2000; Williamson, Snyder, and Omoto, 2000).

Findings such as these on the experiences stage of the volunteer process have clear implications for the practice of volunteerism. To the extent that volunteer service organizations can structure their programs to encourage volunteers to construe their volunteer experiences as matching their motivations for volunteering, the organizations may·effectively increase the likelihood that their volunteers will be satisfied volunteers. Leaders in organizations can also play a key role in creating and communicating frames for understanding and construing volunteer experiences. That is, not only can programs be organized around or designed to meet certain needs, but leaders can also reinforce the perceptions of congruence between volunteer motivations and experiences. For example, leaders can deliver messages (through one-on-one or group meetings with volunteers, newsletter articles, service recognition ceremonies, and so on) that characterize or emphasize certain motivationally consistent aspects of volunteer experiences. The combined effect of these programs and messages should be more satisfied and longer-serving volunteers.

However, it is important to recognize that no matter what a leader or organization does, volunteers' experiences may not be wholly positive and satisfying and may include some negative aspects. In our research on AIDS volunteerism, some volunteers reported feelings of stigmatization and discomfort resulting from their work as AIDS volunteers. Many reported that the reactions of members of their own social networks caused them to feel embarrassed, uncomfortable, and stigmatized because of their AIDS volunteerism (Omoto, Snyder, and Crain, 2003a, 2003b; Snyder, Omoto, and Crain, 1999). This stigmatization appears to come from volunteering to work in an AIDS-related context; hospice volunteers—who perform many of the same functions as AIDS volunteers but whose clients are suffering from terminal diseases other than AIDS—report significantly lower feelings of stigmatization from the work they do (Omoto, Snyder, and Crain, 2003b). Thus it may be that the association of HIV disease with marginalized and already stigmatized members of society leads to a "spillover" stigmatization of AIDS volunteers. As we shall see, such stigmatization may have considerable consequences and may have implications for the practice of volunteerism.

Consequences of Volunteerism

Among the issues at the consequences stage, our research questions have focused on changes in attitudes, knowledge, and behavior among volunteers as a result of their service, as well as their ultimate longevity of service and their perceived and judged effectiveness as volunteers. Volunteers may play roles in changing social attitudes and beliefs about HIV disease and PWAs and in creating new systems of service delivery; these broader social consequences are also of interest at the consequences stage. In longitudinal research with repeated measurements over time, we have found that volunteers are indeed changed by their experiences, with, for example, increases in knowledge about safer sex practices, less stereotyped beliefs about PWAs, and significantly greater comfort with AIDS and AIDS-related issues (Omoto and Snyder, 1999; Omoto, Snyder, Chang, and Lee, 2001). In their own self-reports, moreover, volunteers reveal that their experiences have powerfully affected and changed them (Omoto and Snyder, 1995).

In exploring longevity of service, we have found that the duration of service of the members of one group of AIDS volunteers was related to their satisfaction with their work, the amount of support they perceived from their social network, and the motivations they reported for becoming AIDS volunteers (Omoto and Snyder, 1995). Specifically, volunteers served longer to the extent that they were more satisfied with their work, had less social support, and reported stronger, and particularly self-focused, motivation for volunteering. The fact that greater social support was actually related to shorter length of service is consistent with our findings about the stigmatization of AIDS volunteers. If being a volunteer disrupts harmonious relations with members of one's social network and if these social network members respond negatively to this disruption and to the AIDS volunteerism that has occasioned it, volunteers may quit sooner than if their work is supported by others.

In addition, we have conducted several laboratory studies and analyses of longitudinal data from AIDS volunteers, all of which converge to suggest influences of stigmatization across the volunteer process. People who believe that they will be targets of stigmatization for AIDS-related volunteerism are less likely to follow through on their initial intentions to become volunteers, and the individuals who expect the most negative reactions from others are the least likely to complete the training that organizations generally require before they assign volunteers to work on specific tasks. For those who complete training and become AIDS volunteers, greater perceptions of stigmatization is related to an increased likelihood of early termination of service, particularly if the experiences of stigmatization were relatively unanticipated (Omoto, Snyder, and Crain, 2003a, 2003b; Snyder, Omoto, and Crain, 1999).

The findings with respect to volunteers' motivations, although initially surprising to us, are understandable in retrospect. Engaging in volunteerism for reasons related to understanding, personal development, or esteem enhancement all predicted longer duration of service, whereas ratings of the values and community concern motivations were unrelated to longevity of service. Thus volunteers who can and did get something back from their work are likely to stay involved longer. Volunteering for relatively more other-focused reasons, however, may not sustain people in the face of the stress and stigmatization they are likely to encounter as volunteers.

These findings have strategy implications not only for the recruitment of volunteers but also for their training and retention. Volunteers may need to be inoculated against potential stigmatization they might receive because of their work and assisted in seeing the many personal (as well as social) benefits that their volunteer work provides. As noted previously, leaders may be wise to attend to these issues in the structure and development of programs and also by paying careful attention to the messages that they communicate to volunteers about the work that volunteers do. Focusing on these considerations not only informs psychological theory and research on motivation and stigmatization but also should aid in addressing the practical issue of how to increase the satisfaction of volunteers and more effectively retain them in service to aid others and society.

Research on the consequences of volunteerism has also examined the impact of volunteers on the clients that they serve. Such research addresses the question, Do volunteers make a difference? In a study of the helping relationships between AIDS volunteers and their clients, clients with volunteers (relative to those without) had higher psychological functioning, this effect apparently linked to greater active coping, which was in turn promoted by the quality of the relationship between the volunteer and client (Crain, Snyder, and Omoto, 2000). Further, what makes for a high-quality, effective, and productive volunteer-client helping relationship? A critical ingredient seems to be a *psychological sense of community*—the more closely connected volunteers feel to their communities, the more effective they are as volunteers and in encouraging others to become volunteers (Omoto and Snyder, 2002). By the same token, the closer the psychological connection clients feel to their communities, the more they benefit from the services provided by volunteers (Omoto and Snyder, 2002). These issues, we feel, are ripe for additional research exploration. As a greater understanding of the psychological sense of community is achieved, we are confident that it will have important practical implications for leadership strategies at all of the stages of the volunteer process.

Practical Implications of Understanding the Psychology of Volunteerism

Clearly, the emergence of volunteer service organizations in the United States in response to the challenges of the HIV/AIDS epidemic has provided us with opportunities to explore the dynamics of volunteerism as a form of prosocial action and as a case example of people mobilizing themselves to respond to society's problems. The dynamics of volunteerism have also been observed in related studies of other populations of volunteers. For example, it has been possible to develop measures of volunteer motivations for use in diverse samples of actual and prospective volunteers (see Clary and others, 1998) and to demonstrate that messages, whether in videotape or brochure form, designed to motivate people to volunteer are persuasive to the extent that they target the motivations of individual prospective volunteers (see Clary and others, 1994, 1998); that the satisfaction experienced by diverse groups of volunteers is predicted by the match between their motivations and the benefits that they derive from volunteering (Clary and others, 1998; Crain, Omoto, and Snyder, 1998); and that volunteers' intentions to continue volunteering both in the immediate future and over the longer term is predicted by the match between their motivations and the benefits that they perceive to accrue to them as volunteers (Clary and others, 1998).

Research on volunteerism has been informative about the nature of help-ing, especially the forms of helping and prosocial action that are intentional, sustained, and without obligation. We believe that an understanding of the psy-chology of volunteerism offers practical messages as well. Among the practical implications of our research are the lessons that it suggests about the practice of volunteerism, especially in terms of enhancing the recruitment, placement, and retention of volunteers. Systematic attention to the experiences and the motiva-tions of individual volunteers may go a long way toward making the efforts of grass roots and volunteer organizations more effective. Specifically, if organiza-tions dependent on the services of volunteers can identify the motivations of prospective volunteers, they can systematically tailor their recruitment efforts to the actual motivations of potential volunteers. And if organizations attend to the motivations of their actual volunteers, they may be able to match volunteers to assignments that reflect the particular motivations of these volunteers and thereby enhance their effectiveness, satisfaction, and longevity of service.

At a broader level still, studying volunteerism is likely to yield valuable infor-mation of social significance, including how to understand and expand the roles of volunteers and volunteer organizations in confronting and surmounting many of the problems that challenge societies (see Omoto and Snyder, 1993). Quite con-ceivably, a focus on the motivations of volunteers could be one of the foundations for large-scale, mass-media-based campaigns to promote awareness of and inter-est in volunteerism and other forms of involvement of individuals in the affairs of their societies (see Clary and Snyder, 1993; Snyder, Omoto, and Smith, 2003).

Conclusion

A fact of life for organizations and leaders that rely on volunteers is that volunteerism in the United States is changing (Schindler-Rainman, 1990) and becoming increas-ingly episodic: people often volunteer for short periods and then move to something else (American Red Cross, 1988). Much of volunteer turnover is unpreventable; vol-unteers drop out to take new jobs, care for children, deal with family crises, move, or to recover from illness. However, some of the attrition of volunteers is preventable. Studying the processes of volunteerism, we believe, can provide clues to the moti-vations that factor into people's decisions to volunteer, their preferences for certain volunteer tasks, their satisfaction with their experiences as volunteers, their effec-tiveness, and ultimately their continuing involvement as volunteers. In the face of increasing demand for volunteers coupled with a shrinking pool of potential vol-unteers who tend to offer their services episodically, our research on the processes of volunteerism would seem to have important implications for volunteer management and for decreasing preventable attrition in nonprofit organizations.

In fact, we have offered several modest suggestions for the ways in which leaders in organizations who work with volunteers can put into practice some of the lessons we have learned in our research. Our expectation is that some leaders may already be aware of and using these different practices, while others will find great benefit in their adoption. As a general point, though, we believe that wise leaders in nonprofit or volunteer organizations must attend to the concerns at and between the various stages of the volunteer process, as well as between the different levels of analysis that we have outlined, as they seek to optimize the use of volunteers in their organizations.

The challenges faced by leaders in nonprofit and volunteer service organizations are not limited to recruiting volunteers, ensuring their satisfaction, and retaining them. Each of these in itself is a daunting and difficult task. However, a leader's concerns extend beyond volunteers and focus also on the consumers of services (clients), the public perception of the organization, and the long-term viability of the organization and its programs, among many others. We hope that by offering our model of the volunteer process as a heuristic for thinking about the interactive and interdependent issues in volunteer organizations and also by describing the findings of some of our research derived from this model, we can aid in making the work of volunteer organizations more effective and efficient and lighten the load of their leaders.

REFERENCES

American Red Cross. *Volunteer 2000 Study.* Vol. 1, *Findings and Recommendations.* Washington, D.C.: American Red Cross, 1988.

Bebbington, A. C., and Gatter, P. N. "Volunteers in an HIV Social Care Organization." *AIDS Care,* 1994, *6,* 571–585.

Chambré, S. M. "The Volunteer Response to the AIDS Epidemic in New York City: Implications for Research on Voluntarism." *Nonprofit and Voluntary Sector Quarterly,* 1991, *20,* 267–287.

Clary, E. G., and Snyder, M. "A Functional Analysis of Altruism and Prosocial Behavior: The Case of Volunteerism." *Review of Personality and Social Psychology,* 1991, *12,* 119–148.

Clary, E. G., and Snyder, M "Persuasive Communications Strategies for Recruiting Volunteers." In D. R. Young, R. M. Hollister, V. A. Hodgkinson, and Associates, *Governing, Leading, and Managing Nonprofit Organizations: New Insights from Research and Practice.* San Francisco: Jossey-Bass, 1993.

Clary, E. G., Snyder, M., and Stukas, A. A. "Service-Learning and Psychology: Lessons from the Psychology of Volunteers' Motivations." In R. G. Bringle and D. K. Duffy (eds.), *With Service in Mind: Concepts and Models for Service-Learning in Psychology.* Washington, D.C.: American Association of Higher Education, 1998.

Clary, E. G., and others. "Matching Messages to Motives in Persuasion: A Functional Approach to Promoting Volunteerism." *Journal of Applied Social Psychology,* 1994, *24,* 1129–1149.

Clary, E. G., and others. "Understanding and Assessing the Motivations of Volunteers: A Functional Approach." *Journal of Personality and Social Psychology,* 1998, *74,* 1516–1530.

Crain, A. L., Omoto, A. M., and Snyder, M. "What If You Can't Always Get What You Want? Testing a Functional Approach to Volunteerism." Paper presented at the annual meeting of the Midwestern Psychological Association, Chicago, April 1998.

Crain, A. L., Snyder, M., and Omoto, A. M. "Volunteers Make a Difference: Relationship Quality, Active Coping, and Functioning Among PWAs with Volunteer Buddies." Paper presented at the annual meeting of the Midwestern Psychological Association, Chicago, May 2000.

Curtis, J. E., Grabb, E., and Baer, D. "Voluntary Association Membership in Fifteen Countries: A Comparative Analysis." *American Sociological Review,* 1992, *57,* 139–152.

Ferrari, J. R., McCown, W., and Pantano, J. "Experiencing Satisfaction and Stress as an AIDS Care Provider: The AIDS Caregiver Scale." *Evaluation and the Health Professions,* 1994, *16,* 295–310.

Hellinger, F. J. "The Lifetime Cost of Treating a Person with HIV." *Journal of the American Medical Association,* 1993, *270,* 474–478.

INDEPENDENT SECTOR. *Giving and Volunteering in the United States: Findings from a National Survey.* Washington, D.C.: INDEPENDENT SECTOR, 1999.

Kayal, P. M. *Bearing Witness: Gay's Men's Health Crisis and the Politics of AIDS.* Boulder, Colo.: Westview Press, 1993.

Kelly, J. J., Chu, S. Y., Buehler, J. W. "AIDS Deaths Shift from Hospital to Home." *American Journal of Public Health,* 1993, *83,* 1433–1437.

Maio, G. R., and Olson, J. M. (eds.). *Why We Evaluate: Functions of Attitudes.* Mahwah, N.J.: Erlbaum, 2000.

O'Brien, L. T., Crain, A. L., Omoto, A. M., and Snyder, M. "Matching Motivations to Outcomes: Implications for Persistence in Service." Paper presented at the annual meeting of the Midwestern Psychological Association, Chicago, May 2000.

Omoto, A. M., and Crain, A. L. "AIDS Volunteerism: Lesbian and Gay Community-Based Responses to HIV." In G. M. Herek and B. Greene (eds.), *Contemporary Perspectives on Lesbian and Gay Issues.* Vol. 2, *AIDS, Identity, and Community.* Thousand Oaks, Calif.: Sage, 1995.

Omoto, A. M. and Snyder, M. "Basic Research in Action: Volunteerism and Society's Response to AIDS." *Personality and Social Psychology Bulletin,* 1990, *16,* 152–165.

Omoto, A. M., and Snyder, M. "AIDS Volunteers and Their Motivations: Theoretical Issues and Practical Concerns. *Nonprofit Management and Leadership,* 1993, *4,* 157–176.

Omoto, A. M., and Snyder, M. "Sustained Helping Without Obligation: Motivation, Longevity of Service, and Perceived Attitude Change Among AIDS Volunteers." *Journal of Personality and Social Psychology,* 1995, *68,* 671–686.

Omoto, A. M., and Snyder, M. Unpublished data, University of Kansas, 1999.

Omoto, A. M. and Snyder, M. "Considerations of Community: The Context and Process of Volunteerism." *American Behavioral Scientist,* 2002, *45,* 846–867.

Omoto, A. M., Snyder, M., and Berghuis, J. P. "The Psychology of Volunteerism: A Conceptual Analysis and a Program of Action Research." In J. B. Pryor and G. D. Reeder (eds.), *The Social Psychology of HIV Infection.* Mahwah, N.J.: Erlbaum, 1993.

Omoto, A. M., Snyder, M., Chang, W., and Lee, D. H. "Knowledge and Attitude Change Among Volunteers and Their Associates." Paper presented at the annual meeting of the American Psychological Association, San Francisco, August 2001.

Omoto, A. M., Snyder, M., and Crain, A. L. "Hurt Because You Help: Stigmatization as a Barrier to Social Action." Unpublished manuscript, Claremont Graduate University and University of Minnesota, 2003a.

Omoto, A. M., Snyder, M., and Crain, A. L. "On the Stigmatization of People Who Do Good Work: The Case of AIDS Volunteers." Unpublished manuscript, Claremont Graduate University and University of Minnesota, 2003b.

Omoto, A. M., Gunn, D. O., and Crain, A. L. "Helping in Hard Times: Relationship Closeness and the AIDS Volunteer Experience." In V. J. Derlega and A. P. Barbee (eds.), *HIV Infection and Social Interaction.* Thousand Oaks, Calif.: Sage, 1998.

Omoto, A. M., Snyder, M., and Smith, D. M. [Unpublished data.] Lawrence, Kan.: University of Kansas, 1999.

Ouellette, S. C., Cassel, J. B., Maslanka, H., and Wong, L. M. "GMHC Volunteers and Hopes for the Second Decade of AIDS." *AIDS Education and Prevention,* 1995, *7*(5 Suppl.), 64–79.

Piliavin, J. A., and Charng, H. "Altruism: A Review of Recent Theory and Research." *Annual Review of Sociology,* 1990, *16,* 27–65.

Schindler-Rainman, E. "Volunteerism Is Changing!" *Journal of Volunteer Administration,* 1990, *8*(4), 2–6.

Schondel, C., Shields, G., and Orel, N. "Development of an Instrument to Measure Volunteers' Motivation in Working with People with AIDS." *Social Work in Health Care,* 1992, *17,* 53–71.

Schroeder, D. A., Penner, L. A., Dovidio, J. F., and Piliavin, J. A. *The Psychology of Helping and Altruism: Problems and Puzzles.* New York: McGraw-Hill, 1995.

Simon, B., Stürmer, S., and Steffens, K. "Helping Individuals or Group Members? The Role of Individual and Collective Identification in AIDS Volunteerism." *Personality and Social Psychology Bulletin,* 2000, *26,* 497–506.

Smith, D. M., Omoto, A. M., and Snyder, M. "Motivation Matching and Recruitment of Volunteers: A Field Study." Paper presented at the annual meeting of the American Psychological Society, Toronto, June 2001.

Smith, M. B., Bruner, J., and White, R. *Opinions and Personality.* New York: Wiley, 1956.

Snyder, M., and Cantor, N. "Understanding Personality and Social Behavior: A Functionalist Strategy." In D. Gilbert, S. Fiske, and G. Lindzey (eds.), *The Handbook of Social Psychology.* Vol. 1. (4th ed.) New York: McGraw-Hill, 1998.

Snyder, M., Clary, E. G., and Stukas, A. A. "The Functional Approach to Volunteerism." In G. R. Maio and J. M. Olson (eds.), *Why We Evaluate: Functions of Attitudes.* Mahwah, N.J.: Erlbaum, 2000.

Snyder, M. and Omoto, A. M. "Volunteerism and Society's Response to the HIV Epidemic." *Current Directions in Psychological Science,* 1992a, *1,* 113–116.

Snyder, M., and Omoto, A. M. "Who Helps and Why? The Psychology of AIDS Volunteerism." In S. Spacapan and S. Oskamp (eds.), *Helping and Being Helped: Naturalistic Studies.* Thousand Oaks, Calif.: Sage, 1992b.

Snyder, M., and Omoto, A. M. "Doing Good for Self and Society: Volunteerism and the Psychology of Citizen Participation." In M. Van Vugt, M. Snyder, T. Tyler, and A. Biel (eds.), *Collective Helping in Modern Society: Dilemmas and Solutions.* London: Routledge, 2000.

Snyder, M., and Omoto, A. M. "Basic Research and Practical Problems: Volunteerism and the Psychology of Individual and Collective Action." In W. Wosinska, R. Cialdini, and D. Barrett (eds.), *The Practice of Social Influence in Multiple Cultures.* Mahwah, N.J.: Erlbaum, 2001.

Snyder, M., Omoto, A. M., and Crain, A. L. "Punished for Their Good Deeds: Stigmatization of AIDS Volunteers." *American Behavioral Scientist,* 1999, *42,* 1175–1192.

Snyder, M., Omoto, A. M., and Smith, D. M. "The Role of Persuasion Strategies in Motivating Individual and Collective Action." In E. Borgida, J. L. Sullivan, and E. Riedel (eds.), *The Political Psychology of Democratic Citizenship.* Cambridge: Cambridge University Press, 2003.

Stukas, A. A., Snyder, M., and Clary, E. G. "Service Learning: Who Benefits and Why." *Social Policy Report,* 1999, *13,* 1–19.

Turner, H. A., Catania, J. A., and Gagnon, J. "The Prevalence of Informal Caregiving to Persons with AIDS in the United States: Caregiver Characteristics and Their Implications." *Social Science Medicine,* 1994, *38,* 1543–1552.

Williamson, I., Snyder, M., and Omoto, A. M. "How Motivations and Reenlistment Frames Interact to Predict Volunteer Attitudes and Intentions: A Test of the Functional Matching Effect." Paper presented at the annual meeting of the Midwestern Psychological Association, Chicago, May 2000.

Wilson, J. "Volunteering." *Annual Review of Sociology,* 2000, *26,* 215–240.

CHAPTER THIRTEEN

LEADERSHIP, SOCIAL WORK, AND VIRTUAL TEAMS

The Relative Influence of Vertical Versus Shared Leadership in the Nonprofit Sector

Craig L. Pearce, Youngjin Yoo, Maryam Alavi

The environment'" for nonprofit organizations is becoming increasingly challenging. Not only are the technological, competitive, demographic, and legal aspects changing at an ever-increasing pace, but the focus on accountability and results is intensifying. This has ushered in an era of great change for nonprofit organizations (Drucker, 1999). Many are looking for and implementing new ways of organizing in response to these environmental demands. The new organizational forms have been referred to by a variety of terms, including *virtual* (for example, Byrne, 1993; Davidow and Malone, 1992; Grenier and Metes, 1995), and *networked* (for example, De Sanctis and Poole, 1997; Miles and Snow, 1986). Teams are considered the basic building blocks and instrumental to the implementation of new organizational forms. They are viewed as a key current and future organizational trend (Heckscher, 1994). For example, in the networked organizational form, teams are referred to as the "core substructure" (Piore, 1994), the fundamental unit for collective work, "often supplementing or replacing the vertical structures" (De Sanctis and Poole, 1997, p. 161). This trend is occurring in both the nonprofit and for-profit sectors (Pearce, Perry, and Sims, 2001).

As more and more nonprofit organizations are turning to team approaches to organizing, the study of teams and team leadership has become increasingly important. A critical element contributing to the success of teams is team leadership: "One clear message from all the recent interest [in teams] is that there is a strong need for a better understanding of . . . team leadership in a wide variety of contexts" (Hollenbeck, Ilgen and Sego, 1994, p. 5).

In addition to this general transition toward the use of teams in organizations is the increasing use of virtual teams (see, for example, Coutu, 1998; Townsend, De Marie, and Hendrickson, 1998; Warkentin, Sayeed, and Hightower, 1997). Virtual teams will become increasingly important in all types of nonprofit organizations as these organizations strive for ways to reduce service delivery costs while simultaneously enhancing flexibility and response time. Our need to develop an understanding of team leadership in virtual teams in the nonprofit sector is therefore acutely important.

Virtual organizations and networked organizations consist of individuals collaborating and working from physically dispersed locations (Fulk and De Sanctis, 1995) and thus rely on virtual teams for obtaining member participation and coordinating individual effort in productive work. Virtual teams are teams that rarely meet in person but interact over an extended period of time on complex tasks with the aid of technology-mediated communication (Townsend, De Marie, and Hendrickson, 1998). Although virtual teams can improve flexibility and collaboration among organizational members, their use does bring into question the more traditional model of top-down leadership in nonprofits (Shin and McClomb, 1998). For example, unlike face-to-face team environments, members in virtual team environments communicate and collaborate primarily via electronic communication technologies, such as e-mail, groupware, fax, and telephony. Past research has shown that technology-mediated communication differs from face-to-face communication (Kiesler and Sproull, 1992; Watson, De Sanctis, and Poole, 1988). For instance, communication becomes depersonalized and more task-focused in technology-mediated team environments. As communication forms change, leadership forms may change as well.

Mankin, Cohen, and Bikson (1996), for example, have argued that in technology-mediated teams, the role and the quality of leadership can change dramatically. In particular, they note that in technology-mediated teams, leadership can be shared by several team members, with each providing leadership for different aspects of the team's work. Despite the importance of the topic, there is a significant gap in the leadership and information systems literature about the role of leadership in virtual teams, particularly in the nonprofit sector. To begin filling the gap in the literature, we explore, in the research described here, the relative influence of vertical leadership (leadership from the designated team leader) with shared leadership (leadership emanating from the members of the team) in virtual teams in the social work sector.

In this chapter, we briefly review the current paradigm in leadership research and develop the behavioral model of leadership that guides this research. We then illuminate the theoretical roots of the concept of shared leadership. Subsequently, we review the literature that is related to leadership in virtual teams, which leads to several hypotheses. We especially examine two distinct social sources of leadership: leader behavior exhibited by the designated team leader (vertical leadership) and leader behavior exhibited by the team members (shared leadership). We then describe the study design and the results and discuss implications for practice and future research.

Theoretical Background

In this section we develop the theoretical foundation for our study, reviewing first the general literature on leadership, then the literature specific to the concept of shared leadership.

Leadership

In our research, we generally subscribe to Yukl's definition of leadership as "influence exerted . . . over other people to guide, structure, and facilitate relationships in a group or organization" (1998, p. 3). He especially denotes the "manner in which influence is exerted" as an important issue for understanding what is meant by leadership. Thus it is possible to operationalize leadership as consisting of many different types of specific leader behaviors.

Nonetheless, the bulk of current leadership research is undertaken within the paradigm of the transactional-transformational framework. This research stream is rooted in the work of House (1977) and Burns (1978). Burns, in his seminal book on political leadership, described the distinction between transactional and transformational leader behaviors. He defined transactional leaders as those who "approach followers with an eye to exchanging one thing for another" (p. 3). He subsequently developed the concept of the transformational leader. He drew heavily on the work of Maslow (1954) in defining transformational leadership. He described transformational leadership as a situation where "leaders and followers raise one another to higher levels of morality and motivation" (Burns, 1978, p. 20).

The transformational line of research has added greatly to our current understanding of leadership processes and effect. However, one may wonder if the leadership field has coalesced too narrowly around this two-factor theory of leadership. Yukl stated that the transactional-transformational paradigm "is fast becoming a two-factor theory of leadership processes, which is an unwarranted oversimplification of a complex phenomenon" (1989, p. 212). Further, more recently, Yukl declared "Most research and theory on leadership has favored a definition of leadership that emphasizes the primary importance of unilateral influence by a single 'heroic' leader" (1998, p. 504).

Some scholars have claimed that leader behaviors outside of the transactional-transformational research paradigm are becoming increasingly important in organizations (see Bass, 1990; Manz and Sims, 1987, 1989; Pearce and Sims, 2000, 2002; Zey, 1988). For example, Manz and Sims (1989, 2001), have demonstrated the importance of empowering leadership. Cohen, Chang, and Ledford (1997) also concluded that empowering forms of leadership are positively related to team effectiveness, and Zey (1988) concluded that mentoring types of behaviors would become increasingly important in the leader-follower relationship.

Bass concluded that "democratic, participative, and relations-oriented leader behavior was found to contribute to the cohesiveness of groups in a number of studies" and that "supportive leadership [exerts] the most influence on drive and cohesiveness in small and in recently established groups" (1990, p. 610). Moreover, Leana (1985), in a study of groupthink, found that teams with participative leaders generated more alternatives than teams with directive leaders, thus suggesting that for teams with responsibility for creating complex plans, participative leadership may be more appropriate.

Bass and Avolio (1993) stated that one of the major problems in research on leadership is that "rather than build on earlier theories, there is a tendency to discount them for the sake of introducing a 'new way of thinking'" (p. 51). Thus our conceptual model of leadership entails four behaviors that embrace and build on the current dominant leadership paradigm. More specifically, based on the work of Sims and colleagues (Cox and Sims, 1996; Manz and Sims, 1991; Sims and Manz, 1996; Pearce and Sims, 2000, 2002), our theoretical development begins by conceptualizing four types of leader behavior: directive, transactional, transformational, and empowering.

Directive leadership describes the use of legitimate or position power (see, for example, French and Raven, 1959). Directive leadership is theoretically rooted in Theory X management (see McGregor, 1960), task-oriented components of the Michigan Studies (see Bass, 1967), and initiating structure components of the Ohio State Studies (see Fleishman, 1973). We therefore investigate the effect on team outcomes of the leader's assigning goals.

Transactional leadership describes the use of reward power (e.g., French and Raven, 1959). Transactional leadership is in principle rooted in equity theory (see Adams, 1963), expectancy theory (see Vroom, 1964), path-goal theory (see House, 1971), and exchange theory (see Homans, 1958). We therefore also investigate the effect on team outcomes of the leader's use of contingent rewards for performance.

Transformational leadership describes the shifting of followers from their immediate lower-level needs, such as physiological and security needs, to higher-level needs such as a unifying mission. Transformational leadership is theoretically rooted in the sociology of charisma (see Weber, 1924/1946), charismatic leadership (see House, 1977; Hunt, 1999), and transformational leadership (see Bass, 1985; Burns, 1978; Hunt and Conger, 1999). We therefore also investigate the effect on team outcomes of the leader's providing a vision regarding the purpose of the team.

Empowering leadership describes the focus on developing self-leadership (Manz and Sims, 1980) and internal motivation of followers (see Deci and Ryan, 1985). Empowering leadership is theoretically rooted in behavioral self-management (see Thorenson and Mahoney, 1974), cognitive behavior modification (see Meichenbaum, 1974), social cognitive theory (see Bandura, 1986), and participative goal setting (see Locke and Latham, 1990). We therefore also investigate the effect on team outcomes of the leader's encouraging self-leadership.

Shared Leadership

Most research on leader behavior has focused on the behaviors of an elected or appointed leader of some organization or group (see Bass, 1990). However, this does not mean that leadership cannot be displayed by people other than the designated leader (see Pearce and Conger, 2003).

The idea of shared leadership is deeply rooted in the organizational science literature. Mary Parker Follett (1924), with her concept of "the law of the situation," was one of the first writers to suggest that leadership could come from people other than the designated leader. According to Follett, in any situation, one should not simply rely on the designated leader but should look for leadership from the person who has the most knowledge about the situation at hand. In this regard, knowledge, not hierarchy, becomes the basis for leadership. Unfortunately, her ideas remained dormant for many decades.

Recently, however, a small group of scholars have been making advances in the empirical study of shared leadership (for example, Avolio, Jung, Murry, and Sivasubramaniam, 1996; Ensley and Pearce, 2000; Pearce, 1997; Pearce and Sims, 2002). For example, Avolio and colleagues (1996) found shared leadership in teams of undergraduate students doing community volunteer work to be positively correlated with self-reported ratings of effectiveness. Further, Pearce (1997) found shared leadership to be predictive of team dynamics and team effectiveness, and Pearce and Sims (2002) found shared leadership to be more predictive than vertical leadership of the effectiveness of work teams responsible for implementing innovation. Finally, Ensley and Pearce (2000) found shared leadership to be a more useful predictor of team effectiveness than the more traditional vertical leadership in top management teams of entrepreneurial firms. In addition to these empirical studies, several scholars have made conceptual advances for the study and practice of shared leadership (for example, Ensley, Pearson, and Pearce, 2003; Pearce and Conger, 2003; Pearce, Perry, and Sims, 2001; Perry, Pearce, and Sims, 1999; Seers, 1996). In fact, Pearce, Perry, and Sims (2000) specifically articulate the benefits and application of shared leadership in the nonprofit sector. According to them, if anything, we should expect shared leadership to be even more efficacious in nonprofit organizations than in the for-profit sector.

Leadership in Computer-Mediated Environments

While much research has been done on the group processes and outcomes of technology-mediated teams (see, for example, Beauclair, 1989; Euske and Dolk, 1990; Lewis and Keleman, 1990; Pinsonneault and Kraemer, 1990), the results do not clearly indicate the role of leadership in geographically dispersed virtual teams. Yoo and Wheeler (1995) theorized about the effect of group decision support software (GDSS) technology on various types of leadership. They argued that anonymity, richness of the communication medium, task structuring, and the facilitator of GDSS technology influence the effectiveness of leadership behaviors. Recently, Sosik and his colleagues (Sosik, Avolio, and Kahai, 1997; Sosik, 1997) investigated the effect of transactional and transformational leadership behavior in GDSS environments. They found that in GDSS environments, transformational leadership does improve group members' idea generation and group potency. They further found that GDSS anonymity increased the effect of transformational leadership relative to transactional leadership on group effectiveness. Although not conducted in the leadership research context, numerous previous studies examining group interaction and the effects of communication modality have found that use of computers equalizes the participation rates of group members (see Huber, 1990; Rice, 1984; Sproull and Kiesler, 1991). Group members participated in the group decision-making process and influenced final outcomes more equally in computer-mediated environments than in face-to-face environments (see Weisband, Schneider, and Connolly, 1995, for an exception). If we apply these findings in the context of leadership, one can argue that the traditional leadership style (heroic vertical leadership) may not be as effective in the virtual team setting as it is in face-to-face environments.

Hypotheses: Vertical Versus Shared Leadership

Leader behaviors have been closely linked to team outcomes in a number of studies in all types of organizations (see Bass, 1990; Yukl, 1998). For example, the goal-setting literature has demonstrated the powerful effect that the setting of goals can make on subsequent subordinate outcomes (see, for example, Locke and Latham, 1990). Thus the leader behavior of providing direction seems likely to affect subsequent team outcomes. Moreover, a wealth of literature has shown how the leader behavior of providing contingent rewards is more likely to result in desired behavior (see, for example, Sims, 1977). In addition, recent leadership research has demonstrated how, by providing a compelling vision, a leader can affect subsequent team outcomes (see, for example, Bass and Avolio, 1993). Finally, emerging research on empowering leadership suggests that encouraging follower self-leadership has a positive effect on team outcomes (see Cohen, Chang, and Ledford, 1997). As mentioned earlier, research on leadership in technology-mediated team environments has shown that certain leadership behaviors can have an effect on team outcomes. In total, it seems that leader behavior, in its many forms, is likely to affect the subsequent outcomes of the virtual teams of social workers in this study. This leads us to our first hypothesis:

HYPOTHESIS 1: VERTICAL LEADERSHIP IS A USEFUL PREDICTOR OF TEAM OUTCOMES.

Although there has been a wealth of empirical literature on the effect of vertical leadership on subsequent team outcomes, there is a paucity of empirical research on the effect of shared leadership on team outcomes. However, the initial evidence (Avolio, Jung, Murry, and Sivasubramaniam, 1996; Ensley and Pearce, 2000; Pearce, 1997; Pearce and Sims, 2002) suggests that shared leadership should be an important predictor of team outcomes for virtual teams of social workers. Moreover, the substitutes for leadership literature suggests that the geographical separation of the leader from the team negates the potential effect of the vertical leader on the team (Kerr and Jermier, 1978). The important question then is, What takes the place of the influence of the vertical leader in virtual teams? Mankin, Cohen, and Bikson (1996) claimed that it is possible for team members to share leadership in technology-mediated teams. Lipnack and Stamps (1993) suggested that dispersed teams require multiple leaders, and Haywood (1998) stated that all members of dispersed teams "need to understand how to motivate and influence other team members" (p. 101). Further, as suggested by Euske and Dolk (1990), hierarchical, bureaucratic controls need to be supplanted by norm-based control mechanisms in geographically dispersed, technology-mediated groups. Since norm-based controls are similar to shared leadership, in that they are a source of influence that stems from the team as a whole, it seems likely that shared leadership will yield an effect on the outcomes of the virtual teams of social workers in this study. Thus we arrive at our second hypothesis:

HYPOTHESIS 2: SHARED LEADERSHIP IS A USEFUL PREDICTOR OF TEAM OUTCOMES.

It seems likely that both social sources of leadership should have important causal effects on the outcomes of the teams, however, the precise nature of these relationships is unclear. The importance of this issue was highlighted by Yukl (1998), who designated the most important current controversy in leadership theory and research as "heroic versus shared leadership." He states, "The extent to which leadership can be shared, . . . the success of shared leadership, and the implications [of shared leadership] for design of organizations are important and interesting questions that deserve more research. As yet, we have only begun to examine these research questions" (p. 504). Although Yukl apparently posed this question in the context of traditional face-to-face teams, the answer to this question seems to be even more pertinent to virtual teams due to the geographical and temporal separations between the leader and the team members. Therefore, the purpose of this research is to examine each source, both independently and jointly, to tease out the empirical nature of its effects on the team outcomes in this study. Since we do not have a definitive theoretical basis about the relative usefulness of these two sources of leadership in virtual teams, we treat this as a research question to be explored:

RESEARCH QUESTION: WHICH SOCIAL SOURCE OF LEADERSHIP, VERTICAL OR SHARED, IS A MORE USEFUL PREDICTOR OF TEAM OUTCOMES?

Finally, smaller groups are generally found to be more effective than larger groups on a number of criteria (Levine and Moreland, 1990). For example, several researchers (Pinto and Crow, 1982; Markham, Dansereau, and Alutto, 1982; Kerr, 1989) found members of smaller groups to cooperate more, participate more, and be more satisfied than members of larger groups. Smaller groups have also been found to experience fewer coordination problems and less social loafing than larger groups (Albanese and Van Fleet, 1985; Gooding and Wagner, 1985; Harkins and Szymanski, 1987). Thus team size may be a covariate of leadership and the outcomes of the virtual teams of social workers we studied in this research. We therefore included team size as a control variable in this study.

Method

In this section we describe the participants in the research, review the psychometric properties of the measures we used, and describe the data analysis procedures we employed.

Sample

The teams in this study were made up of social workers who were participants in an educational program. The action-learning project for each team involved the development of a community revitalization plan. Team members were carefully selected so that no two team members were in the same geographical location and so that the teams were as heterogeneous as possible. Participants were given ten weeks to complete the plan via e-mail, groupware, fax, and telephone. The sample consisted of 121 men and 85 women. The average age was forty-nine. Forty-eight participants had bachelor's degrees, 117 had master's degrees, and three had doctorates. Thirty-eight individuals held other degrees, such as law and community college degrees. There were no statistically significant differences among the teams in terms of age, experience, or self-reported computer efficacy. There were a total of twenty-eight teams participating in the study. The average team size was seven members (SD = 1.26).

Measures

All measures, with the exception of team size, were collected using 5-point Likert-type scales. To enhance interpretability, the leadership data and team outcomes data were collected at different points in time. We collected leadership data in week 8 to allow sufficient time for team development, display, and observation of leader behavior by team members while still affording a significant time lag for the collection of team outcome variables. Team outcome variables were collected at the end of the project, at the conclusion of week 10.

Due to the large number of items in this study (see Bentler and Chou, 1987), we examined each group of scale variables with an exploratory factor analysis employing principal components analysis with varimax rotation. Exploratory factor analysis was conducted at the item level, and scales were constructed by unit-weighting the items from these factors. These scales were then examined for internal consistency, reliability, and interrater consensus within the team unit of analysis. To assess the internal consistency of each scale, the Cronbach alpha procedure (Cronbach, 1951) was used. To assess the appropriateness of aggregating individual responses to the team level, the James, Demaree, and Wolf (1984) procedure $r_{wg(j)}$ was used. This procedure produces a measure of consensus among respondents and "provides the justification for aggregation" (Koslowski and Hattrup, 1992, p. 162).

Leader Behavior

Each team formally elected a leader. Team members' perceptions of leader behavior were elicited with a questionnaire formatted such that individuals responded to each question twice: once for their team leader (vertical leadership) and once for their team members as a whole (shared leadership). A similar double response format had been used successfully in previous research in the measurement of vertical and shared leadership (Pearce and Sims, 2002).

Therefore, the first step in developing the leader behavior questionnaire used in this research was to begin with the Cox and Sims (1996) questionnaire, which was conceptualized as four leader behavior strategies (directive, transactional, transformational, and empowering). We selected four subscales from this instrument to examine in the current study.

The factor structures for vertical and shared leadership are presented in Table 13.1. In all cases, all items loaded consistent with our a priori predictions. Reliability for each scale was equal to or greater than .82 and is presented at the bottom of the factor analysis. The $r_{WG(j)}$ for each scale was equal to or greater than .70 and is also presented at the bottom of the factor analysis.

Team Size

Team size was a measure of the number of individuals in each team.

Team Outcomes

We assessed four types of team outcomes: potency, social integration, problem-solving quality, and perceived effectiveness. To assess team potency, we used seven of the eight items recommended by Guzzo, Yost, Campbell, and Shea (1993) and slightly modified the items to reflect the nature of the current study. To assess social integration, we used the positively worded items from the Smith and colleagues (1994) study and likewise modified the items to reflect the nature of the current study. To assess problem-solving quality and perceived effectiveness, we used items from Green and Taber's scheme for rating satisfaction with group problem-solving outcomes and processes (1980).

The final factor structure for team outcomes is presented in Table 13.2. It was necessary to delete one item from our measure of problem-solving quality ("How would you describe your project team's problem-solving process?" rated on a scale of 1 = understandable through confusing = 5) because it loaded on an inappropriate factor and one item from our measure of perceived effectiveness ("How satisfied or dissatisfied are you with the quality of your group's solution?") because it loaded on an independent factor. Otherwise, all items loaded consistent with our a priori predictions. Reliability for each scale was equal to or greater than .88 and is presented at the bottom of the factor analysis in Table 13.2. The $r_{WG(j)}$ for each scale was equal to or greater than .89 and is also presented at the bottom of the factor analysis.

TABLE 13.1. VERTICAL (SHARED) LEADER BEHAVIOR FACTOR LOADINGS.

Factor Name and Items[b]	Factor Loadings[a]							
	I	(I)	II	(IV)	III	(III)	IV	(II)
I (I). Empowering Leadership								
My team leader urges me to assume responsibilities on my own	.82	.88	.25	.13	.00	.00	.16	.13
My team leader encourages me to find solutions to my problems without his or her direct input	.79	.82	.00	.13	.19	.11	.12	.00
My team leader encourages me to search for solutions to my problems without supervision	.74	.61	.16	.31	.18	.28	.15	.13
My team leader advises me to solve problems when they pop up without always getting a stamp of approval	.73	.79	.23	.00	.24	.34	.28	.29
II (IV). Directive Leadership								
My team leader sets the goals for my performance	.21	.10	.86	.85	.16	.29	.24	.11
My team leader establishes the goals for my work	.20	.31	.84	.71	.13	.00	.27	.35
My team leader establishes my performance goals	.25	.17	.82	.74	.18	.20	.18	.30
III (III). Transactional Leadership								
My team leader urges me to reward myself with something I like when I have successfully completed a major task	.00	.20	.17	.17	.90	.85	.15	.17
My team leader encourages me to treat myself to something I enjoy when I do a task especially well	.00	.00	.00	.00	.84	.77	.24	.35
My team leader encourages me to give myself a pat on the back when I meet a new challenge	.37	.39	.35	.22	.71	.73	.00	.00
My team leader gives me special recognition when my work performance is especially good	.52	.55	.24	.26	.59	.58	.12	.00
IV (II). Transformational Leadership								
My team leader provides a clear vision of who and what our team is	.00	.00	.20	.20	.23	.16	.86	.89
My team leader provides a clear vision of where our team is going	.24	.12	.23	.19	.15	.13	.82	.88
Because of my team leader, I have a clear vision of our team's purpose	.39	.28	.33	.26	.13	.23	.67	.79
Eigenvalues	6.69	6.40	1.61	1.08	1.41	1.28	1.08	1.89
Variance (%)	47.8	45.7	11.5	7.7	10.1	9.1	7.7	13.5
Alpha	.85	.86	.91	.82	.87	.86	.85	.90
$r_{WG(J)}$	.76	.71	.72	.70	.73	.74	.93	.93

[a]Factors are presented in the order of extraction from the analysis of vertical leadership. The roman numerals in parentheses indicate the order of extraction from the analysis of shared leadership.

[b]Items appear as worded for description of the vertical leader.

TABLE 13.2. TEAM OUTCOMES FACTOR LOADINGS.

	Factor Loadings			
Factor Names and Items	**I**	**II**	**III**	**IV**
I. Potency				
This team feels it can solve any problem it encounters	.86	.24	.15	.00
This team believes it can become unusually good at producing high-quality work	.83	.25	.30	.14
This team expects to be known as a high-performing team	.83	.17	.26	.20
This team feels it can solve any problem it encounters	.81	.32	.19	.20
This team believes it can be very productive	.80	.23	.28	.00
This team can get a lot done when it works hard	.69	.51	.20	-.00
No task is too tough for this team	.66	.45	-.00	.00
II. Social Integration				
Relationships between members of the team are positive and rewarding	.31	.78	.22	.24
The members of the team really stick together	.20	.78	.17	.25
The members of the team are always ready to cooperate and help each other	.40	.71	.15	.00
The members of the team get along together well	.52	.65	.24	-.00
III. Problem-Solving Quality				
How would you describe your project team's problem-solving process?				
1 = Coordinated . . . through . . .Uncoordinated = 5	−.33	−.17	**−.80**	−.26
1 = Fair . . . through . . . Unfair = 5	.13	−.26	**−.79**	−.15
1 = Efficient . . . through . . . Inefficient = 5	.39	−.13	**−.74**	−.26
IV. Perceived Effectiveness				
To what extent do you feel committed to the group's solution?				
1 = Not at all . . . through . . .To a very great extent = 5	.00	.12	.23	**.91**
To what extent are you confident that the group solution is correct?				
1 = Not at all . . . through . . . To a very great extent = 5	.00	.16	.22	**.88**
Eigenvalue	8.69	1.95	1.11	0.85
Variance explained	54.33	12.20	6.92	5.26
Alpha	.94	.88	.87	.88
$r_{WG(J)}$	.91	.94	.89	.96

Data Analysis

Multiple regression analysis was used to examine the effects of vertical and shared leadership on the subsequent outcomes in the teams in this study. First, we examined the effect of the four vertical leadership behaviors on team outcomes, independent of shared leadership (hypothesis 1). Next, we examined the effect of the four shared leadership behaviors on team outcomes, independent of vertical leadership (hypothesis 2). Finally, employing usefulness analysis (Farh, Podsakoff, and Organ, 1990), we examined the relative usefulness of vertical and shared leadership in explaining unique variance in our outcome variables. In all regression equations, team size was entered as a control variable.

Results

Means, standard deviations, and intercorrelations among the study variables are shown in Table 13.3. For all the regression analyses, we first controlled for the effect of team size. Thus for hypotheses 1 and 2, it is the change in R^2 after the effect of size that is the relevant statistic.

We first examined the effect of vertical leadership, independent of shared leadership, on team outcomes. The results of the four multiple regression models, one for each of the measures of team outcomes, are found in the upper part of Table 13.4. The appropriate test statistics for this hypothesis are the ΔR^2 statistics found on line two of the table. The ΔR^2 for the model of potency was .19, the ΔR^2 for social integration was .14, the ΔR^2 for problem-solving quality was .13, and the ΔR^2 for perceived effectiveness was .20. No statistically significant support was found for hypothesis 1, which stated that vertical leadership would affect team outcomes.

We next examined the effect of shared leadership, independent of vertical leadership, on team outcomes. The results of the four multiple regression models, one for each of the measures of team outcomes, are found in the lower part of Table 13.4. The appropriate test statistics for this hypothesis are the ΔR^2 statistics found on line 5 of the table. The ΔR^2 for the model of potency was .43 ($p < .01$), the ΔR^2 for social integration was .49 ($p < .01$), the ΔR^2 for problem-solving quality was .35 ($p < .05$), and the ΔR^2 for perceived effectiveness was .26. Thus supporting hypothesis 2, the four shared leadership behaviors examined simultaneously explained significant amounts of variance in potency, social integration, and problem-solving quality but not in perceived effectiveness.

An important research question in this study was determining the *relative* usefulness of vertical and shared leadership, when examined simultaneously, in explaining team outcomes. To do this, hierarchical regression models were specified

TABLE 13.3. MEANS, STANDARD DEVIATIONS, AND INTERCORRELATIONS AMONG STUDY VARIABLES.

Variable	Mean	SD	1	2	3	4	5	6	7	8	9	10	11	12
1. Directive Behavior (Vertical)	2.73	.65												
2. Transactional Behavior (Vertical)	2.90	.44	.13											
3. Transformational Behavior (Vertical)	3.46	.58	.67**	.13										
4. Empowering Behavior (Vertical)	3.43	.48	.59**	.30	.71**									
5. Directive Behavior (Shared)	2.43	.57	.55**	-.03	.38**	.33*								
6. Transactional Behavior (Shared)	2.83	.50	-.11	.70**	.05	.11	.16							
7. Transformational Behavior (Shared)	3.08	.74	.16	-.07	.49**	.17	.66**	.35*						
8. Empowering Behavior (Shared)	3.26	.55	.28	.27	.51**	.71**	.45**	.57**	.57**					
9. Team Size	7.39	1.26	-.21	-.27	-.15	-.09	-.05	-.32*	-.14	-.11				
10. Potency	3.76	.56	-.09	-.14	.18	.17	.34*	.23	.64**	.45**	-.09			
11. Social Integration	3.89	.50	-.13	-.04	.14	.09	.39*	.43*	.67**	.51**	-.12	.87**		
12. Problem-Solving Quality	3.97	.80	-.13	.11	.11	.16	.07	.50**	.31	.46**	.02	.57**	.61**	
13. Perceived Effectiveness	4.05	.43	-.14	.24	.14	.18	.00	.43*	.18	.33*	.10	.18	.34*	.68**

*$p < .05$; **$p < .01$.

TABLE 13.4. HIERARCHICAL REGRESSION ANALYSIS OF THE RELATIVE CONTRIBUTIONS OF VERTICAL AND SHARED LEADERSHIP TO THE VARIANCE EXPLAINED.

Line	Step	Independent Variable	Potency			Social Integration			Problem-Solving Quality			Perceived Effectiveness		
			R^2	ΔR^2	Percentage of Variance	R^2	ΔR^2	Percentage of Variance	R^2	ΔR^2	Percentage of Variance	R^2	ΔR^2	Percentage of Variance
1	1	Team Size	.01	.01	0	.01	.01	0	.00	.00	00	.01	.01	03
2	2	Vertical Leadership	.20	.19	32	.16	.14	23	.13	.13	28	.21	.20	57
3	3	Shared Leadership	.63*	.43**	68	.62*	.46**	74	.49	.36*	73	.35	.15	43
4	1	Team Size	.01	.01	00	.01	.01	01	.00	.00	00	.01	.01	03
5	2	Shared Leadership	.43*	.43*	68	.50**	.49**	79	.35*	.35*	71	.27	.26	74
6	3	Vertical Leadership	.63*	.19	32	.62*	.12	19	.49	.14	29	.35	.09	26

Note: Due to rounding, the total of R^2 and ΔR^2 may not equal 100.

*$p < .05$; **$p < .01$.

where the order of entry for vertical and shared leadership was manipulated and examined for each of the dependent variables in the study. The appropriate test statistics are the ΔR^2 statistics found in line 3 (for vertical leadership) compared to the ΔR^2 statistics found in line 6 (for shared leadership). In every case, shared leadership accounted for more unique variance explained than vertical leadership did.

Discussion

Virtual teams are becoming an increasingly important form of organization (Coutu, 1998; De Sanctis and Poole, 1997; Townsend, De Marie, and Hendrickson, 1998; Warkentin, Sayeed, and Hightower, 1997) that holds considerable promise for enhancing the effectiveness of nonprofit organizations. We believe this is the first study to empirically compare vertical versus shared leadership in virtual teams in the nonprofit context. Overall, the results show that shared leadership is a more useful predictor of team outcomes than vertical leadership. In fact, vertical leadership was not found to be an important predictor of any of our measures of team outcomes. Had we had simply followed the traditional model of leadership research and merely examined the effect of vertical leadership, we would have erroneously concluded that leadership is unimportant for these teams (see Pfeffer, 1977). Conversely, our results seem to suggest that Kerr and Jermier (1978) were correct in identifying the spatial distance between leaders and followers as an important contextual variable for the examination and exercise of leadership. Our results suggest that an alternative form of leadership—shared leadership—affects the dynamics of the team when the team is geographically dispersed.

We also wished to examine the relationships between the four leader behaviors and team outcomes. Since we found a high degree of multicollinearity among the leader behaviors, we examined partial correlations (with the effects of team size partialed out) rather than focusing on regression beta weights. These relationships are shown in Table 13.5.

None of the vertical leader behaviors were significantly related to any of the outcome measures. However, shared leader behaviors were significantly related to many of the outcome measures. For example, shared directive leadership was positively related to potency ($r = .34, p < .05$) and social integration ($r = .38, p < .05$). Shared transactional leadership was positively related to social integration ($r = .41, p < .05$), problem-solving quality ($r = .52, p < .01$), and perceived effectiveness ($r = .48, p < .01$). Shared transformational leadership was positively related to potency ($r = .63, p < .01$) and social integration ($r = .67, p < .01$). Finally, shared empowering leadership was positively related to potency ($r = .44, p < .01$), social integration ($r = .50, p < .01$), problem-solving quality ($r = .46, p < .01$), and perceived effectiveness ($r = .35, p < .05$).

TABLE 13.5. PARTIAL CORRELATIONS (CONTROLLING FOR TEAM SIZE) BETWEEN LEADERSHIP AND TEAM OUTCOMES.

	Potency	Social Integration	Problem-Solving Quality	Perceived Effectiveness
Vertical Leadership				
Directive	−.11	−.16	−.14	−.13
Transactional	−.17	−.08	.11	.27
Transformational	.17	.13	.11	.15
Empowering	.17	.08	.16	.19
Shared Leadership				
Directive	.34*	.38*	.07	.06
Transactional	.21	.41*	.52**	.48**
Transformational	.63**	.67**	.31	.19
Empowering	.44**	.50**	.46**	.35*

$*p < .05; **p < .01.$

Overall, these results indicate that shared leadership, in its many forms, may be an important predictor of team outcomes.

Practical Implications

There are several important practical implications of this research for social work and nonprofit organizations, especially in regard to team training and design considerations. First, for nonprofit organizations looking for ways to enhance flexibility and responsiveness to client needs while reducing costs associated with travel, virtual teams appear to show great promise. Virtual teams also open the possibility for volunteers who are not located in the same place to actively collaborate on projects. Virtual teams might also enhance the transfer of knowledge between teams and organizations.

Interestingly, the form of leadership that appears to work best in these types of teams is shared leadership, which has been a relatively neglected area of research. This seems consistent with Euske and Dolk's argument (1990) that norm-based control would supplant bureaucratic control in geographically separated, technology-mediated groups. In fact, not only did shared leadership tend to do a very good job of explaining the outcomes of our teams, but also it seemed to do a much better job of explaining team outcomes than the more traditional vertical leadership. Thus shared leadership seems a good candidate for incorporation into leadership and teamwork training programs for social work or other nonprofit organizations that are implementing virtual teams.

The four leader behaviors examined in this research—directive, transactional, transformational, and empowering—do not seem to be equally important when it comes to explaining team outcomes. Whereas shared directive, transactional, and transformational leadership displayed positive effects on some team outcomes, shared empowering leadership displayed positive effects on all four of our outcome measures. Thus it appears that for these types of teams, substantial gains could be realized from increased emphasis on shared leadership in general and shared empowering leadership in particular. We might speculate that shared empowering leadership is particularly efficacious because of the nature of non-profit work: nonprofit work is generally performed by individuals who are strongly motivated by the mission of the organization and thus desire empowerment and influence over the course of their contributions.

Future Research

Several avenues for future research are readily identifiable. First, the identification of shared leadership in the virtual teams in the social work context is an important step in a new direction for teams and leadership theory. However, while the current study heeded the advice of Hunt (1996) and Pinsonneault and Kraemer (1990) and focused on leadership as a team-level phenomenon, there are clearly other important antecedents of team outcomes. For instance, future research might examine the specific effects of various types of technology on the quality of team dynamics and team effectiveness. Alternatively, future research might examine the effect of virtual teams on client perceptions of service. Clients might view virtual service as less personal or less compassionate, and this will be an important consideration in the implementation of virtual teams. Future research might also examine the effect of virtual teams on the members of those teams. It is possible that the use of virtual teams may lead to psychological effects in individuals (for example, empowerment versus deindividuation). Future research would also be useful for understanding the potential effect of the use of virtual teams on the organizations in which they operate (for example, organizational culture).

Also, while this research identified an important role for an alternative social source of leadership in virtual teams in the nonprofit sector, it will be interesting to see how shared leadership affects other important virtual team outcome variables in both the nonprofit and for-profit worlds. Another area of interest will be to see if there is an interaction effect between vertical and shared leadership. Also of interest will be the causal relationship between vertical and shared leadership—does engaging in certain vertical leadership behaviors affect the display of certain shared leadership behaviors or vice versa?

Limitations

This research, like any, is not without limitations. First, the sample was drawn from virtual teams in the social work context, and therefore the results may not generalize to other types of organizations or other forms of teams. Second, our sample size was not large. Future research should attempt to collect larger data sets. Third, while the selection of measures for this research was relatively broad, it was not exhaustive. Fourth, all team outcome measures were perceptual measures. It is possible that investigations of different measures might produce different results. Finally, although the leaders of these teams were elected, they had no formal authority over the team members. Thus these results may not translate into more "formalized" teams. However, the increasing use of temporary teams and task forces, in which team leaders, particularly in the nonprofit sector, often have little formal authority, suggests that the results may have broad application.

Conclusion

Teams have become an increasingly important component in both nonprofit organizations (see, for example, Kakabadse, Kakabadse, and Myers, 1996) and for-profit organizations (see, for example, Dumaine, 1994), and virtual teams are an emerging phenomenon in all types of organizations (see, for example, Coutu, 1998; De Sanctis and Poole, 1997; Sosik, Avolio, and Kahai, 1997; Townsend, De Marie, and Hendrickson, 1998; Warkentin, Sayeed, and Hightower, 1997). This does not appear to be a fad but rather a trend that is likely to continue well into the future (Heckscher, 1994). With this increasing emphasis on virtual teams has come an increasing need to better understand team leadership in these types of teams (see, for example, Hollenbeck, Ilgen, and Sego, 1994). Therefore, this research proposed and examined a nontraditional social source of leadership and its effect on the outcomes of virtual teams in the social work context.

This research has yielded several significant contributions. First, this study examined a unique form of nonprofit teams that have been described as the key organizational unit in the organization of the future (Piore, 1994) and thus provided some insight into teams that are geographically dispersed and interact primarily through technology-mediated mechanisms. Second, the range of leader behaviors and team outcomes examined was rather broad. Third, this study examined an alternative social source of leadership—shared leadership—and found this alternative source to be quite useful in predicting team outcomes.

Most of all, this research has put the spotlight on an emerging form of leadership (shared leadership) in an emerging form of organization (virtual teams) in the nonprofit sector. Clearly, virtual teams and shared leadership deserve more theoretical, empirical, and practical attention in both the nonprofit and for-profit sectors.

REFERENCES

Adams, J. S. "Toward an Understanding of Inequity." *Journal of Abnormal and Social Psychology,* 1963, *67,* 422–436.

Albanese, R., and Van Fleet, D. D. "Rational Behavior in Groups: The Free Riding Tendency." *Academy of Management Review,* 1985, *10,* 244–255.

Avolio, B. J., Jung, D. I., Murry, W., and Sivasubramaniam, N. "Building Highly Developed Teams: Focusing on Shared Leadership Processes, Efficacy, Trust, and Performance." In M. M. Beyerlein (ed.), *Advances in Interdisciplinary Studies of Work Teams.* Vol. 3. Greenwich, Conn.: JAI Press, 1996.

Bandura, A. *Social Foundations of Thought and Action: A Social Cognitive Theory.* Upper Saddle River, N.J.: Prentice Hall, 1986.

Bass, B. M. "Some Effects on a Group of Whether and When the Head Reveals His Opinion." *Organizational Behavior and Human Performance,* 1967, *2,* 375–382.

Bass, B. M. *Leadership and Performance Beyond Expectations.* New York: Free Press, 1985.

Bass, B. M. *Bass and Stogdill's Handbook of Leadership: Theory, Research, and Managerial Applications.* (3rd ed.) New York: Free Press, 1990.

Bass, B. M., and Avolio, B. J. "Transformational Leadership: A Response to Critiques." In J. G. Hunt, B. R. Baliga, H. P. Dachler, and C. A. Schriesheim (eds.), *Emerging Leadership Vistas.* Lexington, Mass: Heath, 1993.

Beauclair, R. A. "An Experimental Study of GDSS Support Application Effectiveness." *Journal of Information Science,* 1989, *15,* 321–332.

Bentler, P. M., and Chou, C. P. "Practical Issues in Structural Modeling." *Sociological Methods and Research,* 1987, *15,* 78–117.

Burns, J. M. *Leadership.* New York: HarperCollins, 1978.

Byrne, J. A. "The Virtual Corporation." *Business Week,* Feb. 8, 1993, pp. 37–41.

Cohen, S. G., Chang, L., and Ledford, G. E., Jr. "A Hierarchical Construct of Self-Management Leadership and Its Relationship to Quality of Work Life and Perceived Work Group Effectiveness." *Personnel Psychology,* 1997, *50,* 275–308.

Coutu, D. L. "Organization: Trust in Virtual Teams." *Harvard Business Review,* 1998, *76,* 20–21.

Cox, J. F., and Sims, H. P., Jr. "Leadership and Team Citizenship Behavior: A Model and Measures." In M. M. Beyerlein (ed.), *Advances in Interdisciplinary Studies of Work Teams.* Vol. 3. Greenwich, Conn.: JAI Press, 1996.

Cronbach, L. J. "Coefficient Alpha and the Internal Structure of Tests." *Psychometrika,* 1951, *16,* 297–334.

Davidow, W. H., and Malone, M. S. *The Virtual Corporation.* New York: HarperCollins, 1992.

Deci, E. L., and Ryan, R. M. *Intrinsic Motivation and Self-Determination in Human Behavior.* New York: Plenum, 1985.

De Sanctis, G., and Poole, M. S. "Transitions in Teamwork in New Organizational Forms." *Advances in Group Processes,* 1997, *14,* 157–176.

Drucker, P. F. *Managing the Nonprofit Organization: Principles and Practices.* New York: Harper Business, 1999.

Dumaine, B. "The Trouble with Teams." *Fortune,* September 4, 1994, pp. 86–92.

Ensley, M. D., and Pearce, C. L. "Assessing the Influence of Leadership Behaviors on New Venture TMT Processes and New Venture Performance." Paper presented at the 20th Annual Entrepreneurship Research Conference, Babson Park, Mass., June 2000.

Ensley, M. D., Pearson, A., and Pearce, C. L. "Top Management Team Process, Shared Leadership, and New Venture Performance: A Theoretical Model and Research Agenda." *Human Resource Management Review,* 2003, *13*(6), 1–18.

Euske, K. J., and Dolk, D. R. "Control Strategies for Group Decision Support Systems: An End-User Computing Model." *European Journal of Operational Research,* 1990, *46,* 247–259.

Farh, J., Podsakoff, P. M., and Organ, D. W. "Accounting for Organizational Citizenship Behavior: Leader Fairness and Task Scope Versus Satisfaction." *Journal of Management,* 1990, *16*(4), 705–721.

Fleishman, E. A. "The Description of Supervisory Behavior." *Journal of Applied Psychology,* 1973, *37,* 1–6.

Follett, M. P. *Creative Experience.* London: Longman, 1924.

French, J.R.P., and Raven, B. (eds.). *The Bases of Social Power.* Ann Arbor: University of Michigan, Institute for Social Research, 1959.

Fulk, J., and De Sanctis, G. "Electronic Communication and Changing Organizational Forms." *Organization Science,* 1995, *6,* 337–349.

Gooding, R. Z., and Wagner, J. A. "A Meta-Analytic Review of the Relationship Between Size and Performance: The Productivity and Efficiency of Organizations and Their Subunits." *Administrative Science Quarterly,* 1985, *30,* 462–481.

Green, S. G., and Taber, T. D. "The Effects of Three Social Decision Schemes on Decision Group Process." *Organizational Behavior and Human Decision Performance,* 1980, *25,* 97–106.

Grenier, R., and Metes, G. E. *Going Virtual.* Upper Saddle River, N.J.: Prentice Hall, 1995.

Guzzo, R. A., Yost, P. R., Campbell, R. J., and Shea, G. P. "Potency in Groups: Articulating a Construct." *British Journal of Social Psychology,* 1993, *32,* 87–106.

Harkins, S. G., and Szymanski, K. "Social Loafing and Social Facilitation: New Wine in Old Bottles." In C. Hendrick (ed.), *Review of Personality and Social Psychology: Group Process and Intergroup Relations.* Vol. 9. Thousand Oaks, Calif.: Sage, 1987.

Haywood, M. *Managing Virtual Teams: Practical Techniques for High-Technology Project Managers.* Boston: Artech House, 1998.

Heckscher, C. *White-Collar Blues: Management Loyalties in an Age of Corporate Restructuring.* New York: Basic Books, 1994.

Hollenbeck, J. R., Ilgen, D. R., and Sego, D. J. "Repeated Measures Regression and Mediational Tests: Enhancing the Power of Leadership Research." *Leadership Quarterly,* 1994, *5,* 3–23.

Homans, G. C. "Social Behavior as Exchange." *American Journal of Sociology,* 1958, *63,* 597–606.

House, R. J. "A Path Goal Theory of Leader Effectiveness." *Administrative Science Quarterly,* 1971, *16,* 321–338.

House, R. J. "A 1976 Theory of Charismatic Leadership." In J. G. Hunt and L. L. Larson (eds.), *Leadership: The Cutting Edge.* Carbondale: Southern Illinois University Press, 1977.

Huber, G. P. "A Theory of the Effects of Advanced Information Technologies on

Organizational Design, Intelligence, and Decision Making. *Academy of Management Review,* 1990, *15,* 47–71.

Hunt, J. G. *Leadership: A New Synthesis.* Thousand Oaks, Calif.: Sage, 1996.

Hunt, J. G. "Transformational/Charismatic Leadership's Transformation of the Field: A Historical Essay." *Leadership Quarterly,* 1999, *10,* 129–135.

Hunt, J. G., and Conger, J. A. "From Where We Sit: An Assessment of Transformational and Charismatic Leadership Research." *Leadership Quarterly,* 1999, *10,* 335–344.

James, L. R., Demaree, R. G., and Wolf, G. "Estimating Within-Group Interrater Reliability With and Without Response Bias." *Journal of Applied Psychology,* 1984, *69,* 85–98.

Kakabadse, A., Kakabadse, N., and Myers, A. "Leadership and the Public Sector: An Internationally Comparative Benchmarking Analysis." *Public Administration and Development,* 1996, *16,* 377–396.

Kerr, N. L. "Illusions of Efficacy: The Effects of Group Size on Perceived Efficacy in Social Dilemmas." *Journal of Experimental and Social Psychology,* 1989, *25,* 374–403.

Kerr, S., and Jermier, J. M. "Substitutes for Leadership: Their Meaning and Measurement." *Organizational Behavior and Human Performance,* 1978, *22,* 375–403.

Kiesler, S., and Sproull, L. S. "Group Decision Making and Communication Technology." *Organizational Behavior and Human Decision Processes,* 1992, *52,* 96–123.

Koslowski, S. W., and Hattrup, K. "A Disagreement About Within-Group Agreement: Disentangling Issues of Consistency Versus Consensus." *Journal of Applied Psychology,* 1992, *77,* 161–167.

Leana, C. R. "A Partial Test of Janis's Groupthink Model: Effects of Group Cohesiveness and Leader Behavior on Defective Decision Making." *Journal of Management,* 1985, *11,* 5–17.

Levine, J. M., and Moreland, R. L. "Progress in Small Group Research." *Annual Review of Psychology,* 1990, *41,* 585–634.

Lewis, L. F., and Keleman, K. S. "Experiences with GDSS Development: Lab and Field Studies." *Journal of Information Science,* 1990, *16,* 195–205.

Lipnack, J., and Stamps, J. *The TeamNet Factor: Bridging the Power of Boundary Crossing into the Heart of Your Business.* Essex Junction, Vt.: Wright, 1993.

Locke, E. A., and Latham, G. P. *A Theory of Goal Setting and Task Performance.* Englewood Cliffs, N.J.: Prentice-Hall, 1990.

Mankin, D., Cohen, S. G., and Bikson, T. K. *Teams and Technology.* Boston: Harvard Business School Press, 1996.

Manz, C. C., and Sims, H. P., Jr. "Self-Management as a Substitute for Leadership: A Social Learning Theory Perspective." *Academy of Management Review,* 1980, 5, 361–367.

Manz, C. C., and Sims, H. P., Jr. "Leading Workers to Lead Themselves: The External Leadership of Self-Managing Work Teams." *Administrative Science Quarterly,* 1987, *32,* 106–129.

Manz, C. C., and Sims, H. P., Jr. *SuperLeadership: Leading Others to Lead Themselves.* Upper Saddle River, N.J.: Prentice Hall, 1989.

Manz, C. C., and Sims, H. P., Jr. "SuperLeadership: Beyond the Myth of Heroic Leadership." *Organizational Dynamics,* 1991, *19,* 18–35.

Manz, C. C., and Sims, H. P., Jr. *The New SuperLeadership: Leading Others to Lead Themselves.* San Francisco: Berrett-Koehler, 2001.

Markham, S. E., Dansereau, F., and Alutto, J. A. "Group Size and Absenteeism Rates: A Longitudinal Analysis." *Academy of Management Journal,* 1982, *25,* 921–927.

Maslow, A. H. *Motivation and Personality.* New York: HarperCollins, 1954.

McGregor, D. *The Human Side of Enterprise.* New York: McGraw Hill, 1960.

Meichenbaum, D. *Cognitive-Behavior Modification: An Integrative Approach.* New York: Plenum Press, 1974.

Miles, R. E., and Snow, C. C. "Network Organization: New Concepts for New Forms." *California Management Review,* 1986, *28,* 62–73.

Pearce, C. L. "The Determinants of Change Management Team Effectiveness: A Longitudinal Investigation." Unpublished doctoral dissertation, University of Maryland, 1997.

Pearce, C. L., and Conger, J. A. (eds.) *Shared Leadership: Reframing the Hows and Whys of Leadership.* Thousand Oaks, Calif.: Sage, 2003.

Pearce, C. L., Perry, M. L., and Sims, H. P., Jr. "Shared Leadership: Relationship Management to Improve NPO Effectiveness." In T. D. Connors (ed.), *The Nonprofit Handbook: Management.* New York: Wiley, 2001.

Pearce, C. L., and Sims, H. P., Jr. "Shared Leadership: Toward a Multilevel Theory of Leadership." In M. M. Beyerlein, D. A. Johnson, and S. T. Beyerlein (eds.), *Advances in Interdisciplinary Studies of Work Teams.* Greenwich, Conn.: JAI Press, 2000.

Pearce, C. L., and Sims, H. P., Jr. "The Relative Influence of Vertical versus Shared Leadership on the Longitudinal Effectiveness of Change Management Teams." *Group Dynamics: Theory, Research, and Practice,* 2002, *6,* 172–197.

Perry, M. L., Pearce, C. L., and Sims, H. P., Jr. "Empowered Selling Teams: How Shared Leadership Can Contribute to Selling Team Outcomes." *Journal of Personal Selling and Sales Management,* 1999, *19*(3), 35–52.

Pfeffer, J. "The Ambiguity of Leadership." *Academy of Management Review,* 1977, *2,* 104–112.

Pinsonneault, A., and Kraemer, K. L. "The Effects of Electronic Meetings on Group Processes and Outcomes: An Assessment of the Empirical Research." *European Journal of Operational Research,* 1990, *46,* 143–161.

Pinto, L. J., and Crow, K. E. "The Effects of Congregations Within the Same Denomination." *Journal of Scientific Study of Religion,* 1982, *21,* 304–316.

Piore, M. J. "Corporate Reform in American Manufacturing and the Challenge to Economic Theory." In T. J. Allen and M. S. Scott Morton (eds.), *Information Technology and the Corporations of the 1990s.* New York: Oxford University Press, 1994.

Rice, R. E. "Mediated Group Communication." In R. E. Rice (ed.), *The New Media.* Thousand Oaks, Calif.: Sage, 1984.

Seers, A. "Better Leadership Through Chemistry: Toward a Model of Emergent Shared Team Leadership." In M. M. Beyerlein (ed.), *Advances in Interdisciplinary Studies of Work Teams.* Vol. 3. Greenwich, Conn.: JAI Press, 1996.

Shin, J., and McClomb, G. E. "Top Executive Leadership and Organizational Innovation: An Empirical Investigation of Nonprofit Human Service Organizations (HSOs)." *Administration in Social Work,* 1998, *22*(3), 1–21.

Sims, H. P., Jr. "The Leader as Manager of Reinforcement Contingencies: An Empirical Example and a Model." In J. G. Hunt and L. L. Larson (eds.), *Leadership: The Cutting Edge.* Carbondale, Ill.: Southern Illinois University Press, 1977.

Sims, H. P., Jr. and Manz, C. C. *Company of Heroes: Unleashing the Power of Self-Leadership.* New York: Wiley, 1996.

Smith, K. G., and others. "Top Management Team Demography and Process: The Role of Social Integration and Communication." *Administrative Science Quarterly,* 1994, *39,* 412–438.

Sosik, J. J. "Effects of Transformational Leadership and Anonymity on Idea Generation in Computer-Mediated Groups." *Groups and Organizational Management,* 1997, *22,* 460–487.

Sosik, J. J., Avolio, B. J., and Kahai, S. S. "Effects of Leadership Style and Anonymity on Group Potency and Effectiveness in a Group Decision Support Systems Environment." *Journal of Applied Psychology,* 1997, *82,* 89–103.

Sproull, L., and Kiesler, S. *Connections: New Ways of Working in the Networked Organization.* Cambridge, Mass.: MIT Press, 1991.

Thorenson, E. E., and Mahoney, M. J. *Behavioral Self-Control.* Austin, Tex.: Holt, Rinehart and Winston, 1974.

Townsend, A. M., De Marie, S. M. and Hendrickson, A. R. "Virtual Teams: Technology and the Workplace of the Future." *Academy of Management Executive,* 1998, *12*(3), 17–29.

Vroom, V. H. *Work and Motivation.* New York: Wiley, 1964.

Warkentin, M. E., Sayeed, L., and Hightower, R. "Virtual Teams Versus Face-to-Face Teams: An Exploratory Study of a Web-Based Conference System." *Decision Sciences,* 1997, *28,* 975–996.

Watson, R. T., De Sanctis, G., and Poole, M. S. "Using a GDSS to Facilitate Group Consensus: Some Intended and Unintended Consequences." *MIS Quarterly,* 1988, *12,* 463–480.

Weber, M. "The Sociology of Charismatic Authority." In H. H. Mills and C. W. Mills (eds.), *From Max Weber: Essays in Sociology.* New York: Oxford University Press, 1924/1946.

Weisband, S. P., Schneider, S. K., and Connolly, T. "Computer-Mediated Communication and Social Information: Status Salience and Status Differences." *Academy of Management Journal,* 1995, *38,* 1124–1151.

Yoo, Y., and Wheeler, B. C. "The Impact of Group Support Systems on Leadership Behavior." *Proceedings of Inaugural Conference of Association for Information Systems,* 1995, 264–266.

Yukl, G. A. *Leadership in Organizations.* (2nd ed.) Upper Saddle River, N.J.: Prentice Hall, 1989.

Yukl, G. A. *Leadership in Organizations.* (4th ed.) Upper Saddle River, N.J.: Prentice Hall, 1998.

Zey, M. G. "A Mentor for All Reasons." *Personnel Journal,* 1988, *67,* 46–51.

PART FIVE

NONPROFIT LEADERSHIP TOOLS AND TECHNIQUES

A leader has to engage people in facing the challenge, adjusting their values, changing perspectives, and developing new habits of behavior.
RONALD A. HEIFETZ, *LEADERSHIP WITHOUT EASY ANSWERS* (P. 276)

The leader's role as a visionary, as a strategist, as a change agent, as one who uses tools to achieve greater effectiveness, and as one who is committed to developing leadership within his or her organization is the subject of the chapters in Part Five.

The exploration and testing of different models of leadership and leadership development and their application are primary elements of these chapters—the authors provide tools designed to help leaders in nonprofit organizations craft visions, inspire action, and empower others to achieve their organizational mission and goals.

CHAPTER FOURTEEN

LEADERSHIP OF THE NONPROFIT STRATEGY DEVELOPMENT PROCESS

Thomas J. Reynolds

A fundraising leader is different from other corporate leaders in that he or she must be competent enough to interact directly with and manage a great many functional areas of the organization, ranging from communications (public relations and advertising) to market research and the sales function, on a daily basis. Moreover, beyond the management of all of these day-to-day tactical responsibilities, the executive director of a nonprofit is responsible for CEO duties, primarily providing strategic direction. Clearly, leadership of a nonprofit calls for a true Renaissance person.

Given the limited number of hours in the day, month, and year, the immediate concerns of these tactical responsibilities must often take precedence over the time necessary to thoroughly develop strategy. And with the additional constraint of the limited time available for board member participation, the area of strategy often gets very short shrift. Put simply, strategy defines the job of the corporate CEO and is clearly his or her primary responsibility. For the nonprofit CEO, however, the multiplicity of functional areas in the organization that require regular attention severely limits the time available to devote to strategy. In fact, of all functions provided by the executive director, strategy may be the single most important function and yet the least focused on. Therein lies the problem that this chapter will attempt to address.

Direction

Board members are expected to contribute, in terms of both strategic direction and methods of strategy implementation. The impact they make determines how successful their organization or fundraising campaign will be. But what information do they have to guide their decision making? Do all board members operate on the same basic knowledge? Is this information accurate and relevant to the task at hand? Is the use of this information to derive strategy applied in a consistent and thoughtful manner? That is, does each board member understand the relevance of this key information to the strategy development process?

To get the most from the board and thereby maximize the organization's success, the executive director must organize and manage to this end. Doing so requires a systematic means of summarizing relevant information, in an updatable format, that can be used to ground all strategy development initiatives. This process of data organization also serves to focus the organization's staff on the key issues, as well as to provide them with a methodology to contribute and thereby gain a better understanding of the overall mission.

Imagine for a moment that you are an investment banker preparing a summary on "NewCo, Inc.," for potential investors. What information would be necessary to evaluate the marketplace and provide a basis for assessing the viability of NewCo's business strategy? Using this perspective for providing the necessary background material for investors (remember, all constituents of a nonprofit are investors), a list of questions need to be answered in detail. Without consistent, well-thought-out answers to these questions, it is unlikely that an optimal strategy can be developed. In fact, in my experience, when these questions are asked of both staffers and board members, the answers show little consistency (Norvell and Reynolds, 2003). So if we are successful in developing an investment banker "book" on our organization, we will not only have the ability to ground our strategic decisions in a common base but also have the common thread to bind the staffers (paid and nonpaid) more closely, and more productively, to our long-term goals.

Strategic Process: Development and Implementation

The centerpiece of the strategic process is the development of key questions that must be answered as the basis of our "investment book." Fifteen of these questions, with some insights as to how they should be positioned, will be presented shortly. However, the management process and how to work through it is worth an initial review. Basically, there are four action steps that should be considered.

1. The executive director should finalize the questions and assign them to staff members for answering. A minimum of three staff members should answer each question. So for the fifteen questions we will review, forty-five answers will be sought, balanced across the staff. The executive director should formally answer each question as well, yielding a total of four unique answers per question.

2. The executive director should review all the answers and build a presentation that can be reviewed in a staff work session or retreat. Each question should be reviewed, considering each of the different perspectives, and finalized. The work product from the work session or retreat should be the complete "book."

3. A retreat or several meetings of the board should be conducted to review the "book" with the purpose of seeking input to refine it. A valuable by-product of this discussion is the familiarization of all board members with the central tenets that underlie the strategy development process. As the board members discuss each question and answer, many ideas will emerge. These should be recorded and discussed, and a written summary should be prepared.

4. The executive director should produce a final version of the "book" and recommendations as to the organization's strategy, noting a rationale for each. This document should then be reviewed and discussed by the board, with two desirable outcomes: signoff on the strategy and the development of specific implementation ideas. (The final document, once approved, should be made available to the staff.)

Strategy "Framing" Questions

Listed here are fifteen essential questions for strategy development. Of course, more questions can be added to address unique circumstances. It is important to realize that all answers must be well thought out and carefully phrased. (Answers that do not reflect the necessary depth of thinking will likely result in a strategy that is equally shallow.) For each question, a descriptive narrative of the kinds of information needed will be presented.

Overview

These questions are intended to provoke discussion about the fundamentals underlying the nonprofit enterprise.

1. What business is your organization really in?

In answering this question, typologies like "museum" or "repertory theater" may not be perfectly appropriate. In the case of a museum, thinking solely about acquiring and presenting artifacts limits your vision. For example, if you were the director at the Smithsonian, you might want to focus on the key deliverable activities of education or research and what these activities provide or mean.

Or if you were the director of a repertory theater and thought you were simply in the business of presenting plays to the public, your perspective, and therefore your vision, is lacking. A broader vision, something on the order of a "cultural force," may define strategies that better match the true mission and subsequent "business you are really in." For example, if one thinks the primary mission is to exemplify, drive, and thereby lead cultural change, the focus becomes one of reaching and therefore attracting larger and larger audiences. This introduces the consideration of such things as the commissioning of new plays, some of which may never reach the stage but nevertheless encourage playwrights to continue the creative process. One might also consider providing a teaching conservatory that trains individuals who are interested in theater as a career. An education outreach to schools also comes to mind, one that is intended to stimulate the imagination of youth and introduce them to the acting profession. In terms of the marketing domain, one may move beyond direct fundraising activities to considering a black tie gala that focuses on celebrating the importance of arts in our culture (though the fundraising is, of course, never neglected). Basically, what is suggested here is thinking about the broader definition of the organization's mission and ways to provide leadership in reaching these goals. Leadership requires vision, and developing strategic vision means first thinking more broadly about the definition of the true mission.

2. How are the competitive nonprofits in your region doing, and why is this so?

This question is intended to get at both competition (initially) and relative assessment. The first step is thinking through who the competition is. Achieving agreement on this point is often difficult. Do you define competition by "deliverables," by "share of wallet" for common constituents, or by the potential impact of the nonprofit on the community? Detailing the rationale for the classification used, as required by the "why" part of the question, will be useful in the future to explain one of the fundamental assumptions on which the strategic thinking was based.

Should a college consider itself in a competitive situation with other colleges, thereby defining competition in terms of deliverables? Maybe; maybe not. Consider Chapman University in Orange County, an affluent area of southern California. It would appear that it has defined competition in terms of potential impact on the community and has gone about explaining this "leverageable" strategic perspective to its constituents. When Chapman defines itself in this way, it competes with local nonprofits, making it a highly desirable choice for creating value in the community. The fact is that Chapman is on the verge of successfully completing a three-year $200 million capital campaign. Does Chapman directly compete with Claremont McKenna, the prominent academic institution directly to the north? Probably not, except perhaps in local "share of wallet."

Assessing the success of Chapman, then, should be undertaken relative to its strategic competitive class or set. In this case, it is organizations that affect Orange County, not simply universities in the geographical area. Relative to this classification, one sees the truly great accomplishment that Chapman has attained, rather than the inappropriate conclusion that would be reached by contrasting Chapman to, say, the University of Southern California or the Claremont Colleges. Importantly, the "why?" here is that the success of Chapman, nearly bankrupt not too long ago, was achieved by thinking about its strategic mission, which was defined as contributing to the success of Orange County.

3. What are your organization's current mission, vision, and goals? What role have these played in attracting volunteer and financial support, and is this optimal for the future?

It is to be hoped that the present mission, vision, and goals are straightforward and easy to summarize with little disagreement. However, in the case of the seat-of-the-pants management style, the debate that ensues should point the interested parties toward the importance and value of the strategy development process as well as perhaps the status of the current leadership.

Once the underpinnings of the current strategy have been summarized, the issue of optimality should launch a healthy debate on the future direction of the organization. This should further provide support for the process and the need to clearly answer the remaining questions before a definitive evaluation of strategic options can be undertaken.

Also, it is likely that if some time is spent debating question 1, about what business your organization is in, the contrasting discussion relative to the previously stated mission and goals will give rise to significant questioning. It is recommended that these criticisms be recognized briefly, but the primary focus of the exercise should be to answer all the questions before new strategy development becomes the issue at hand. Participants in the process should be reminded that these questions provide the foundation for strategy development, and not until all are answered can one formally begin to generate options for consideration and evaluation.

Competitive and Self-Assessment

These questions are intended to focus on the metrics involved in assessing performance as well as the leader's position on the key performance measures.

4. Who is your primary competition, and how are you doing (compared to your competitors) on the key performance measures you monitor? Why?

Narrowing the competition to a "primary" grouping is the initial step. Defining the performance measures is step 2. For example, such measures as annual budget, relative annual budget growth, total number of donors, and annual growth in donors exemplify the types of summary statistics that could be used. A chart representing a summary matrix of primary competition (rows) by key performance measures (columns) should be constructed. (Staffers should be encouraged to determine new metrics that they think more directly reflect the performance of the competition.)

As alternative strategic options are weighed, it is sometimes advisable to reconstruct this summary matrix as a method for focusing on the strength of the newly defined competitive set. Once a final strategic direction has been determined, the final summary matrix should be revisited, reflecting the relevant competitive set.

5. What specifically do you do well, and what do you wish you could do better?

Answering this question ordinarily requires the main portion of a day's meeting activity. Consider the following diagrammatic scenario. Construct a two-dimensional graph, labeling one axis "What you do" and the other axis "How well you do it." On the "What you do" axis, label one extreme "Right things" and the other extreme "Wrong things." On the "How well you do it" axis, label the extremes "Well" and "Poorly."

What this gives you is essentially a game board on which you can graphically position the organization as a whole, as well as all major activities of the organization, including donor acquisition, upgrading, and major gifts. Each participant in this process should be provided with a list of all major activities to be rated and then asked to place them on their worksheets. The moderator, who summarizes each person's response, should then prepare a summary sheet for each activity and engage the group in a discussion focusing on each topic individually. This one exercise, using this type of graphic management tool, given enough time and involvement by the leadership group, should generate virtually all the positions, issues, and related ideas for the development of a strategic plan.

Figure 14.1 shows such a matrix mapping "donor solicitation" for participants A, B, C, and D. We see that person A thinks everything is going pretty well, both in terms of what we are doing and how well we are doing it. This could be summarized as good strategy and good execution. Persons B and D think we are doing the right things, but our execution is lacking—good strategy and mediocre execution—

FIGURE 14.1. DONOR SOLICITATION MATRIX.

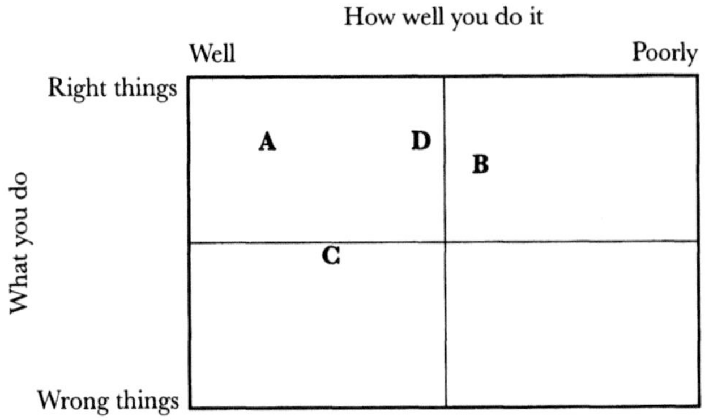

How well you do it

| | Well | | Poorly |

Right things

A   D
                    B

What you do

C

Wrong things

meaning they think something additional is needed. And person C is not so sure that what we are doing is right, but we are doing it OK. This orientation represents position of unsure or questionable strategy but good execution.

As you can imagine, working through each key activity and discussing the pros and cons of both strategy and execution permit pointed and productive discussions to take place. This management tool, when executed correctly, has the possibility of getting to the heart of all key organizational initiatives. An important ingredient of success involves asking each participant to explain, with specifics, the reasons behind their positioning on both axes. Once put on the table, these underlying reasons can be discussed, weighing the pro and con comments about each. After some discussion and debate, a group consensus will likely emerge. Once all key areas have been reviewed and discussed in detail, a final revisiting of each area will often yield group consensus. (A question worth asking at the conclusion of discussing each activity is, "Are there any organizations you can cite as examples of 'doing it right'?") If consensus cannot be reached, the result is a list of key strategic issues to be more formally debated, researched, and resolved prior to the development of the strategic plan.

Finances

These questions ask for a summary of your financial status or perspective, past, present, and future.

6. What is your current financial position, and how did you get there?

Current financial statements should be constructed that summarize the organization's cash flow, reserves, endowment, and tangible assets. Also, a chronological history should be organized, including budgets and reflecting income growth, key events, such as capital campaigns and extraordinary gifts, and so forth.

7. Is demand for your services likely to increase or decrease? If it is likely to increase, how will you finance your growth?

In answering this question, it may be helpful to break down your answer into the following categories: constituent growth or decline (existing services to existing markets), market initiatives (existing services to new markets—for example, new geographical or demographic segments), and diversification (new services to new markets). In this case, "new" means new to your organization, not necessarily new to the world.

Marketing and Communication

These questions serve as the foundation of strategy development as well as the bridge to implementing decisions. They ask for the identification of the target market and the appropriateness of the current communication strategies for each, as well as the underlying bases for future communication strategy development.

8. Who are your key constituents, in terms of both service and support?

In answering this question, it is important to distinguish between the service and support groups. For example, a hospital may list as service constituents such groups as patients, physicians, and nursing and other staff (including volunteers). As support groups, the hospital may list vendors, media, and other sources of support (such as doctors' spouses).

9. What do you want each constituency to do; that is, what key behaviors would you like to influence?

This question is intended to get at the behaviors that drive success and, if possible, a way to measure them. Continuing the hospital service example, focusing on satisfaction with medical treatment delivered, skill competence and growth, and efficiency, respectively, illustrate the types of items that can be included. Metrics for these may range from attitudinal scales to types of advances with respect to the medical facility and practices to length-of-stay statistics. Specifically for the patient constituency, metrics that involve traditional consumer measurements such as awareness, trial, and repeat should be developed.

In terms of support organizations, again using the hospital example, the level of involvement and contribution to the overall mission of the organization should be summarized, along with financial and subjective evaluations.

10. What positioning advantages do you have, how did you get them, and are they leverageable—and if so, how?

The initial goals of this question are to determine both the power of the organization's image and the loyalty that has been achieved among key constituent groups. Secondarily, the question asks for the reasons or causes that have resulted in the positioning advantage you enjoy. And third, the leverageability issue refers to an estimate of the organization's ability to use these perceptual assets in gaining momentum by promoting them.

To illustrate, consider the situation of a fifty-year-old, state-run public broadcasting organization (both radio and television) that was headquartered in a century-old school building. The facilities were so limited that one of the broadcast studios was in a closet. Clearly, new facilities were needed, but the state was not willing to fund this effort. When probed about "positioning advantages," the board summarily recognized three: a very significant viewership, a large membership roster that provided modest operating support, and a significant amount of high-quality programming, at least on par with the networks.

So even without a history of individual gift support, the key defining traits were more than sufficient to demonstrate the clear case for the importance of the product or service as determined by the need manifested in the marketplace. The result is that the public broadcasting authority presented its case to corporate and philanthropic leaders, who agreed to fund a new $9.5 million headquarters building.

11. What is your current communication strategy, and how effective is it with regard to your key constituencies?

What is the strategic intent of your current communication strategy; that is, what do you want people to think about you (your current intention), and why is that important or personally relevant to them? What are the elements of the marketing mix that are accomplishing your strategy? Provide some estimate of how well each is working.

Human Capital

These questions focus on both the positives and the negatives of staffing issues.

12. How are you organized, and who provides significant leadership in the organization?

Answering the organizational aspects can be accomplished by providing a diagrammatic chart. In addition, describe how staff and volunteers participate in major activities of the organization. Indicate the major activities for which each of the staff is responsible. With regard to the leadership component, a summary of positives of key staff, including contributions and initiatives, should be developed.

13. What personnel resources and constraints do you have?

This question should be answered by summarizing your current staffing levels by functional area, providing an overall evaluation of your key people and also of gaps that show where you need help. Of course, much of the "where you need help" issue depends on future strategic initiatives determined as a result of this process. However, general areas of strength and weakness should be addressed here, for the purpose of acquainting the board with the true organizational situation.

Decisions

These questions finalize the framing of strategy, namely, the prioritizing of the key issues to be addressed as well as the status of the necessary information required.

14. What is your current information infrastructure, and how well does it work?

Answering this question need not focus on the age of the platform used or the timeliness of the reports. Rather, this question should be used to provide a brief description of your overall information needs, capabilities, and gaps. Specific recommendations as to potential solutions related to the gaps, with costs, should be included.

15. What key decisions have to be made in the next twelve months? Twenty-four months? Prioritize these decisions.

The reality is that most nonprofit organizations focus on one issue: launching and managing a capital campaign. Many decisions have to be made prior to this effort.

Organized by time frame, a list of the prioritized decisions should be drawn up, indicating who needs to make them and what information is needed prior to making the decision. Relevant information regarding each decision, such as staffing constraints, legal constraints, or a competitor's preemptive position, should be included.

Obviously, a great many of the decisions are affected by the strategic direction output from this very exercise. However, connecting or linking the general nature of the decisions with the strategic output is enough. The primary emphasis here is on knowing the steps in the implementation process. When the preliminary outline is completed, it is often advisable to undertake a reality check, perhaps by employing an outside firm to conduct a feasibility study in order to reveal false assumptions and oversights. This is a wise investment. Once the realities and timing of implementation are factored in as the extension of a well-grounded and well-specified strategy, the basis for generating and sustaining enthusiasm in the organization should be in place.

The end product of the "briefing book" is only as good as the process of involving all members of the board of directors and key members of management in its construction. Once this background is complete, strategy development becomes an ongoing methodology rather than an intermittent project of coming up with hit-or-miss ideas for what can or should be done.

Strategic Direction

The creation of a nonprofit at a given point in time is driven by a specific need, which is then tackled in a specific way. But as time passes, things change. Paramount among these changes is the dynamic of the marketplace. Moreover, new volunteers and staff bring the leavening of different attitudes and practices to the process. As a result, the practices can end up driving the mission. In other words, tactics come to frame and implicitly define the strategy. Many nonprofits, unfortunately, end up following this model due to the combination of a lack of well-articulated strategy and the inability of the board to have enough of the required information presented to it in a consistent, cogent manner, so that the board members can actively participate in the strategy development and assessment process.

Peter Drucker has long emphasized the centrality of strategy to organizational success. One could also say that one key definition of leadership involves providing the expertise, process, and energizing momentum that leads to strategy development. The intended contribution of this chapter is in providing the process template that can be merged with the know-how and motivational force of the executive director. In my experience, strategy does drive success, and the best way to develop strategy is by providing those involved with a consistent set of questions and answers that frame their understanding of the situational variables that define the marketplace environment.

Conclusion

All nonprofits need to develop an appreciation of the power of strategy, learn how to develop their own unique strategic direction, and institutionalize a way to periodically reassess it. Strategy is the common denominator that weds vision to plans. Leadership is about vision, and communicating vision has to be in the language of strategy.

Reference

Norvell, J., and Reynolds, T. J. *The Art and Science of Philanthropic Fund Raising.* Denver, Colo.: Quantum Press, 2003.

CHAPTER FIFTEEN

A LEADERSHIP MODEL
FOR NONPROFIT PROJECTS

Victor Sohmen

Where there is no vision, the people perish.

PROVERBS 29:18

Although people around the world are becoming ever more interdependent, we continue to live in a world of diversity and of unique individualism. Nationalism and individuality continue to dominate the geopolitical landscape. Globalization has challenged leaders to be more creative, collaborative, and tenacious than ever before. Further, businesses and organizations are in a state of flux and have to constantly attune themselves to multiple environmental forces to survive, compete, and grow. This dynamic environment calls for a creative approach to nonprofit leadership, one that identifies, integrates, and synergizes diverse internal and external factors.

Increasingly, in our resource-constrained world, nonprofit enterprises (NPEs) are blessed with volunteers and modestly paid employees, many of them temporary. In such a milieu, the preferred method of operating appears to be that of *organizing by projects,* that is, spawning nonprofit projects with specific task and production mandates under strict constraints of time, cost, and performance. Launching such projects has become a response to both strategic and operational problems in both businesses and NPEs because of the inherent flexibility of project organizations. In today's environment, success is increasingly a function of how effectively the work groups in an organization achieve common goals. This chapter looks at strategic visioning, mentoring, and organizational transformation by capitalizing on the synergy created when specific leadership traits and approaches are combined in nonprofit projects.

To accomplish the complex goals of such a project effectively, an astutely configured nonprofit project leadership structure is imperative. A project leader is most of all a strategist: someone who thinks across and around the complex terrain of a project with the broadest possible vision and then successfully persuades people to follow. The leader must see the overall picture and should seek the best interests of the parent organization. Further, valuable knowledge acquired in a nonprofit project needs to be retained and reused in subsequent projects by the parent NPE. The combination of complexity, flexibility, and volunteerism points to three distinct necessities: in terms of structure, the nonprofit project organization demands a network configuration for fluid communication throughout the project, with the project manager at the center. As for strategy, a sustained vision toward accomplishing the NPE's strategic objectives is called for. Further, creative capture, absorption, and reuse of project-generated knowledge for the parent NPE is also of strategic consequence.

Though there is no dearth of leadership models, ranging from the one-dimensional (for example, visionary or charismatic) to the multidimensional (such as, for example, transformational or connective), there has been little evidence in the literature of the development of a nonprofit leadership model for projects launched by NPEs. The focus of this chapter is the development of a nonprofit project leadership (NPL) model that helps ordinary people of diverse backgrounds do extraordinary things under the project constraints of time, cost, and quality. The project manager would essentially be a change agent practicing operational democracy as a savvy coordinator, skilled negotiator, and cross-functional communicator. This leader would have a spirit of servanthood, reflecting behavioral integrity and empathy with followers and project stakeholders. This could be accomplished by synthesizing three modern, powerful, and overlapping leadership models: transformational, visionary, and servant. The purpose of such a model is to promote strategic visioning, organizational transformation, and morale building in the NPE's nonprofit projects. A strategic, visionary perspective is taken because the leader must think beyond the project at hand and view the broader, strategic interests of the parent NPE.

The first model considered is transformational leadership (TL). Transformational leaders cast themselves into a dynamic and uplifting relationship with followers. This results in transforming followers in a holistic way by raising their levels of motivation and morality. Studies have found significant and positive relationships between TL and the extent of effort followers are willing to exert, satisfaction with the leader, ratings of job performance, and perceived effectiveness (Avolio, 1999; Bass, 1990, 1998). In essence, transformational leadership elevates followers to becoming wholesome leaders themselves, and the leaders in turn become moral agents (Burns, 1978). TL holds great promise for advancing projects, NPEs, and society because it can cause fundamental change, answer deeper social issues, and facilitate paradigm shifts. In addition, projects are intensely goal-oriented and hence are ideal tools to vigorously accomplish the strategic objectives of the NPE.

Figure 15.1 depicts the typical project as a flat, networked structure that promotes focused interdisciplinary interactions to accomplish tasks creatively, systematically, and speedily. This portends a shift from permanent structures to more project-oriented and temporary ones. Thus there are clusters of focal interest at different levels and locales of the NPE, depending on how resources are allocated to support these projects. As leaders, project managers plan, coordinate, and control these projects, economizing on the parent NPE's limited resources toward timely and successful project outcomes.

The postmodern epoch encourages smaller, skilled work groups and rapid technological innovations (Huzzard, 2000). This is evident in modern projects. Figure 15.2 shows an NPE that is projectized through launching multiple projects. The boundary of the NPE is depicted as a broken line in the figure because the hierarchically structured parent can be expected to become more flexible and less pyramidal. Rigid and vertical functional boundaries are thus broken down. Consequently, synergies and economies of scale can be expected, concurrent with projectization and the dissolution of functional boundaries.

NPEs and Nonprofit Projects

The nonprofit enterprise is a complex organizational form operating across diverse services, products, and markets. The NPE typically has branches operating in different locations to promote logistical, commercial, and scale economies. The overall structure can be an integrated network model (Bartlett and Ghoshal, 1993). Consequently, the subsidiaries of the NPE develop strategic links with regional entities and may well spawn nonprofit projects with a multicultural mix. For instance, a Canadian NPE operating in Sweden may have projects with personnel of Scandinavian and North American nationalities. This multicultural mix in nonprofit projects can also present challenges for the leadership that could benefit from the nonprofit leadership model developed in this chapter.

Nonprofit projects, then, are temporary group constellations that work horizontally and break through conventional boundaries of specialization and differentiation (Hedlund, 1994). Essentially, these temporary entities are organized by NPEs, typically composed of altruistic team members selected for their expertise, idealism, and local knowledge. The parent NPE launches nonprofit projects in order to tap into local resources, take advantage of logistical and scale

FIGURE 15.1. FLAT-NETWORKED NONPROFIT PROJECT.

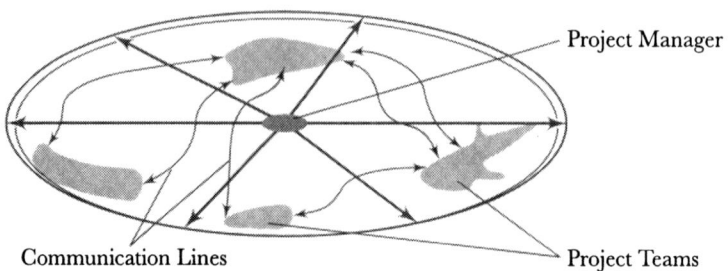

Project Manager

Communication Lines

Project Teams

FIGURE 15.2. PROJECTIZATION OF THE NONPROFIT ENTERPRISE (NPE).

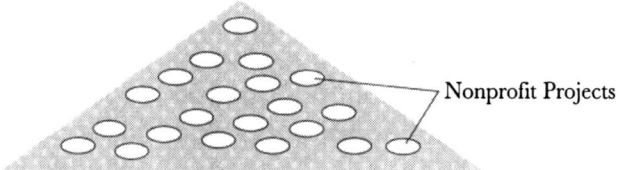

Nonprofit Projects

economies, harness regulatory advantages, effect technology transfers, and marshal operational synergies. Similar to their business counterparts, nonprofit projects are also time-constrained, especially through intensified competition for scarce resources and time-sensitive markets. It is apparent that leading a nonprofit project, populated by volunteers and idealistic participants, would require a highly evolved and multidimensional leadership style.

Transformational Leadership

The idea of transformational leadership was first developed by James McGregor Burns in 1978 and later extended by Bernard Bass, among others. Burns and Bass based their work on political leaders, army officers, and business executives. TL focuses on humanistic rather than authoritative, patriarchal, and conformist styles and is founded on the belief that inner development is the first step to outward leadership action (King, 1994). Transformational leaders are concerned about doing the right things and being role models for followers to emulate in a cascading effect. They engage their followers as whole persons and are not interested merely in management by exception based on transactions and exchanges with followers, as in transactional leadership. The attitudes and behaviors of followers change in response to the leader's conduct. With its emphasis on vision, development of the individual, and empowerment, this has become a popular model of leadership in business organizations. Theories of transformational leadership have focused on identifying a range of leadership behaviors that contributes to effective performance (Bass, 1990; Conger and Kanungo, 1988; Kouzes and Posner, 1995). Although these theories differ slightly in the leadership behaviors they distinguish, they share a number of common themes.

Transformational leaders articulate a vision; use lateral or nontraditional thinking, encourage individual development, give regular feedback, use participative decision making, and promote a cooperative and trusting work environment. The scales developed by Bass (1990, 1998) and by Kouzes and Posner (1995) together provide an assessment of transformational leadership. Empirical research has revealed that TL is positively related to self-confidence, feminine attributes, pragmatism, and nurturance and negatively related to criticalness and aggression (Ross and Offermann, 1997). The crucial test of TL, according to Burns (1978), is social change: followers are trained by example to become leaders, and the leaders themselves become moral agents. Thus followers are in a synergistic, reflexive relationship with their transformational leaders.

Transformational leadership is a superior form of leadership that occurs when leaders "broaden and elevate the interests of their employees, when they generate awareness and acceptance of the purposes and mission of the group, and when they stir their employees to look beyond their own self-interest for the good of the group" (Avolio, 1999; see also Bass, 1990). Transformational leaders have a strong, positive impact on individual, team, and company performance; they develop people to higher levels of individual and group performance; they are seen as more effective and satisfying to work for; and they produce performance beyond expectations all around.

Certain contextual factors, such as the structure of the organization, could facilitate the emergence and impact of transformational leadership. Burns (1978) claimed that it is motivating, uplifting, and ultimately "moral, in that it raises the level of human conduct and ethical aspirations of both the leader and the led." Such a leader aligns overall vision with followers' needs and aspirations, propagates open communication, and generates team motivation. Further, he or she is a prudent risk taker who builds confidence and promotes team building. Transformational leaders generate sufficient energy to launch and sustain a transformation process in the organization. They are thus able to articulate a compelling and credible vision and get everyone to focus on the new critical path.

From the examination of transformational leadership so far, it appears that it telescopes several one-dimensional leadership models, thereby acquiring flexibility and breadth. "Idealized influence," "inspiring motivation," "intellectual stimulation," and "individualized mentoring"—all constructs of transformational leadership—are reflected in earlier, one-dimensional leadership models. Transactional leadership, with its concept of contingent exchanges and management by exception, seems to be at the core of transformational leadership. However, TL also incorporates elements of charismatic leadership and visionary leadership (House and Shamir, 1993), with a strong emphasis on the mentoring of followers (see Figure 15.3). This multiple composition gives TL depth and multidimensionality.

Visionary Leadership

Visionary leadership emphasizes connecting individuals to the leader's vision. In VL, leaders ethically employ the talents of others to achieve strategic goals. The VL model (see Exhibit 15.1) therefore emphasizes working with and through a diverse workforce. Visionary leadership creates conditions for followers to get excited about—passionate impulses inside themselves that need exploration and

FIGURE 15.3. ESSENTIAL COMPONENTS OF TRANSFORMATIONAL LEADERSHIP.

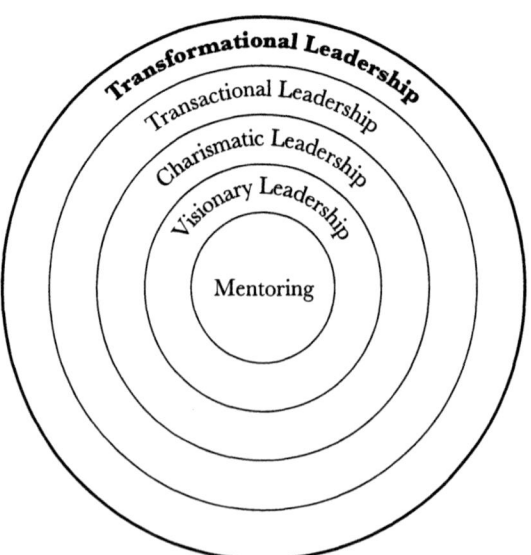

EXHIBIT 15.1. VISIONARY LEADERSHIP MODEL.

1. Sharing the vision
2. Competence in skills
3. Building trust
4. Enthusiastic enterprise
5. Service-oriented actions
6. Integrity in relationships
7. Wisdom in strategy
8. Humility in approach
9. Empowerment of followers
10. Persistent goal orientation

nurture. Not only does visionary leadership arouse passions, but it also provides the context for those passions to come to fruition. In a projectized environment, this means that an intrinsically motivated leader creates long-term, cohesive coalitions with motivated followers that are self-empowering. Such a visionary leader articulates goals to which people will readily commit themselves.

Dynamic leadership requires vision, for it is the vision that supplies meaning and purpose to the work of the nonprofit organization. Forging a shared vision with followers by communication of the vision truly empowers people to act. According to Mintzberg and Westley (1989), visionary leadership is dynamic and involves a three-stage process:

1. *Imaging* the desired future for the organization
2. *Communicating* the shared vision
3. *Empowering* followers to enact the vision

According to Manasse (1986), vision includes the "development, transmission, and implementation of the image of a desirable future. It is the force which molds meaning for the people of an organization." The process of developing a shared vision promotes collegial and collaborative relationships among project participants. Current leadership literature frequently characterizes the leader as the visionary who has a vision of the organization's purpose. In *Leadership Is an Art,* De Pree (1989) asserts that "the first responsibility of a leader is to define reality." Bennis (1990) writes that leaders "manage the dream."

Visionary leaders not only develop a common vision but also nurture the human resources of their organizations. They facilitate the development of individual potential by providing an environment that promotes individual contributions to the common purpose. Collaborative relationships are formed and maintained to sustain the shared vision. Visionary leaders form teams, instill team dynamics and cohesion, develop the skills of individuals, and provide the necessary resources to accomplish the shared vision.

We live in an increasingly interdependent world where, to quote the English poet John Dunne, "no man is an island." It must be remembered that despite differences, human beings everywhere have similar basic traits that make them human. Thus diverse people, having very different needs and coming from a variety of backgrounds, can find a common platform to develop a sense of belonging to the project community. This is a key factor in welding project players to the leader's vision and infusing a sense of common purpose among them.

This interdependence calls on visionary leaders to create and build on the bedrock of a common ethos shared by all. In a nonprofit project, it means a passionate commitment to the project goals by project participants of all stripes. After all, a project is a temporarily organized, goal-oriented coalition. In visionary leadership, therefore, we see an attraction between, and the coexistence of, two opposite forces—interdependence and diversity. This is vital for the successful execution of nonprofit projects with multiskilled players. On the part of the leader, coherent and meaningful action based on consensual decision making is called for: persuasion, negotiation, and mediation must replace coercive, unilateral, and autocratic decision making. Through devolution of authority, visionary leaders bring others into the leadership process. They serve as role models, encouraging participants to voluntarily make collective sacrifices.

VL is also about mentorship of followers to train a crop of future leaders. It looks to the future, allying to worthy and ennobling goals that could outlast the leader. The visionary leader sets an example for the followers as one who values ethics while excelling in negotiation, mediation, and political skills. Finally, the visionary leader builds a reputation for authenticity through consistency of words and deeds.

Servant Leadership

Leadership has historically been associated with seeking and gaining power. Many famous "leaders" have used coercion, fear, and intimidation to achieve their objectives. Servant leadership is refreshingly revolutionary. This concept goes against the grain of common wisdom about organizations and power. Its philosophy is rooted in the example of Jesus in the Bible, for example, when he washed his disciples' feet: "If I then, your Lord and Teacher, have washed your feet, you also ought to wash one another's feet. For I have given you an example, that you should do as I have done to you" (John 13:14–15).

This essential Christological tenet, which puts serving the greater needs of others above one's own as the primary goal of leadership, was introduced as a viable leadership theory by Robert K. Greenleaf. In a groundbreaking 1970 tract titled *The Servant as Leader*, Greenleaf described how caring for and nurturing the members of a group can occur through the practice of SL. The idea of the leader as a servant first came partly out of Greenleaf's extensive experience working for AT&T in the areas of management research, education, and development. He has also described some of the characteristics and activities of servant leaders, providing examples to show that individual efforts, inspired by vision and a servant ethic, can cumulatively make a substantial difference in the quality of society. According to Greenleaf, true leaders are chosen by their followers. True leadership emerges from those whose primary motivation is a deep and selfless desire to help others. He discussed the skills necessary to be a servant leader—the importance of awareness, foresight, and listening. Greenleaf also compared coercive, manipulative, and persuasive power—the last being the best. Since the 1980s, servant leadership has become widely recognized in leadership and management writings and in organizational practice.

SL emphasizes increased service to others, a holistic approach to work, promoting a sense of community, and the sharing of power in decision making. The essence of this credo is ennobling and-long lasting. The best test of SL involves asking the following questions: Do the individuals served realize their aspirations and grow as persons? Do they become more autonomous and more likely to become servants themselves? Moreover, what is the effect on the least privileged in society? Will they benefit? (Greenleaf, 1970). SL crosses national and cultural boundaries. It is being applied by a wide variety of people working with businesses, nonprofit enterprises, hospitals, governments, churches, universities, and foundations. The result is the enrichment of the lives of both leader and followers. This is a postbureaucratic paradigm. The most successful leaders are revolutionaries who step outside routine bureaucratic structures and develop solutions that are new, fresh, and innovative (Gabris, Maclin, and Ihrke, 1998). Nonprofit enterprises are accountable to a host of governmental and private stakeholders for the deployment of their limited, publicly committed resources. It is therefore a poignant necessity to adopt a multidimensional, flexible, yet robust model of nonprofit project leadership.

The triangulation of transformational, visionary, and servant leadership styles is pragmatic, for several reasons. The flat organizational structure of projects in general calls for an egalitarian, participative approach to leadership, as underscored in these three models. In addition, addressing the challenge of obtaining diversity in a typical nonprofit project means that value systems that are commonly accepted and admired by people around the world are to be exhibited by the leader. As the three models are adaptable to constantly changing environments while focusing on superior performance, their amalgamation would contribute significantly to the proposed model. It may also be noted that the purpose of launching nonprofit projects is to take advantage of extraordinary skills across traditional boundaries for value-added, competitive output. As the TL, VL, and SL models are perhaps individually insufficient to meet the comprehensive challenges of highly complex nonprofit projects, they are viewed synoptically. However, all three models expect leaders to keep in view the long-term, strategic perspective, which has crucial implications for nonprofit project leadership.

The NPE is best served when the leaders of its nonprofit projects serve as strategists attuned to the visionary objectives of the parent organization. The military meaning of the word *strategy* can be traced back to the word's Greek ancestor *strategema*, which is itself based on *strategein,* meaning "to act as a general." *Strategein* in turn comes from *strategos* ("general"), which derives from *stratos* ("army") and *agein* ("to lead"). Thus there is a strong correspondence between strategy and leadership. Of all strategic priorities of an organization, leadership style is the most crucial. Strategic time scales are being dramatically compressed today from the standard model of five to seven years, with business conditions changing every eighteen to thirty-six months (King, 1994). In triangulating the three models of leadership to construct an NPL model, we would be wise to focus on the personal values of the leader as the core issue and motivating force.

Values underlie thoughts that stimulate human behavior and set prescriptive and enduring standards that have cognitive, affective, and behavioral components (Rokeach, 1973). They form the core of our personality, influencing the choices we make, the people we trust, the appeals we respond to, and the way we invest our time and energy (Posner and Schmidt, 1992). Transformational leaders rate themselves high on purpose in life, personal efficacy, interpersonal control, and social self-confidence; followers rate these leaders high on interpersonal control (Sosik and Megerian, 1999). Values serve as blueprints or foundations for making decisions, solving problems, and resolving conflicts (Kouzes and Posner, 1995). The personal values of both leaders and followers are influenced by national culture, social institutions, and family (Finkelstein and Hambrick, 1996; Hofstede, 1980). This has important implications for NPL, which must negotiate a diversity of facets.

There are two dominant value cultures: one has a short-term perspective motivated by material and monetary gain; the other is long-term, being spiritually and morally driven (Lloyd, 1998; Oster, 1991). The leaders and followers of nonprofit enterprises are in the latter value culture. This is because they are driven by altruistic aims in serving the NPE. The three leadership styles discussed in this chapter—transformational, visionary, and servant leadership—emphasize the leader's moral and ethical character. The focus is strategic rather than short-term and expediency-driven. Further, in the flat and networked organizational structure of nonprofit projects, position power is practically invalid. The leader has to *earn* the respect, loyalty, and admiration of the followers by being a role model who genuinely cares for them.

Nonprofit projects involve a large number of diverse people interacting simultaneously, with consequently increased complexity. Therefore, trust, loyalty, and credibility have exceptional value in nonprofit projects. Obviously, values that are universally accepted, respected, and emulated have to be championed by the nonprofit project leader. The most critical values of good leaders are honesty and integrity, and these values serve as the essence of high-impact leadership. Indeed, these are common to the TL, VL, and SL styles. All three promote trust, empowerment, and respect. Trust has to be won through a consistent display of behavioral integrity, honesty, and commitment. Empowerment involves entrusting rank-and-file participants with authority and responsibility to enable them to realize and extend their potential. It means that the project leader must be secure enough to delegate power throughout the networked and flat project structure. In nonprofit project environments, empowerment is a practical necessity. Respect involves honoring others and believing in them to help them be the best they can be. It also means humility on the part of the leader to acknowledge mistakes and be willing to learn from others. This is prudent in the complex and fast-paced environment of a nonprofit project, where the leader cannot have all the answers.

Transformational leaders are likely to be guided by universal values such as the human rights to security, equality, and harmony, respect for the individual, and personal development (Burns, 1978). They value collective welfare more than their personal welfare. According to a recent study using the Rokeach Scale, they give importance to such ideals as "a world at peace" and "freedom" (Krishnan, 2001). This suggests that rather than go by defined national boundaries, transformational leaders allow themselves to be guided by broader, change-oriented values such as fairness and enriching experiences. This is also evident in visionary and servant leadership styles. These enriching values are imperative to leadership in nonprofit projects. The leaders lift project performance to levels beyond anticipated targets through increased motivation. In the resource-constrained project environment, such lofty inspiration of followers is a necessity to synergize performance. Exhibit 15.2 summarizes the key distinctions and commonalities of the TL, VL, and SL models.

A Model of Nonprofit Project Leadership

The rapid changes in the global environment have also affected the leadership process. Leadership today must be visionary, developmental, and service-oriented. It should also be ethical, stimulating, facilitative, and clear in establishing expectations (Avolio, 1999). Undoubtedly, the requirements are multidimensional and even daunting, commensurate with the complexity of our world today.

The proposed model of nonprofit project leadership consists of ten factors (see Exhibit 15.3). This model is tentative, given that its psychometric properties

EXHIBIT 15.2. COMPARISON OF THE TRANSFORMATIONAL, CONNECTIVE, AND SERVANT LEADERSHIP MODELS.

Leadership Model	Distinctive Features	Common Features
Transformational	Idealized influence Inspiring vision Intellectual stimulation Individualized development	Visionary outlook Charisma Nonhierarchical Learning-focused Mentorship of followers
Visionary	Inspiring vision Competence building Trust building Integrity in relationships	Empowering of people Fostering new leaders Fairness and democracy Long-term, strategic view Focus on obtaining superior results
Servant	Grassroots democracy Leader as servant first Spirituality- and ethics-based Balance of power and responsibility	

have not been empirically tested. It does, however, capture the essence of the TL, VL, and SL models, geared toward a nonprofit project. In essence, it is strategic and value-oriented. The model has the built-in flexibility to be change-oriented for nonroutine situations, as well as communication-driven, and cross-cultural in philosophy. A fundamental requirement of leaders in all settings is the capacity to establish trust. The leader leads by example and shows competence in tactical tasks to promote confidence in the overall strategy. Figure 15.4 depicts the triangulation of the three leadership models in order to forge a NPL model.

The NPL model captures the essence of successful nonprofit leadership in the twenty-first century. Leading idealistic people with altruistic motives calls for vision, empathy, and enthusiasm. These features are captured and nurtured in the NPL model.

Conclusion

This chapter brings to the surface interesting dimensions of nonprofit leadership at the intersection of vision, altruism, and nonprofit enterprise. Its purpose is to broaden leaders' worldviews and to enable them to become ethically motivated change agents in an increasingly projectified society. There is a great ne-

EXHIBIT 15.3. TEN ESSENTIAL FACTORS
OF THE NONPROFIT PROJECT LEADERSHIP MODEL.

The nonprofit project leadership model can be described by the following essential factors, derived largely from the three models (TL, VL, SL) triangulated:

1. The leader is at the center of a flat, networked, and complex project organization.
2. The style of the leader is visionary, charismatic, service-oriented, and nurturing.
3. The leader models deep respect for, and appreciation of, people of all cultures and skills.
4. Being competent and knowledgeable, the leader stimulates others and is a constant learner.
5. The leader plays a pivotal role in operationalizing the nonprofit parent's strategy.
6. The leader is a skilled communicator, negotiator, and conflict manager.
7. The leader mentors followers and encourages them to interact creatively with each other.
8. The leader initiates and nurtures profound connectivity with followers and stakeholders.
9. The leader inspires trust and respect among followers by exhibiting behavioral integrity.
10. The leader selflessly converts followers into leaders, keeping the long term in view.

cessity today to enhance skills in leading nonprofit projects. It has been postulated that a multidimensional leadership model is needed to match the complexity of NPL. The model also serves to advance studies in the area.

Leaders with the broadest and most flexible leadership repertoire are the ones most likely to meet the complex challenges of our turbulent times. As projects have become widespread phenomena around the globe, the need for a nonprofit project leadership model is critical for the NPEs that spawn these projects. No single style of leadership in isolation may be appropriate or even effective, as cultural backgrounds of transient participants vary widely. In this chapter, three styles of leadership, each with elements universally acknowledged to be laudable leadership traits, have been triangulated. The result is a plausible abstraction of the essentials of leadership in nonprofit projects, using a ten-factor framework.

In this context, transformational leadership is seen as an extension of transactional leadership, focusing on the transformation of followers. Visionary leadership emphasizes the energizing of a common vision among all participants. Servant leadership helps the leader earn the respect and loyalty of followers through humility and self-sacrifice. It is not difficult to see the impact of the three leadership styles in combination, as they are not mutually exclusive. The NPL

FIGURE 15.4. NONPROFIT PROJECT LEADERSHIP MODEL.

model is gilded with encouragement for leaders to be culturally sensitive, fair-minded, and competent, yet willing to learn from followers. The result is the multidimensional ten-factor model that can be applied to leadership of nonprofit projects. This model remains to be empirically tested.

The core values of nonprofit project leaders are the motive forces that drive their mission and enable them to be laudable role models. These include honesty, transparency, and integrity. As the NPE is idealized by the public, the behavioral integrity of the leader inspires trust and respect. In turn, the respect and equality shown to all as the cornerstone of the leader's interpersonal attitude enables followers to grow without fear and realize their legitimate aspirations. The followers are thus empowered to develop and to be trained as excellent leaders in their own right. Ultimately, the best leader is one who takes a strategic view attuned to organizational goals, selflessly converts followers into future leaders, and leaves a lasting imprint on the minds and hearts of peers and followers alike.

References

Avolio, B. J. *Full Leadership Development: Building the Vital Forces in Organizations.* Thousand Oaks, Calif.: Sage, 1999.

Bartlett, C. A., and Ghoshal, S. "Beyond the M-Form: Towards a Managerial Theory of the Firm." *Strategic Management Journal,* 1993, *14,* 23–46.

Bass, B. M. "From Transactional to Transformational Leadership: Learning to Share the Vision." *Organizational Dynamics,* 1990, *18*(3), 19–36.

Bass, B. M. *Transformational Leadership: Military and Educational Impact.* Mahwah, N.J.: Erlbaum, 1998.

Bennis, W. "Managing the Dream: Leadership in the Twenty-First Century." *Training: The Magazine of Human Resource Development,* 1990, *27*(5), 44–46.

Burns, J. M. *Leadership.* New York: Harper & Row, 1978.

Conger, J., and Kanungo, R. N. "Behavioral Dimensions of Charismatic Leadership." In J. Conger and R. N. Kanungo (eds.), *Charismatic Leadership: The Elusive Factor in Organizational Effectiveness.* San Francisco: Jossey-Bass, 1988.

De Pree, M. *Leadership Is an Art.* New York: Doubleday, 1989.

Finkelstein, S., and Hambrick, D. *Strategic Leadership: Top Executives and Their Effects on Organizations.* St. Paul, Minn.: West Publishing Company, 1996.

Gabris, G. T., Maclin, S. A., and Ihrke, D. M. "The Leadership Enigma: Toward a Model of Organizational Optimism." *Journal of Management History,* 1998, *4*(4), 334–349.

Greenleaf, R. K. *The Servant as Leader.* New York: Paulist Press, 1970.

Hedlund, G. "A Model of Knowledge Management and the N-Form Corporation." *Strategic Management Journal,* 1994, *15*, 73–90.

Hofstede, G. *Culture's Consequences.* New York: Sage, 1980.

House, R. J., and Shamir, B. "Toward the Integration of Transformational, Charismatic, and Visionary Theories." In M. M. Chemers and R. Ayman (eds.), *Leadership Theory and Research: Perspectives and Directions.* San Diego: Academic Press, 1993.

Huzzard, T. *Labouring to Learn: Union Renewal in Swedish Manufacturing.* Umeå, Sweden: Boréa Bokförlag.

King, S. "What Is the Latest on Leadership?" *Management Development Review,* 1994, *7*(6), 7–9.

Kouzes, J. M., and Posner, B. Z. *The Leadership Challenge.* San Francisco: Jossey-Bass, 1995.

Krishnan, V. R. "Value Systems of Transformational Leaders." *Leadership & Organization Development Journal,* 2001, *22*(3), 126–131.

Lloyd, B. "Leadership Values and Society: Trends and Priorities for the New Millennium." *Leadership & Organization Development Journal,* 1998, *14*(4/5), 220–224.

Manasse, A. L. "Vision and Leadership: Paying Attention to Intention." *Peabody Journal of Education,* 1986, *63*(1), 150–173.

Mintzberg, H., and Westley, F. "Visionary Leadership and Strategic Management." *Strategic Management Journal,* 1989, *10*, 17–32.

Oster, M. J. *Vision-Driven Leadership.* San Bernardino, Calif.: Here's Life Publishers, 1991.

Posner, B. Z., and Schmidt, W. H. "Values and the American Manager: An Update Updated." *California Management Review,* 1992, Spring, 80–94.

Rokeach, M. *The Nature of Human Values.* San Francisco: Jossey-Bass, 1973.

Ross, S. M., and Offermann, L. R. "Transformational Leaders: Measurement of Personality Attributes and Work Group Performance." *Personality and Social Psychology Bulletin,* 1997, *16*(4), 693–703.

Sosik, J. J., and Megerian, L. E. "Understanding Leader Emotional Intelligence and Performance: The Role of Self-Other Agreement on Transformational Leadership Perceptions." *Group and Organization Management,* 1999, *24*, 367–390.

CHAPTER SIXTEEN

USING PROFESSIONAL EVALUATION TO IMPROVE THE EFFECTIVENESS OF NONPROFIT ORGANIZATIONS

Stewart I. Donaldson

A hallmark of American society today is the pervasiveness of nonprofit organizations explicitly designed to meet the needs and promote the welfare of its citizens. Oster (1995) reported that while nonprofit organizations dominate some sectors (such as human services, religion, and the arts) and share other markets with for-profit corporations (for example, health care and education), most are now experiencing unprecedented levels of competition, requiring their leaders to seek new strategic management methods and tools to enhance both efficiency and effectiveness. The purpose of this chapter is to discuss and illustrate how leaders of nonprofit organizations can benefit from using some of the latest advancements in the profession of evaluation to improve organizational effectiveness.

Professional Evaluation

The profession of evaluation has grown by leaps and bounds in recent years. For example, in 1990, there were perhaps five major evaluation professional associations, whereas today there are more than forty worldwide, linked in an international evaluation association network enabling global cooperation (Mertens, 2003). Donaldson and Scriven (2003a) have described this recent growth as the second major boom in evaluation. While the first bull market in evaluation was driven by the need to evaluate large-scale federal social programs initiated in the 1960s and 1970s, during the Great Society era of American history, the second boom seems to be occurring largely in the nonprofit sector. That is, a wide range of federal agencies, state governments, and philanthropic organizations now encourage and often require a large number of the nonprofit organizations they support to systematically evaluate their efforts.

Contrary to what some leaders of nonprofits may expect or believe, there are many different views about how best to conduct evaluations today. For example, some evaluators still simply employ traditional social science research methods without much concern for or awareness of modern theories of evaluation practice or the latest developments in the profession (in fact, many who represent themselves as evaluators are not members of evaluation professional associations and may have little formal training in evaluation). It is also generally well known that some evaluations and evaluators are affected by economic pressures or the desire of their clients to look good, which can result in highly biased or erroneous evaluations (Scriven, 1991). Furthermore, many nonprofit organizations still rely on relatively untrained staff to conduct in-house data collection and evaluations. Internal evaluation by program staff can be useful under some circumstances but is often limited and sometimes misleading because it is difficult to be objective and to present bad news to those with more power in one's work organization (unless staff are highly trained and experienced).

Even within the range of acceptable professional standards for evaluation, there continues to be lively and sometimes contentious debates about how best to practice evaluation in modern organizations (Donaldson and Scriven, 2003a). Leaders of nonprofits must now select from a smorgasbord of options for hiring professional evaluators to improve their organizations. For example, some of the most popular evaluation approaches today include results-oriented management (Wholey, 2003), empowerment evaluation (Fetterman, 2003), utilization-focused evaluation (Patton, 1997), inclusive evaluation (Mertens, 2003), transdisciplinary evaluation (Scriven, 2003), social experimentation and quasi-experimentation (Shadish, Cook, and Campbell, 2001; Lipsey and Cordray, 2000), fourth-generation evaluation (Lincoln, 2003), realist evaluation (Mark, 2003), and theory-driven evaluation (Crano, 2003; Donaldson, 2003). Because professional evaluation now offers a range of acceptable approaches and perspectives, it is critical that leaders of nonprofit organizations not assume that all potential evaluators of their organizations are alike or that they offer similar services that may vary only in cost. In fact, I would argue that evaluator or evaluation team selection has become one of the most important factors in determining whether or not a nonprofit organization will become more effective by using evaluation.

Fortunately, there are now widely accepted sets of standards for good evaluation—guiding principles and ethical standards that evaluators should be expected to follow (see Shadish, Newman, Scheirer, and Wye, 1995, Joint Committee on Standards for Educational Evaluation, 1994; Patton, 2001). For example, evaluators of non-profit organizations should be expected to follow the following guiding principles:

- *Systematic inquiry:* Evaluators conduct systematic, data-based inquiries about whatever is being evaluated.
- *Competence:* Evaluators provide competent performance to stakeholders.
- *Honesty and Integrity:* Evaluators ensure the honesty and integrity of the entire evaluation process.
- *Respect for people:* Evaluators respect the security, dignity, and self-worth of the respondents, program participants, clients, and other stakeholders with whom they interact.
- *Responsibility for general and public welfare:* Evaluators articulate and take into account the diversity of interests and values that may be related to the general and public welfare.

Consistent with these principles is the need for evaluators to fully discuss all aspects of the evaluation process with the leaders and other relevant members of nonprofit organizations (Donaldson, 2001b).

Professional evaluation has the potential to help leaders of nonprofit organizations dramatically improve organizational functioning. For example, professional evaluation can help nonprofit leaders make better decisions about service, policy, and organizational direction; build knowledge and skills and develop a capacity for evaluative thinking; facilitate continuous quality improvement and organizational learning; provide accountability to funders; and justify the organization's value to investors, volunteers, staff, and prospective funders and supporters.

However, beyond the standard discussion of the benefits of evaluation in general should be a detailed discussion of the potential and likely benefits of "this particular evaluation for this particular organization at this time in its history." In addition, potential risks of conducting the evaluation should be fully explored. For example, it is important to consider who could be negatively affected by the evaluation, how much time and resources may be taken away from the services under investigation while the evaluation is being conducted, and the facts that the evaluation process could be uncomfortable or disruptive for some organizational members (see Donaldson, Gooler, and Scriven, 2002), that the evaluation itself could change behavior in unpredictable ways, and that evaluation findings could turn out to be very negative and have repercussions for staff and the organization. A major benefit of this discussion is that the evaluators and nonprofit organizational leaders can develop an evaluation plan designed to minimize the potential risks and maximize the potential benefits of the evaluation. In summary, when evaluators and nonprofit leaders (and relevant organizational members) fully explore the potential benefits and costs of doing a specific evaluation, expectations and plans become more realistic, and the evaluation is much more likely to lead to improvements in organizational effectiveness (see Donaldson, 2001b).

Evaluating Nonprofit Organizations

Nonprofits are a diverse class of organizations sharing tax-exempt status and a nonfinancial bottom line. One rather large subcategory of nonprofit organizations is what some refer to as human service organizations (Hasenfeld, 1983, 1992)—organizations designed to change and improve the lives of human beings (for example, cure a patient, educate a child, prevent an adolescent from using drugs or engaging in risky sexual behavior, or developing the knowledge and skills of working professionals). Whereas some scholars tend to use the descriptors "nonprofit organization" and "human service organization" interchangeably (see, for example, Drucker, 1990), I recognize that some nonprofits are not human service organizations and some human service organizations are not nonprofits. Nevertheless, most of the examples and analyses I have selected to focus on in this chapter are relevant to nonprofit human service organizations. However, I will refer to nonprofit organizations (NPOs) and their leaders more generally, recognizing that some adaptations may be needed for nonprofits that do not provide human services.

Evaluation is a tool that can be used to improve various components or subsystems of NPOs. For example, evaluation can be used to improve an NPO's mission, goals, human resource selection and management, policies, proposals, products, organization-environment relations (including fundraising), client-organization relations, board functioning, and the like. Although all of these components are important in the achievement of organizational effectiveness, they are not sufficient. That is, at the core of most NPOs is a transformation technology that is responsible for changing human beings from a present state or status to a desired state or status. Hasenfeld (1983) provided a typology of these transformation technologies, which include the following:

- *People-processing technologies:* These attempt to transform clients by conferring on them a social label and a public status that evoke desirable reactions from other social units (e.g., gifted child ready for an accelerated education program or cancer patient in need of special treatment).
- *People-sustaining technologies:* These attempt to prevent, maintain, and retard the deterioration of the personal welfare of well-being of clients (for example, nursing home care for the elderly and income maintenance services for the poor).

- *People-changing technologies:* These aim at altering the personal attributes of clients in order to improve their well-being (for example, through education, counseling services, and personal and career development).

As part of their mission, NPOs typically describe their purpose and raison d'être through their transformation technologies ("to prevent drug abuse," "to promote healthy child-rearing practices," "to mentor and educate tomorrow's leaders"). To be recognized as effective, NPOs must be able to demonstrate that the clients they serve are indeed better off after receiving their services. Professional evaluation is the most effective tool for determining if an NPO is effective, as well as for improving the many efforts needed to become and remain effective.

Common Challenges in Achieving Organizational Effectiveness

Evaluators of the effectiveness of NPOs have been haunted by a history of disappointing results, sometimes referred to as a "parade of null effects" (see Donaldson, 2003). That is, many evaluations over the past three decades have shown that NPOs are not as effective as they claim or desire to be. Fortunately, this has driven the profession of evaluation to develop evaluation methods and approaches to help identify and solve challenges encountered in the past. A synthesis of the past three decades of evaluation reveals at least five common problems that evaluators of NPOs must overcome (Donaldson, 2003):

- Inadequate service, transformation technology, or program conceptualization
- Poor service implementation
- Insensitive evaluation
- Poor relations between evaluators and NPO leaders and staff
- Barriers preventing cumulative knowledge and wisdom

The evaluation approach discussed here, theory-driven evaluation, has been developed to help organizations make sure their services are well-designed and based on sound theory and research, implemented with high fidelity, and evaluated in a manner that minimizes the chances of design sensitivity and validity errors, empowers stakeholders to use findings to continuously improve their efforts, and advances cumulative knowledge and wisdom about improving NPOs and the lives of their clients.

Theory-Driven Evaluation

Theory-driven evaluation is a relatively recent theory of evaluation practice that builds on hard-won lessons from the practice of evaluation over the past three decades (Chen, 1990; Chen and Rossi, 1983, 1987; Donaldson, 2001a, 2003). Shadish, Cook, and Leviton (1991) refer to theory-driven evaluation as one of the most advanced forms of evaluation theory—Stage III Evaluation Theory. They describe how it has integrated and synthesized previous approaches to develop a contingency approach to evaluation practice, acknowledging that some evaluation approaches and methods work well under some circumstances but fail under others. This approach to evaluation practice has become quite popular in recent years (Crano, 2003; Donaldson, 2002) and now provides a foundation for some of the most widely used textbooks on evaluation (including Rossi, Freeman, and Lipsey, 1999, and Weiss, 1998).

Although the details of how to conduct a theory-driven program evaluation are beyond the scope of this chapter, these issues have been described in detail elsewhere (see Chen, 1990; Donaldson, 2001a; Donaldson and Gooler, 2002b, 2003; Fitzpatrick, 2002; Rossi, Freeman, and Lipsey, 1999). Simply stated, theory-driven evaluation is a comprehensive approach that involves three general steps:

1. Developing program theory
2. Formulating and prioritizing evaluation questions
3. Answering evaluation questions

In other words, evaluators typically work with leaders and members of nonprofit organizations to develop a common understanding of how an organization intends to improve the functioning of its clients or solve a particular social or human problem. This common understanding helps evaluators and members of the NPO identify and prioritize evaluation questions. Evaluation questions of most interest are then answered using the most rigorous methods possible, given the practical constraints of the evaluation context.

Developing Program Theory

The first task of a systematic theory-driven evaluation is to develop a conceptual framework or program theory specifying how a NPO intends to solve the problem of interest and meet the needs of its target population. In some cases, this may be purely the NPO's service designers' view of the transformation technology or technologies, ideally based on systematic needs assessment. However, often this view is implicit, and the task is to make it explicit and testable.

Fortunately, it is often possible and highly desirable to base the conceptual framework on multiple sources of information such as prior theory and research in the service domain (see Donaldson, Street, Sussman, and Tobler, 2001), implicit theories held by those closest to the operation of the services (program personnel such as health educators or other human service providers), observations of the services in action, and in some cases exploratory research to test critical assumptions about the nature of the transformation technologies. This process seems to work well when evaluators and NPOs' leaders and members approach it as an interactive and nonlinear exercise (Donaldson and Gooler, 2002b; Fitzpatrick, 2002). Once a program theory or competing program theories have been developed, they are used to make informed choices about evaluation questions and methods.

It is important to note that the first step in theory-driven evaluation often reveals that a NPO's programs or services are not ready for implementation and evaluation. Program theory development can be used to aid evaluability assessment procedures (cf. Wholey, 2003), which are used to determine whether a program is ready to be evaluated which involves the use of time consuming and costly procedures. Therefore, developing program theory has the potential to save substantial time and resources by redirecting efforts toward further program development and/or implementation activities, as opposed to moving directly to summative evaluation that would simply expose null effects.

Formulating and Prioritizing Evaluation Questions

Formulating, prioritizing, and answering important evaluation questions are core tasks of theory-driven evaluation. First, well-developed program theories are used to identify a wide range of potential evaluation questions. Relevant stakeholders and evaluators typically generate an exhaustive list of possible questions. The group then attempts to prioritize these questions so that it is clear which questions are of most value. Differences of opinion about the value of each question across the relevant NPO members are noted and factored into final decisions about which questions to answer and which methods to use to answer those questions.

Answering Evaluation Questions

In many respects, theory-driven evaluation is method-neutral and creates a superordinate goal that helps evaluators get past old debates about which evaluation methods are superior (for example, the qualitative-quantitative debate; see Reichardt and Rallis, 1994). That is, from the contingency point of view, the theory-driven approach argues that quantitative, qualitative, or mixed designs are neither superior nor applicable in every evaluation situation (Chen, 1997). Instead, methodological choices are informed by program theory, by specific evaluation questions ranked in order of priority, and by practical constraints (Donaldson, 2003). Therefore, the final step in theory-driven evaluation involves determining what type of evidence is needed to answer questions of interest with an acceptable level of confidence.

The details of this step vary considerably across NPO evaluations. In some cases, the group will accept nothing short of evidence based on a large-scale randomized experiment. In other cases, rich description developed through qualitative methods is preferred over experimental designs. Furthermore, unless data collection resources are plentiful, compromises are made to determine the most convincing design within resource and practical constraints. Unfortunately, guidelines for making these decisions are rather complex and beyond the scope of this chapter. It may be said, however, that many factors typically interact to determine how to collect the evidence needed to answer the key evaluation questions (for example, design feasibility issues, resources, stakeholder preferences, and evaluator expertise and preferences).

As was mentioned previously, theory-driven evaluation has become quite popular in recent years, and there is now a range of examples demonstrating how it pays off in practice (see Birckmayer and Weiss, 2000; Donaldson, 2003). To further illustrate the theory-driven evaluation approach, I will discuss a rather large-scale project that used evaluation to improve the effectiveness of over forty nonprofit organizations funded to promote health through work.

Developing Nonprofits to Promote Health Through Work

The nature of one's work (for example, whether one has a job or one's working conditions on the job) is often a substantial determinant of health status, well-being, and overall quality of life (Donaldson, Gooler, and Weiss, 1997). Based on this premise, the California Wellness Foundation launched the five-year, $20 million statewide Work and Health Initiative to promote the health and well-being of California workers and their families through work. The mission of the Work and Health Initiative was to improve the health of Californians by funding more than forty nonprofit organizations to positively influence health through employment-related approaches (see Donaldson and Gooler, 2002a, 2002b).

Evaluation Approach

The California Wellness Foundation (CWF) was also deeply committed to the science of promoting health and well-being through work (Donaldson, Gooler, and Weiss, 1998). As part of this commitment, systematic evaluation by an external evaluation team was commissioned to guide the strategic development and management of each program in the initiative, as well to inform the direction of the entire initiative. The initiative evaluator served as an integrating, synthesizing force in evaluating goals, objectives, strategies, and outcomes central to the long-term impact of the initiative. Cross-cutting goals and synergies were identified, enhanced, and evaluated in an effort to maximize the overall impact of the initiative (the whole was expected to be greater than the sum of the parts). In addition, the initiative evaluator developed evaluation systems that provided responsive evaluation data for each NPO. Those data were used to continually improve and evaluate NPO effectiveness.

To ensure that the perspectives and problem-solving needs of all with a vested interest in the initiative programs (for example, the CWF, grantees, program administrators, staff, and program recipients), collectively known as stakeholders, were understood and addressed, the evaluation team adopted a participatory theory-driven evaluation approach (see Chen, 1990; Donaldson, 1995, 2001b, 2003). This approach rested on developing program theories for each NPO and using empirical feedback to guide service development. Each program theory was based on the stakeholders' experience with how these types of services seem to work, prior evaluation research findings, and more general theoretical and empirical work related to the phenomena under investigation. Such frameworks provided a guiding model around which evaluation designs were developed to specifically answer key evaluation questions as rigorously as possible, given the practical constraints of the evaluation context. Given the high potential for environmental factors to confound the estimates of program effects, this "conceptual mapping" approach helped identify and examine sources of variance and isolate the effects of the factors that each NPO was attempting to influence. In addition, this approach increased understanding about how services worked and under what circumstances they worked.

Finally, data collection efforts were based on the premise that no single data source was a bias-free or completely accurate representation of reality. Evaluation plans were designed to specifically encourage each grantee to use multiple methodological strategies with different strengths and weaknesses to answer evaluation questions (Chen, 1997; Cook, 1985; Donaldson, 2002; Shadish, 1993). A special effort was made to understand cross-cultural and language concerns so that the methodologies employed were sensitive enough to detect effects when they existed. In addition to evaluating outcomes and impacts, evaluation efforts were both formative (aimed at developing and improving services from an early stage) and process-oriented (geared toward understanding how a program achieves what it does over time). Evaluation efforts also identified cross-cutting goals and synergies within and across NPOs to facilitate success of the overall initiative.

Program Development and Evaluation Process

The evaluation design for each NPO was developed through a collaborative process that included the CWF staff, project coordination teams, leaders of the community-based NPOs, and other community stakeholders. The evaluation team engaged stakeholders in a participatory process that involved constructing models of how their services work and then used those models to guide question formation, data gathering, and evaluation. To achieve this, the evaluation team facilitated numerous meetings and discussions of the program models and theories of change, evaluation design, data collection methods, feedback loops, and evaluation reports. Specific attention was given to identifying and measuring realistic outcomes and indicators that would result from specific service efforts. In addition, each evaluation was tailored to answer questions deemed of most importance by each project team. As such, each initiative program evaluation was designed to include methods and techniques that can be used for understanding lessons learned and providing external feedback to enhance continuous quality improvement and long-term program success.

To support continuous program improvement throughout the life of the initiative, the evaluation team created three primary vehicles for providing continuous service improvement feedback over time: midyear evaluation reports, year-end evaluation reports, and annual 360-degree feedback from grantees (see Mersman and Donaldson, 2000); that is, NPO leaders were given the opportunity each year to evaluate the evaluation team and foundation staff. In addition, these evaluations were supplemented with several interim evaluation reports and frequent telephone and e-mail communications designed to provide timely feedback throughout the year.

Resulting Program Theories

There is often confusion about the nature of program theory (Donaldson, 2001a, 2002; Weiss, 1997). For some evaluators and program stakeholders, the term seems to conjure up images of broad social science theories rather than rather small and specific theories of treatments, services, or interventions (Donaldson, 2002; Lipsey, 1993). The following definitions of program theory capture the essence of how the term is used in this chapter:

> The construction of a plausible and sensible model of how a program is suppose to work (Bickman, 1987).
>
> A set of propositions regarding what goes on in the black box during the transformation of input to output, that is, how a bad situation is transformed into a better one through treatment inputs (Lipsey, 1993).
>
> The process through which program components are presumed to affect outcomes and the conditions under which these processes are believed to operate (Donaldson, 2001a).

It is highly desirable if program theory is rooted in, or at least consistent with, behavioral or social science theory or prior research (see Donaldson, Street, Sussman, and Tobler, 2001). However, often sound theory and research are not available for the problem of concern. Other sources of information can also be used to develop program theory, including implicit theories held by individuals close to the operation of the program, observations of the services being delivered, documentation of service operations, and exploratory research to test critical assumptions about the nature of the services or transformation technologies. (For discussions on how to use these sources, see Donaldson, 2001a, and Rossi, Freeman, and Lipsey, 1999.) The goal is to develop, in collaboration with key NPO members and other relevant stakeholders, a parsimonious program theory (or competing theories to be tested) that captures the main factors that link services with presumed outcomes. This program theory can then be used to generate and prioritize evaluation questions. To illustrate outcomes of this process in practice, I will present parsimonious versions of the program theories used to evaluate the NPOs involved in two of the four areas that made up the Work and Health Initiative.

Winning New Jobs Program Theory

One of the demonstration programs was the Winning New Jobs (WNJ) program. The mission of WNJ was to provide job search training to five thousand unemployed and underemployed Californians over a four-year funding period. The WNJ program is based on a theory-based intervention, JOBS, which was developed and initially tested in a randomized trial in Michigan (Price, Friedland, Choi, and Caplan 1998; Vinokur, van Ryn, Gramlich, and Price, 1991). Using systematic organizational readiness assessments, three NPOs in diverse California communities were selected to implement the WNJ program (Donaldson, Gooler, and Weiss, 1998).

The core program theory that was developed using the process described earlier and was then used to guide the evaluation of WNJ is shown in Figure 16.1. Participants attended a one-week workshop designed to improve job search self-confidence, job search skills, and problem-solving strategies including inoculation against setbacks. These skills and psychological factors are presumed to facilitate reemployment and improve mental health. Furthermore, the WNJ program is hypothesized to have impacts at multiple levels: participant (with respect to increased job search self-efficacy and reemployment), organization (staff skill development, reputation enhancement), community (increased access to job search services), and the policy environment (financial support for continuation of program).

This conceptualization of the WNJ program was used to develop and prioritize evaluation questions and to guide data collection. For example, extensive standardized eligibility, demographic, pretest, posttest, and employment follow-up data were collected at each site. Various types of qualitative implementation and outcome data were also collected. Databases tracking participants in other parts of the country and world were available for comparison purposes. This collection of databases was used for both formative and summative evaluation of the WNJ program.

Computers in Our Future Program Theory

The second demonstration project was called Computers in Our Future (CIOF). The CIOF project funded eleven NPOs to create fourteen CIOF community computing centers (CCCs) in eleven low-income California communities. The fourteen CCCs were designed to demonstrate innovative, creative, and culturally sensitive strategies for using computer technology to meet the economic, educational, and development needs of their local communities. The CIOF program explored and demonstrated ways in which CCCs can prepare youth and young adults aged fourteen through twenty-three to use computers to improve their educational and employment opportunities, thereby improving their own health and well-being and that of their families and communities.

Organizational readiness criteria were used to select eleven NPOs to accomplish these goals. These NPOs were diverse with respect to organizational type, geographical location, and populations served. Collectively, these centers were designed to provide access to more than two hundred computer workstations statewide. With respect to open-access service goals, each site collectively committed to providing unrestricted open access to 27,705 Californians (approximately 6,900 individuals per year, statewide). Similarly, the NPOs committed to providing technology training and work experiences to more than 4,300 youth and young

FIGURE 16.1. WINNING NEW JOBS PROGRAM THEORY.

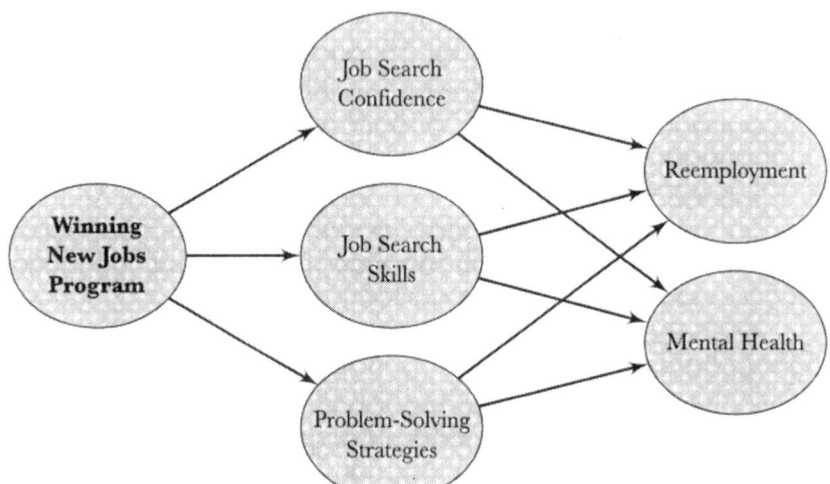

adults over the four-year program period. With extensive input from NPO leaders, the funder, and the CIOF program coordination team, we constructed a guiding program theory of how the CIOF program is presumed to work.

Figure 16.2 shows that participation in the CIOF program is believed to lead to improved attitudes toward computers, technology skills, career development knowledge, job search skills, and basic life skills. These acquired skills and knowledge are presumed to facilitate the pursuit of more education, internship opportunities, and better employment options, which over the long term is expected to improve participants' health status. This program theory has been used to identify a number of evaluation questions and the types of data needed to answer these questions and verify whether these relationships do indeed exist. Extensive standardized demographic, center utilization, pretest, posttest, and follow-up data were collected from each site. Various types of qualitative implementation and outcome data were also collected. Data were used for both formative and summative evaluations of the CIOF program.

Findings and Lessons Learned

The evaluation findings (Donaldson and Gooler, 2002a) and some of the key lessons learned from these evaluations of NPOs (Donaldson and Gooler, forthcoming) have been presented in detail elsewhere. In brief, these evaluations of NPOs illustrated

FIGURE 16.2. COMPUTERS IN OUR FUTURE PROGRAM THEORY.

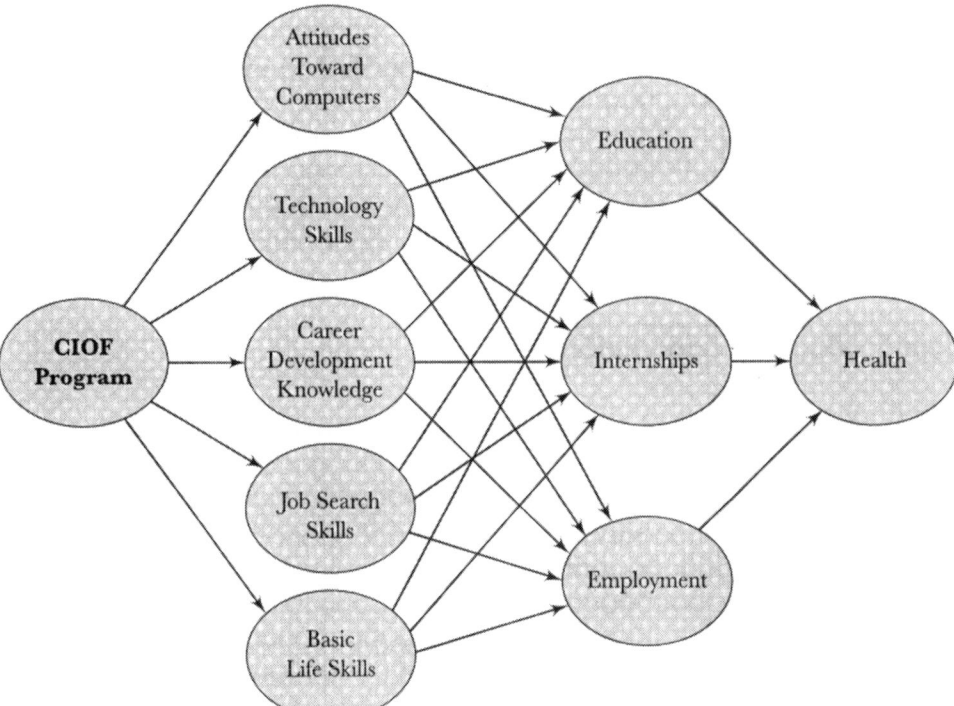

that when evaluators and NPO leaders and members work together to explore and maximize the potential benefits and minimize the potential risks of each evaluation and participate in all phases of a theory-driven evaluation process, professional evaluation became viewed and used as powerful tool for creating strategic advantage and improving NPO effectiveness. Further, these evaluations demonstrated that theory-driven evaluation is feasible to use in NPOs, can be inclusive and empowering to NPO members, provides valid data and critical information to improve strategic decision making, builds organizational knowledge and learning, can be used to improve organizational effectiveness at many levels, and legitimates NPOs to outside supporters and potential funders and supporters.

It is important to note that theory-driven evaluation is just one of several modern professional evaluation approaches that nonprofit leaders should consider using to improve organizational effectiveness (Donaldson and Scriven, 2003b). As described earlier, a serious and forthright discussion with potential evaluators should provide enough information to NPO leaders that they become aware of potential benefits and risks and are able to make an informed decision about which evaluation team and approach to use to meet their particular needs. Again, the examples presented here illustrate how professional evaluation can be used to determine if an NPO is fulfilling its core mission or achieving its desired bottom line (improving the lives of its clients) and how to improve its degree of success. Professional evaluation can also be used to improve the various components of NPO effectiveness, such as human resource performance (performance of leaders, staff, and volunteers), resource procurement, and board performance.

The Evaluation Imperative

Some evaluation scholars have argued strongly in recent years that disciplined, professional evaluation (planned, systematic, funded evaluations adhering to professional guidelines and standards) is the obligation of all leaders (see, for example, Sanders, 2001; Scriven, 2003). Leaders of nonprofit organizations owe this level of professionalism and accountability to their clients, employees, volunteers, and society at large. That is, it is no longer acceptable for NPO leaders to avoid or resist using professional evaluation to improve their services and transformation technologies, to prevent null and harmful effects from adversely affecting their clients, and to account for the resources they receive from the supporters of their mission and organization. Professional evaluation services are becoming more widely available throughout the world (Donaldson and Scriven, 2003b). It is my hope that this chapter inspires or motivates NPO leaders to use this powerful tool to more effectively carry out their noble work of preventing or ameliorating human suffering and promoting human welfare.

References

Bickman, L. "The Functions of Program Theory." *New Directions for Program Evaluation,* 1987, *33,* 5–18.

Birckmayer, J. D., and Weiss, C. H. "Theory-Based Evaluation in Practice. What Do We Learn?" *Evaluation Review,* 2000, *24,* 407–431.

Chen, H. T. *Theory-Driven Evaluations.* Thousand Oaks, Calif.: Sage, 1990.

Chen, H. T. "Applying Mixed Methods Under the Framework of Theory-Driven Evaluations." *New Directions for Evaluation,* 1997, *74,* 61–72.

Chen, H. T., and Rossi, P. H. "Evaluating with Sense: The Theory-Driven Approach." *Evaluation Review,* 1983, *7,* 283–302.

Chen, H. T., and Rossi, P. H. "The Theory-Driven Approach to Validity." *Evaluation and Program Planning*, 1987, *10*, 95–103.

Cook, T. D. "Post-Positivist Critical Multiplism." In R. L. Shotland and M. M. Mark (eds.), *Social Science and Social Policy.* Thousand Oaks, Calif.: Sage, 1985.

Crano, W. D. "Theory-Driven Evaluation and Construct Validity." In S. I. Donaldson and M. Scriven (eds.), *Evaluating Social Programs and Problems: Visions for the New Millennium.* Mahwah, N.J.: Erlbaum, 2003.

Donaldson, S. I. "Worksite Health Promotion: A Theory-Driven, Empirically Based Perspective." In L. R. Murphy, J. J. Hurrel, S. L. Sauter, and G. P. Keita (eds.), *Job Stress Interventions.* Washington, D.C.: American Psychological Association, 1995.

Donaldson, S. I. "Mediator and Moderator Analysis in Program Development." In S. Sussman (ed.), *Handbook of Program Development for Health Behavior Research and Practice.* Thousand Oaks, Calif.: Sage, 2001a.

Donaldson, S. I. "Overcoming Our Negative Reputation: Evaluation Becomes Known as a Helping Profession." *American Journal of Evaluation*, 2001b, *22*, 355–361.

Donaldson, S. I. "Theory-Driven Program Evaluation in the New Millennium." In S. I. Donaldson and M. Scriven (eds.), *Evaluating Social Programs and Problems: Visions for the New Millennium*. Mahwah, N.J.: Erlbaum, 2003.

Donaldson, S. I., and Gooler, L. E. *Summary of the Evaluation of the California Wellness Foundation's Work and Health Initiative.* Claremont, California: Institute for Organizational and Program Evaluation Research, Claremont Graduate University, 2002a.

Donaldson, S. I., and Gooler, L. E. "Theory-Driven Evaluation of the Work and Health Initiative: A Focus on Winning New Jobs." *American Journal of Evaluation*, 2002b, *22*(3), 341–346.

Donaldson, S. I., and Gooler, L. E. "Theory-Driven Evaluation in Action: Lessons from a $20 Million Statewide Work and Health Initiative." Forthcoming.

Donaldson, S. I., Gooler, L. E., and Scriven, M. "Strategies for Managing Evaluation Anxiety: Toward a Psychology of Program Evaluation." *American Journal of Evaluation*, 2002, *23*(3), 261–273.

Donaldson, S. I., Gooler, L. E., and Weiss, R. "Promoting Health and Well-Being Through Work: Science and Practice." In X. B. Arriaga and S. Oskamp (eds.), *Addressing Community Problems: Psychological Research and Intervention.* Thousand Oaks, Calif.: Sage, 1997.

Donaldson, S. I., and Scriven, M. "Preface." In S. I. Donaldson and M. Scriven (eds.), *Evaluating Social Programs and Problems: Visions for the New Millennium.* Mahwah, N.J.: Erlbaum, 2003a.

Donaldson, S. I., and Scriven, M. "Diverse Visions for Evaluation in the New Millennium: Should We Integrate or Embrace Diversity?" In S. I. Donaldson and M. Scriven (eds.), *Evaluating Social Programs and Problems: Visions for the New Millennium.* Mahwah, N.J.: Erlbaum, 2003b.

Donaldson, S. I., Street, G., Sussman, S., and Tobler, N. "Using Meta-Analyses to Improve the Design of Interventions." In S. Sussman (ed.), *Handbook of Program Development for Health Behavior Research and Practice.* Thousand Oaks, Calif.: Sage, 2001.

Drucker, P. F. *Managing the Nonprofit Organization: Practices and Principles.* New York: Harper-Collins, 1990.

Fetterman, D. "Empowerment Evaluation Strikes a Responsive Cord." In S. I. Donaldson and M. Scriven (eds.), *Evaluating Social Programs and Problems: Visions for the New Millennium.* Mahwah, N.J.: Erlbaum, 2003.

Fitzpatrick, J. "Dialogue with Stewart Donaldson." *American Journal of Evaluation*, 2002, *23*(3), 347–365.

Hasenfeld, Y. *Human Service Organizations.* Upper Saddle River, N.J.: Prentice Hall, 1983.

Hasenfeld, Y. "The Nature of Human Service Organizations." In Y. Hasenfeld (ed.), *Human Services as Complex Organizations.* Thousand Oaks, Calif.: Sage, 1992.

Joint Committee on Standards for Educational Evaluation. *The Program Evaluation Standards: How to Assess Evaluations of Educational Programs.* Thousand Oaks, Calif.: Sage, 1994.

Lincoln, Y. S. "Fourth-Generation Evaluation in the New Millennium." In S. I. Donaldson and M. Scriven (eds.), *Evaluating Social Programs and Problems: Visions for the New Millennium.* Mahwah, N.J.: Erlbaum, 2003.

Lipsey, M. W. "Theory as Method: Small Theories of Treatments." *New Directions for Program Evaluation*, 1993, *57*, 5–38.

Lipsey, M. W., and Cordray, D. "Evaluation Methods for Social Intervention." *Annual Review of Psychology*, 2000, *51*, 345–375.

Mark, M. M. "Toward an Integrative View of the Theory and Practice of Program and Policy Evaluation." In S. I. Donaldson and M. Scriven (eds.), *Evaluating Social Programs and Problems: Visions for the New Millennium.* Mahwah, N.J.: Erlbaum, 2003.

Mersman, J. L., and Donaldson, S. I. "Factors Affecting the Convergence of Self-Peer Ratings on Contextual and Task Performance." *Human Performance*, 2000, *13*, 299–322.

Mertens, D. M. "The Inclusive View of Evaluation: Visions for the New Millennium." In S. I. Donaldson and M. Scriven (eds.), *Evaluating Social Programs and Problems: Visions for the New Millennium.* Mahwah, N.J.: Erlbaum, 2003.

Oster, S. M. *Strategic Management for Nonprofit Organizations: Theory and Cases.* New York: Oxford University Press, 1995.

Patton, M. Q. *Utilization-Focused Evaluation: The New Century Text.* (3rd ed.) Thousand Oaks, Calif.: Sage, 1997.

Patton, M. Q. "Evaluation, Knowledge Management, Best Practices, and High-Quality Lessons Learned." *American Journal of Evaluation*, 2001, *22*, 329–336.

Price, R. H., Friedland, D. S., Choi, J. N., and Caplan, R. D. "Job-Loss and Work Transitions in a Time of Global Economic Change." In X. B. Arriaga and S. Oskamp (eds.), *Addressing Community Problems: Psychological Research and Intervention.* Thousand Oaks, Calif.: Sage, 1998.

Reichardt, C. S., and Rallis, S. F. (eds.). "The Qualitative-Quantitative Debate: New Perspectives." *New Directions for Program Evaluation*, 1994, *61*(entire issue).

Rossi, P. H., Freeman, H. E., and Lipsey, M. W. *Evaluation: A Systematic Approach.* (6th ed.) Thousand Oaks, Calif.: Sage, 1999.

Sanders, J. R. "A Vision for Evaluation." *American Journal of Evaluation*, 2001, *22*, 363–366.

Scriven, M. *Evaluation Thesaurus.* (4th ed.) Thousand Oaks, Calif.: Sage, 1991.

Scriven, M. "Evaluation in the New Millennium: The Transdisciplinary Vision." In S. I. Donaldson and M. Scriven (eds.), *Evaluating Social Programs and Problems: Visions for the New Millennium.* Mahwah, N.J.: Erlbaum, 2003.

Shadish, W. R. "Critical Multiplism: A Research Strategy and Its Attendant Tactics." *New Directions for Program Evaluation*, 1993, *60*, 13–57.

Shadish, W. R., Cook, T. D., and Campbell, D. T. *Experimental and Quasi-Experimental Designs for Generalized Causal Inference.* Boston: Houghton-Mifflin, 2001.

Shadish, W. R., Cook, T. D., and Leviton, L. C. *Foundations of Program Evaluation: Theories of Practice.* Thousand Oaks, Calif.: Sage, 1991.

Shadish, W. R., Newman, D. L., Scheirer, M. A., and Wye, C (eds.). "Guiding Principles for Evaluators." *New Directions for Program Evaluation*, 1995, *66*(entire issue).

Vinokur, A. D., van Ryn, M., Gramlich, E., and Price, R. H. "Long-Term Follow-Up and Benefit-Cost Analysis of the JOBS Program: A Preventive Intervention for the Unemployed." *Journal of Applied Psychology*, 1991, *76*, 213–219.

Weiss, C. H. "How Can Theory-Based Evaluation Make Greater Headway?" *Evaluation Review*, 1997, *21*, 501–524.

Weiss, C. H. *Evaluation: Methods for Studying Programs and Policies*. (2nd ed.) Upper Saddle River, N.J.: Prentice Hall, 1998.

Wholey, J. S. "Improving Performance and Accountability: Responding to Emerging Management Challenges." In S. I. Donaldson and M. Scriven (eds.), *Evaluating Social Programs and Problems: Visions for the New Millennium*. Mahwah, N.J.: Erlbaum, 2003.

CHAPTER SEVENTEEN

LEADERSHIP ASSESSMENT AND DEVELOPMENT

Recommendations for a New Assessment Model

Paul M. Arsenault

The advertising slogan "You've come a long way, baby" can be applied to leadership. Over the past twenty years, substantial progress has been made in our understanding of leadership. The most important component of the progress has been a shift in the concept of leadership. The traditional industrial paradigm—that leadership is defined only by the leader's traits or qualities (Clark and Clark, 1990) or is shaped by a situation—has been diminishing in value. The postindustrial perspective envisions leadership as action-oriented, thus putting the focus on the interaction between multiple factors that occur within the leadership process (Rost, 1991). These factors include the follower, organizational culture and the performance of the organization. Avolio (1999) describes this process as a "full range of leadership" that includes inputs (people and resources), process (the system or context), and outcomes.

A New Paradigm for Organizational Leadership Development

A more systematic way of thinking has come about because of the many dramatic changes in society that have affected organizations both nonprofit and for-profit. Changes such as the transformation from hierarchical, command-and-control organization models to ones that are flexible, centerless, and networked (Pasternack and Viscio, 1998), finding common ground among diverse cultures and in-terest groups, a growing gap between the haves and have-nots (Foster, 2000), and the increasing value of information have led researchers and practitioners to con-clude that leadership has to be much more flexible, subjective, and complex. The realities of the twenty-first century are requiring even more changes in leadership. Organizations now insist that leadership be oriented to constant change, handling uncertainty, and welcoming innovation, a trend that all indicators show will con-tinue. In addition, leaders at all levels will be less vested with formal authority, more opportunistic, and encouraged to act as agents of "positive deviation" by instigat-ing small wins and furthering learning (Meyerson, 2001). The traditional belief that leaders have to be larger than life (Kotter, 1988) is not relevant in twenty-first-century organizations. All these trends and changes have strong relevance to non-profit organizations and how future leadership in the nonprofit sector is developed and sustained.

This paradigm shift in the conceptualization of leadership has significantly transformed thinking on how to develop future leaders. The transformation has overcome two traditional beliefs. The first belief is that leaders are born with the right stuff (McCall, 1998) and therefore do not need any additional qualities. The second belief is that if there is a need for developing leaders, the development will based on the traditional concepts of training in which the teacher controls the de-velopment process (Pedler and Boydell, 1980) and development focuses only on the individual and is primarily done inside the classroom.

The new leadership development paradigm contradicts these traditional be-liefs. Developing nonprofit leaders who embody the leadership qualities just de-scribed will require that individuals set their own goals and evaluate their own success. The new paradigm will require individuals to become agents of their own development (Pedler and Boydell, 1980). McCall (1998) adds that individuals should have personalized developmental plans in order to know where they are, how far they have come, and how they can improve. As shown in Figure 17.1, the plan should consist of four ability levels, with the bottom two focusing on indi-vidual competencies (knowing oneself) and interpersonal skills (coaching). The complexity of the new leadership also requires that leadership development go beyond just the individual level. Conger and Benjamin (1999) add two more de-velopmental levels: socialization, which is instilling the values and visions of the organizational culture, and developing capabilities of implementing strategic change, both critical components of nonprofit leadership.

There are important differences between nonprofit and for-profit organiza-tions that need to be addressed. For example, in for-profits, leaders are expected to develop; this is encouraged by the organization and is usually paid for by the company because there is a belief that it will eventually contribute to the bottom

FIGURE 17.1. THE NEW LEADERSHIP DEVELOPMENT MODEL.

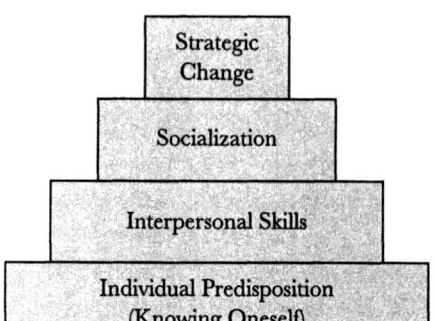

line. Also, in larger for-profits, getting leadership training is the method for advancing. Having the encouragement, in addition to having the organizational resources supporting training and development, is not necessarily the case in nonprofits, where leadership development is more often left up to the individual, especially in small, low-budget nonprofits. Among the larger nonprofits, budgets contain funding for training, but budgetary allocations for training are far less common for midsize and smaller organizations. When times are tough, training and staff leadership development is one of the first line items to be cut. Given the challenges of the economy, it is highly unlikely that there is an adequate amount of funding budgeted and spent for leadership development training. If training is funded, it is most often task-focused (for example, teaching fundraising techniques) or, if for the top executive, focused on survival techniques.

The other significant change is that development is based on action learning and not formal learning. Action learning, defined as a continuous process of learning and reflecting supported by colleagues, with a focus on getting things done (Revans, 1980), does not happen in the classroom; it occurs while working on future-oriented scenarios (Dixon, 1994), on special job assignments (Ready, 1994), and in team-based training (Conger and Benjamin, 1999). Applied to the nonprofit sector, the elements of action learning as defined here can be structured in strategic planning processes with future-oriented strategy development, cross-functional or collaborative work assignments, and staff and volunteer teams focused on problem solving and program development from a system perspective rather than a narrow functional perspective.

This new paradigm for leadership development requires a shift from a one-size-fits-all training program to a program that is custom-designed—one that takes advantage of the varied learning opportunities within the nonprofit organization.

Managers of organizations are now realizing that successful development of leaders will be beneficial only in the presence of the following:

- A full endorsement of senior-level managers (Zenger, Ulrich, and Smallwood, 2000). For the nonprofit, this means the top leadership, often the combined support of the top professional and the top volunteer leaders.
- A clear-cut business objective (Zenger, Ulrich, and Smallwood, 2000; Conger and Benjamin, 1999). Leadership development must be a component of the nonprofit organization's overarching goals and specifically a human resource development objective, regardless of the nonprofit's size.
- A more systematic approach or process (Brown, 1999). As a key organizational goal and a specific objective for human resources, leadership development becomes a functional part of the organization's ongoing human development and strategic processes.
- A vision that leadership development is a long-term process, advocating change rather than preserving the status quo. As part of the nonprofit's annual and strategic plans, leadership development is regarded as a crucial component for the success and future existence of the organization, with the nonprofit never losing sight of why it does the work it does and the type of leadership that is needed within the organization to achieve its mission.

Using the Leadership Assessment Process

In light of the vast changes in leadership and leadership development, more focus is now required on how to change the current leadership assessment processes (or performance review processes) to meet the demands of the changes in leadership and leadership development. Traditional processes were inadequate to effectively assess the traditional perspective of leadership, so this methodology is unable to effectively assess the new leadership process that is discussed in this chapter. Examples of the inadequacy are wanting quick results and therefore depending on testing whether people have the needed leadership skills or not (McCall, 1998), measuring leadership on a universal or ideal leadership model instead of a specific leadership model for the organization, and not customizing leadership development by level and organizational circumstances (Conger and Benjamin, 1999).

The following seven recommendations are based on two innovative steps that disrupt the traditional processes. The first step, which involves three recommendations, requires shifting the mental model of the organization that encompasses the central tendencies of beliefs and attitudes of leadership assessment. These prevailing dogmas must be upended for change. The second step, which can be achieved only once the first step has been accomplished, is changing the operating model that entails how leadership assessment is implemented on a day-to-day basis (Hamel, 2000).

Shifting the Mental Model

The three recommendations that require the shifting of the organizational model are the willingness to change, becoming a learning organization, and accepting a new model for assessment.

Recommendation 1: Organizations Must Be Willing to Change

As noted, the rapidly increasing rate of change has put people and organizations under increasing pressure to adapt, lest they go under. What does this mean for the nonprofit organization? It means that while holding on to the values of the nonprofit's mission, the organization must be open to and actively seek alternative ways of thinking and performing and of being in touch with the changing needs of the community it serves. The dilemma is that very few people like change (Barger and Kirby, 1995)—as the old saying goes, the only person who likes change is a baby with a wet diaper (Tubbs, 2001). So the question is, how do you go about changing the individuals' perspective of and capacity to assess their own and the organization's leadership competencies?

Any organization has to recognize that change is going to be resisted by many people, causing stress and anxiety. Barger and Kirby (1995) describe these people as so afraid of change that they need particularly compelling reasons to change because the status quo will look better and better to them once change begins. To overcome this resistance and motivate constructive behavior, Tushman and O'Reilly (2002) offer three practical steps:

1. Generate dissatisfaction with the status quo. Create a credible crisis (for example, a significant funding source loss and a mandate from the board of directors to restructure the organization with existing resources in addition to defining and seeking new funding opportunities; [Nelson, 2002]) that is simple to communicate, and offer a plan to resolve the crisis that is realistic (for example, everyone must be involved in assessing his or her own leadership skills for the future success of the organization). The rationale for this step is to overcome the trouble that people have focusing and listening when facing change. For example, the assessment (action learning) exercise could include a team of board leaders with a team of upper management staff, creating a collaborative assessment ef-

fort that heightens the understanding of all of the implications of every action from a deficit and asset perspective.

2. Build in participation, based on a simple concept that increasing personal participation will increase personal ownership and decrease personal resistance to change. For example, everyone in the organization would be involved in an organizational capacity assessment. Once the assessment team described in step 1 has done its preliminary work, move it to other levels in the organization, describing preliminary plans and seeking input from others within the organization.

3. Recognize and reward desired new behaviors. Design and implement both formal rewards (such as personal time off or a monetary bonus, however small) and informal rewards (such as personal recognition or the right to attend special events) through systems that reward the behaviors and attitudes that are needed for the change.

Recommendation 2: Become a Learning Organization

To develop an effective leadership assessment program demands that learning become paramount within the organization. Learning in an organization is defined as the "means of continuous testing of experience and the transformation of that experience into knowledge" (Ross, Smith, Roberts, and Kleiner, 1994, p. 49). Senge (1990) describes a learning organization as "an organization that is continually expanding its capacity to create the future. For such an organization, it is not enough merely to survive. . . . For a learning organization, 'adaptive learning' must be joined by 'generative learning,' learning that enhances our capacity to create" (p. 14). This process of learning allows for rigorous examination of existing deeply held beliefs, habits, images, and assumptions about assessment that help organizations and their leadership at all levels accept and implement change. Learning will enable organizations to accept the constant change affecting organizations by building new skills and the ability to constantly renew themselves (Green, 2000).

Recommendation 3: Accept a New Model for Leadership Assessment

Rethinking assessment is essential to assessing the new leadership development process. The outdated or current perspective of assessment for most people is the gut-wrenching memory of being graded. This elicits personal feelings of anger and resentment (Roth, 1999). Assessment in this perspective leads to reductionist thinking and to a mechanical notion that people are like machines (Johnson, 1999). Exhibit 17.1 adds some more insight into the current traditions and reinforces the concept of organizational control ("Old") versus individual responsibility for renewal that is defined in the opposite column ("New").

EXHIBIT 17.1. TRADITIONS IN ASSESSMENT: OLD VERSUS NEW.

Old	New
Assessment for auditors	Assessment for understanding
Collecting data for someone else	Collecting data for ourselves
Knowledge is detached and abstracted from people	Embedded in social relationships (knowing exists in a community of actors)
Primary audience is external to organization	Primary audience is internal to organization
Post hoc	Here and now
Presumes "objectivity"	Known to be dependent on development, values, and mental models of those involved
Other-oriented (How are they doing?)	Self-oriented (How am I/are we doing?)
Imposed on people	Invited
Fear of evaluation—predisposes you to self-affirming data	Intent of learning opens you to self-contradicting data
Culture of reports—managing the hierarchy	Culture of review—people reflecting together on their personal roles

Source: Easterday, Reilly, Senge, and Senge, 1998, p. 25.

The elements of traditional thinking described in Exhibit 17.1 do not bode well for assessing the new leadership competency requirements for the rapidly changing environment in which nonprofit organizations now reside. Instead of taking a mechanical point of view, the new process needs to see leadership as a natural process that has no end but constantly evolves (Johnson, 1999). The preferred model of leadership assessment focuses on self-renewal so that people can find out how they are doing, engage in personal reflection, and be understood within the social structure of the organization. Exhibit 17.1 further illustrates the new assessment focus on the here and now, developing the individual for the long term, and the desirability of change.

Nonprofit organizations cannot afford to ignore the importance of the new assessment characteristics described in Exhibit 17.1; in fact, they must be a high organizational priority if the organization is to move beyond survival and thrive. Assessment, as it is being defined here, can be very valuable, especially assessment of the complex and ambiguous leadership process required in an unpredictable and possibly unstable operating environment that will need more than a few measures and benchmarks (Senge, 1999). The value can be expressed in the following ways:

- Effective leadership assessment can inform the organization how best to allocate resources (Senge, 1999).
- An effective assessment process links people, environment, and behavior in an information-based framework (Walsh and Betz, 1995).
- Assessing leader development competencies provides a clear message that leadership development is valued by the organization (Osland, Kolb, and Rubin, 2000).
- Assessment provides systematic observations of differences and change (Walsh and Betz, 1995).

The new definition, therefore, has to be a natural process that allows individuals to see their own progress and that of the organization in order to set standards. The definition to meet these requirements is to include the gathering of information about the assessment results, comparing these results with past ones, having an open discussion about the meaning of the results, and deciding on the implications for improvement (Roth, 1999).

Shifting the Operating Model

The shifting of the operating model requires three key elements: assessment as an integral component of strategic planning, an organization assessment plan, and a leadership plan for each person.

Assessment as an Integral Component of Strategic Planning

The key factor for successful leadership assessment is that the leadership assessment process must be a significant part of the strategic planning process. Traditionally, leadership assessment has not been part of this process, thereby lacking accountability because there were no set goals and outcomes. All too frequently, the primary focus of nonprofit organizations is the development of financial resources. The people and leadership development aspects of the organization's future, at least equal in importance to financial development, is often undervalued. The absence of goals does not give an organization any benchmark as to whether leadership development is accomplishing the task of developing leaders. By linking leadership assessment with the strategic planning process, management will be forced to define and integrate leadership development, the assessment strategy, and goals and objectives for both the organization and the individuals in it.

Once the strategy, goals, and objectives have been set, organizations can design an appropriate assessment plan. The plan should include the following components:

- Desired leadership behaviors and outcomes
- Baselines for these behaviors and outcomes
- Assessment methods and inventories that are going to be used to collect data

Organization Assessment Plan

After leadership assessment has been integrated into the strategic plan, the organization can establish specific goals that are measurable. These goals will determine baselines and identify the organization's desired outcomes for these goals. Here is an example of one organization's goals:

- Provide new learning and leadership opportunities to 20 percent of employees
- Lower employee turnover by 10 percent
- Increase participation in the leadership development program by 15 percent
- Have at least 25 percent of the employees mention in annual survey that every employee should take on more leadership responsibilities
- Reassess goals on a yearly basis, and revise them to reflect whether the goals were met

Individual Leadership Development Plans

Individual development plans are the crowning jewel of an effective leadership assessment process. All the other steps will have to be in place to effectively have a development plan for every member of the organization. The overall goal of these plans is to facilitate development of each person within the organization, based on his or her strengths and weaknesses (areas for development) derived from the assessment process. This process enables individuals to recognize what they do well and why and to improve in areas that are underdeveloped (McCall, 1998). In addition, the assessment process establishes baselines for behaviors and outcomes for future plans.

The success of the individual plans will depend greatly on accepted beliefs, people's attitudes or assumptions, and working with assessment tools provided through outside organizations. These beliefs, attitudes, or assumptions are the following:

- Plans are designed to develop the whole person.
- Progress or lack of progress toward goals in the individual plan is to be tied to the individual's annual review and possible salary increases and bonuses.

- The individual's role is to take responsibility for becoming aware of personal weaknesses and strengths and to develop a course of growth that is tied in to the strategic direction of the organization (McCall, 1998).
- Organizations should, if possible, work closely with assessment companies to individually customize assessment inventories that allow for active feedback process to the individual (Conger and Benjamin, 1999). If working with a company specializing in assessment is not possible, use one or more of the tools indicated in Exhibit 17.2.

The assessment methods should include both qualitative and quantitative methods. (Exhibit 17.2 gives the names and qualities of recommended methods.) These methods are widely used in many organizations;[1] studies show that most organizations use some of these techniques, especially the multisource method (Walker and Smither, 1999; Atwater, 2001). This creative approach will integrate and execute these methods with individual assessment plans that makes the difference in effectively developing leaders (Hewitt Associates, 2002).

The actual plan should be based on a model like Conger and Benjamin's leadership development model (1999), discussed earlier in the chapter. The model ranges from the need to develop individual competencies, interpersonal skills, and understanding of organizational dynamics to implementing strategic change. Individual competencies focus on personal awareness inventories like personality, learning type, motivation, and ability to handle change. Interpersonal skills center on interpersonal and team skills. Included in this focus should be coaching, negotiation, and conflict management skills. The third area will center on strategic development. This area will focus on inventories in the area of leadership and handling organizational and strategic change.

Exhibit 17.3 presents an example of an individual assessment plan. The plan includes the results from the self-assessment,[2] personal reflection, performance appraisals, and multisource feedback and the stated goals given this evaluation. Establishing the individual goals differ somewhat from establishing the organizational goals for leadership development in that not all individual goals can be stated in measurable terms. The individual, with supporting evidence or in agreement with others (specifically, with direct superiors), determines whether any of the individual goals are accomplished. Each individual will revise these plans on a yearly basis to reflect feedback from others. The goals will then be changed, in agreement between the individual and his or her superiors, to align with organizational goals.

The benefits of the individual leadership assessment are twofold: individuals benefit by learning more and becoming more responsible because they are achieving goals that matter to them, and management benefits from knowing more

EXHIBIT 17.2. RECOMMENDED ASSESSMENT METHODS.

Method	Description
Personal reflection (journal writing)	An important feedback process that helps a person gain personal insight; a great means for self-expression
Multisource (360-degree) feedback	A feedback system that allows input from peers and subordinates and not just supervisors (Osland, Kolb, and Rubin, 2000)
Performance appraisal	Provides direct feedback from the supervisor and sets clear expectations for what is expected
Self-assessment inventories (personality or learning style)	Help people recognize their personal characteristics and individual strengths and weaknesses

about its workforce and seeing if its investment is making a difference (Hewitt Associates, 2002).

Now You Are Ready to Do It

There will never be a universal template or one-size-fits-all assessment program for the leadership development process required in an ever-changing environment. Therefore, each organization is going to have to develop its own assessment program, based on its particular goals and objectives. This task can be challenging; it requires taking risks, handling ambiguity, and accepting failure. Mistakes will be made in this never-ending process. So organizations are going to have to just do it and learn from their successes and failures how to improve the assessment program. As John McCain, the senator from Arizona, stated recently in a college graduation speech: "Speaking from experience, failure stinks. But it is not a permanent condition, and what really counts is courage and employing it" (Hunt, 2002).

Conclusion

The need for organizations to assess their leadership development process is key to forward-thinking organizations. The recommendations in this chapter will help organizations go beyond merely being aware of the need for a leadership assessment program to actually implementing one. The bottom line is that a well-thought-out

EXHIBIT 17.3. EXAMPLE OF INDIVIDUAL LEADERSHIP ASSESSMENT PLAN.

Self-Assessment Evaluation

1. Personality type: ENTJ (Myers-Briggs Type Indicator; Myers and Briggs, 2002)
2. Learning style: Accommodator (Kolb Learning Style Inventory; Osland, Kolb, and Rubin, 2000)
3. Leadership style: Spirited (What's My Leadership Style? HRDQ, 2001)
4. Decision-making style: Behavioral (What's My Decision-Making Style? Robbins, 2002)
5. Conflict-handling style: Collaborating and Accommodating (tie; Thomas-Kilmann Conflict Mode Instrument; Thomas and Kilmann, 2000)

Personal Reflection, Peer, and Superior Feedback

Strengths

- Is enthusiastic about learning; looks for learning experiences
- Handles ambiguous situations well; takes calculated risks
- Is innovative
- Is a team player
- Is a good strategic thinker

Weaknesses

- Needs to be less impulsive
- Needs to listen more effectively
- Needs to show more emotion, especially with human problems
- Needs to be more flexible; must not be so hardheaded about personal beliefs

Development Goals

1. Will propose three new projects or ideas to the new development committee
2. Will continue to be an instrumental participant on the strategic planning committee
3. Will publish two or more stories on learning experiences in the organization's newsletter
4. Will model leadership style in two or more leadership development workshops
5. Will be more reflective by considering all sides before making a decision
6. Will be more sensitive to people's problems; will offer emotional support rather than suggest possible solutions
7. Will participate in brainstorming activities and meetings

comprehensive leadership assessment plan that overcomes traditional mental models that are narrow and limiting and becomes a day-to-day component of an organization's strategic plan makes good business sense, whether it is a for-profit or a nonprofit business; such a plan can help any organization determine whether the leadership objectives it adopts are up to the task of ensuring the strength and future sustainability of the organization and its ability to serve the community it is in business to serve.

Author's note: The research for this chapter was supported by a grant from the James MacGregor Burns Center for Leadership at the University of Maryland. The grant supported a study to investigate how to assess the new leadership process and to recommend strategies to answer the question of how the assessment of the leadership development process might be improved. A major assumption was that traditional assessment processes were inadequate to assess the complexity of the new leadership paradigm. As Bryman (1992) stated, traditional leadership assessments are primarily focused on the behaviors or perceptions of a given leader or the causal relationship between group performance and job satisfaction, on the one hand, and leadership style, on the other. This focus is not adequate to effectively assess the new leadership process and development strategies as described in this chapter.

Notes

1. Hewitt Associates (2002), a human resource consultant firm, reported that organizations use a variety of methods to assess leadership. For example, 80 percent rely on evaluations by managers, 58 percent use 360-degree feedback, and 40 percent have self-assessment programs.
2. The self-assessments will usually only be completed once. Assessments on many of the individual competencies like personality and learning style do not change over time. Other assessments will be done at least once a year, preferably twice a year.

References

Atwater, L. "Understanding and Optimizing Multisource Feedback." *Illumine*, 2001, *2*, 4.

Avolio, B. J. *Full Leadership Development: Building the Vital Forces in Organizations.* San Francisco: Jossey-Bass, 1999.

Barger, N. J., and Kirby, L. K. *The Challenge of Change in Organizations: Helping Employees Thrive in the New Frontier.* Palo Alto, Calif.: Davies-Black, 1995.

Brown, P. "New Directions in Leadership Development: A Review of Trends and Best Practices." *Public Manager*, 1999, pp. 37–41.

Bryman, A. *Charisma and Leadership in Organizations.* Thousand Oaks, Calif.: Sage, 1992.

Clark, K. E., and Clark, M. B. *Measures of Leadership.* West Orange, N.J.: Leadership Library of America, 1990.

Conger, J. A., and Benjamin, B. *Building Leaders: How Successful Companies Develop the Next Generation.* San Francisco: Jossey-Bass, 1999.

Dixon, N. M. *The Organizational Learning Cycle: How We Can Learn Collectively.* New York: McGraw-Hill, 1994.

Easterday, B., Reilly, L., Senge, P., and Senge, P. M. "New Traditions in Assessment." In *Assessing to Learn and Learning to Assess.* Society for Organizational Learning, Assessment for Learning Research Initiative, Report of the First Research Forum, Cambridge, Mass., Jan. 14–16, 1998.

Foster, R. "Leadership in the Twenty-First Century: Working to Build a Civil Society." *National Civic Review,* 2000, *89,* 87–93.

Green, F. *10 Things Nonprofits Must Do in the 21st Century.* Los Angeles: California Association of Nonprofits, 2000.

Hamel, G. *Leading the Revolution: How to Thrive in Turbulent Times by Making Innovation a Way of Life.* Boston: Harvard Business School Press, 2000.

Hewitt Associates. "Companies See Limited Success in Developing Leaders, According to Hewitt." Press release, June 5, 2002.

HRDQ. *What's My Leadership Style?* King of Prussia, Pa.: Organization Design and Development, 2001.

Hunt, A. R. "Waiting for the Call." *Wall Street Journal,* May 30, 2002, p. A15.

Johnson, H. J. "Moving Upstream from Measurement: A Former Management Accountant's Perspective on the Great Dilemma of Assessing Needs." In P. Senge and others, *The Dance of Change: The Challenges to Sustaining Momentum in Learning Organizations.* New York: Doubleday, 1999.

Kotter, J. P. *The Leadership Factor.* New York: Free Press, 1988.

McCall, M. W. *High Flyers: Developing the Next Generation of Leaders.* Boston: Harvard Business School Press, 1998.

Meyerson, D. *Tempered Radicals: How People Use Difference to Inspire Change at Work.* Boston: Harvard Business School Press, 2001.

Myers, I. B., and Briggs, K. *Myers-Briggs Indicator.* Palo Alto, Calif.: Consulting Psychologists Press, 2002.

Nelson, S. J. "Do You Know What's in Your Leadership Pipeline?" *Harvard Management Update,* 2002, *7,* 1–3.

Osland, J. S., Kolb, D. A., and Rubin, I. M. *Organizational Behavior: An Experiential Approach.* (7th ed.) Upper Saddle River, N.J.: Prentice Hall, 2000.

Pasternack, B. A., and Viscio, A. J. *The Centerless Corporation: A New Mode for Transforming Your Organization for Growth and Prosperity.* New York: Simon and Schuster, 1998.

Pedler, M., and Boydell, T. "Is All Management Development Self-Development?" In J. Beck and C. Cox (eds.), *Advances in Management Education.* New York: Wiley, 1980.

Ready, D. *Champions of Change.* Lexington, Mass.: International Consortium for Executive Development Research, 1994.

Revans, R. W. *Action Learning.* London: Blond and Briggs, 1980.

Robbins, S. R. *Self-Assessment Inventory 2.0.* Upper Saddle River, N.J.: Prentice Hall, 2002.

Ross, R., Smith, B., Roberts, C., and Kleiner, A. *The Fifth Discipline Fieldbook: Strategies and Tools for Building a Learning Organization.* New York: Currency/Doubleday, 1994.

Rost, J. C. *Leadership for the Twenty -First Century.* New York: Praeger, 1991.

Roth, G. "Cracking the 'Black Box' of a Learning Initiative Assessment." In P. Senge and others, *The Dance of Change: The Challenges to Sustaining Momentum in Learning Organizations.* New York: Doubleday, 1999.

Senge, P. *The Fifth Discipline: The Art and Practice of the Learning Organization.* New York: Doubleday, 1990.

Senge, P. "The Challenge." In P. Senge and others, *The Dance of Change: The Challenges to Sustaining Momentum in Learning Organizations.* New York: Doubleday, 1999.

Thomas, K. W., and Kilmann, R. H. *Thomas-Kilmann Conflict Mode Instrument.* Palo Alto, Calif.: Consulting Psychologists Press, 2000.

Tubbs, S. L. "Leadership and Organizational Change." *Net Results: NASPA's E-Zine for Student Affairs Professionals.* February 27, 2001. [http://www.naspa.org/netresults/article.cfm?ID=151].

Tushman, M. L., and O'Reilly, C. A. *Winning Through Innovation: A Practical Guide to Leading Organizational Change and Renewal.* Boston: Harvard Business School Press, 2002.

Walker, A. G., and Smither, J. M. "A Five-Year Study of Upward Feedback: What Mangers Do with Their Results Matters." *Personnel Psychology,* 1999, *52,* 393–424.

Walsh, W. B., and Betz, N. E. *Tests and Assessment.* (3rd ed.) Upper Saddle River, N.J.: Prentice Hall, 1995.

Zenger, J., Ulrich, D., and Smallwood, N. "The New Leadership Development." *Training and Development,* 2000, *54,* 22–27.

CONCLUSION

SOUL-BASED LEADERSHIP

The Confluence of Ideals, Concepts, and Action

Sarah Smith Orr

Few will have the greatness to bend history itself, but each of us can work to change a small portion of events, and in the total of those acts will be written the history of this generation.

Each time a man stands for an ideal, or acts to improve the lot of others, or strikes out against injustice, he sends forth a tiny ripple of hope.

And crossing each other from a million different centers of energy and daring, those ripples build a current that can sweep down the mightiest walls of oppression and resistance.

Our future may lie beyond our vision, but it is not completely beyond our control. It is the shaping impulse of America that neither fate, nor nature, nor the irresistible tides of history, but the work of our own hands matched to reason and principle will determine our destiny.

ROBERT F. KENNEDY
(June 6, 1966, speech to students,
University of Capetown, South Africa)

Reflecting on the evolution of the nonprofit or social sector and its historical base in our country's democratic system and on Robert Kennedy's statement, we are reminded that just as our nation's beginnings were based on ideals of its founders, each nonprofit organization has been founded on an ideal, often that of one person who led the creation of a collective vision with like-minded individuals. The nonprofit or social sector was one of the nation's key building blocks, initially as a collection of modest neighbor-helping-neighbor actions. Since those humble beginnings, the sector has grown to represent a significant part of the United States' GDP (O'Neill, 2002). (O'Neill reports that there are 1.8 million registered and probably millions of unregistered nonprofit organizations, with

267

annual revenue greater than the GDP of all but six nations, more civilian employees than the federal government and the fifty state governments combined, and a place in virtually every American's life.) Many nonprofit organizations reach well beyond our borders to support social needs in other countries. This phenomenon has not gone unnoticed—international awareness of this sector's uniqueness began early in the nineteenth century. Most individuals who have worked in the nonprofit sector have made reference, at various times, to Alexis de Tocqueville's classic *Democracy in America* (1945 [1835]). Tocqueville was fascinated by the propensity of Americans to create "voluntary associations" or "moral and intellectual associations" and described them as central to our democratic system. Studying the American democratic system, the Frenchman reached the conclusion that no other society embraced voluntarism as it was embraced then, and continues to be embraced, in America. And interest in the commitment and intensity of the "voluntary associations" that make up the nonprofit or social sector today has not waned, as affirmed by O'Neill (2002, p. 34): "The rapid growth of the nonprofit sector in the last half century has led to greatly increased attention from the media, scholars, the government, and the public, as well as from new foreign observers." The contributions of the organizations in the nonprofit or social sector are enormous and reach all parts of society. Although most are likely to be small or midsize, many organizations in the sector have become big businesses. Just as the for-profit sector is closely examining the way it does business, the nonprofit sector should too. The growth of organizations in this sector, from humble beginnings when their mission and purpose were palpable to organizations with large budgets and extended outreach, calls for a pause to examine what the organizations are in the business of doing and just how they might improve the leadership of their businesses—the focus of much of volume.

The purpose of this chapter is to provide a different lens through which to examine the characteristics and acts of nonprofit leaders, returning, in a sense, to the underlying intentions of this sector, and then to align those intentions with designs for healthy and gratifying places to work. Robert Kennedy's statement at the beginning of the chapter will serve as a framework for further conceptual exploration.

Leadership Ideals and Acts

"Each time a man stands for an ideal, or acts to improve the lot of others . . .," Kennedy began. Every nonprofit organization was started by a person with an ideal. Through these initiators' acts, and those of their followers, they want to improve the lot of others; they may have seen or experienced injustices that they feel demand correction or elimination in order to improve the quality of life for people in a particular community. The focus of the founders or initiators of these organizations has served as a source of energy and daring, with the leader of a particular initiative breaking through any number of obstacles to achieve the envisioned outcome. The leader becomes the champion for the cause; the organizational purpose serves as the vehicle to achieve synergy between the cause and others who have an affinity with the ideal. It is the leader's responsibility to create the environment that motivates these followers to work toward the desired end. Consistently, individuals who join the ranks of nonprofit organizations as volunteers or staff are seeking a confluence—an integration of their work and their reason for being with the altruistic purpose or ideal of the organization they are a part of: a gratifying place to work.

Looking into the future and considering the challenging and volatile nature of the world we live and work in, one must wonder: What confluence of skills, values, attitudes, and competencies or set of leadership acts are integral to purposeful, soul-based leadership, the kind of leadership that ensures the existence of a gratifying place to work? Soul-based or purposeful leadership in this context is defined as the kind of leadership that seeks to conjoin the compelling reason people wish to be a part of an organization and devote their energies to it with the organization's cause or reason for being. Why is this important? It is assumed that most nonprofits are founded on a basis of altruism—a cause worth supporting with all one's heart and soul.

Based on more than three decades working as both a professional leader and a volunteer leader in the nonprofit sector, I can attest that one cannot assume that an altruistically founded organization always embodies qualities that match its altruistic intent. Nonprofit organizations are just as vulnerable to external and internal vagaries as for-profit businesses. Although the "for the greater good of society" intent is there, the leadership capabilities necessary for the organization to be healthy and thriving are often either weak or absent. Several contributing factors are frequently seen. The most prevalent center around the existence of a highly competitive environment for scarce resources and the focus of many organizations and their leaders on survival, resulting in budgetary limitations for securing and developing effective leaders (see Chapter Seventeen). Also, in many instances, the continued presence and pervasive (sometimes paralyzing) influence of nonprofit founders or leaders who have abandoned the transformational leadership model is a contributing factor (see Chapters Five and Eight). Too many nonprofit staff members experience burnout and disillusionment resulting from a perceived mismatch between their personal goals and the organization's purpose. What might people who join nonprofit organizations be looking for? In a word, *meaning*—or, put another way, for an organizational with *soul*.

Ellsworth (2002) recognizes that the conversation about work and finding meaning (soul-based work) may be a bit "abstract" for the manager or leader who just wants to get things done. Nonprofit organizations are most often stretched in every way, with many feeling that they have insufficient time or resources to think "outside the box"; they are just trying to survive. Ellsworth provides this perspective: "The historical battle between work as a source of drudgery and alienation, and work as a creative, fulfilling experience continues today" (p. 58). He maintains that an organization has the advantage when its employees are knowledgeable, committed to renewal and learning, creative, more focused on positive than on negative activities, and supported in their pursuits. An environment that fosters these advantageous behaviors is designed and led by people who understand the importance of creating work experiences that transcend the mundane, bringing "added meaning to people's lives and value to the organizations they serve" (p. 59)—in short, organizations with soul.

Organizations with Soul

"Our future may lie beyond our vision, but it is not completely beyond our control. It is the shaping impulse . . . that neither fate, nor nature, nor the irresistible tides of history, but the work of our own hands matched to reason and principle will determine our destiny," Kennedy said.

Bolman and Deal, in *Leading with Soul: An Uncommon Journey of Spirit* (2001) use the word *soul* in relation to how one leads one's personal life along with one's leadership of an organization. In response to what they define as "restlessness" and a feeling among many leaders that "something is missing," they launched their contemporary search into soul and meaning. Of the people they studied, they write, "Some people experienced this gap [something missing] as a haunting sense that somewhere along the line they got off track. They're working harder than ever, but they're not sure why, and they've lost touch with what's really important in life" (p. 5). Their descriptions of many workplaces use expressions such as "devoid of meaning and purpose" and "having little regard for what human beings need in order to experience personal fulfillment and success" (p. 6). They describe the toll that these feelings and experiences take on motivation, loyalty, and performance, a toll that they characterize as "a road to crisis and decay" (p. 6).

Mihalyi Csikszentmihalyi, noted scholar and writer in the study of creativity, flow, and meaning, describes a leader able to inspire as one who can create "an organization that will be a gratifying place to work" (2003, p. 143). Csikszentmihalyi describes the optimal workplace as one that has soul as the key ingredient. "We attribute soul to those entities that use some portion of their energy not only for their own sake, but to make contact with other beings and care for them" (p. 145).

How is soul discernible in the workplace? First, the organization itself, through its leadership, can manifest soul. Second, soul is evident in the leader and his or her capacity to convey a compelling vision and to demonstrate the values and behaviors that can create a soulful organizational environment.

Csikszentmihalyi (2003) maintains that for an organization, soul exists when the system reaches out beyond itself, investing in another system, which ends up creating an entity larger than itself. Gill Hickman, in Chapter Eleven, provides such a model through her "Organizations of Hope" research, illustrating the benefits to all parties involved of the for-profit's investment of time and resources in partnership with a nonprofit addressing a social cause that is aligned with the for-profit's purpose. Another example of organizational soul comes from Frances Hesselbein in Chapter One as she calls on the leaders of the social sector to "take the lead, initiating partnerships with business and government leaders and their enterprises." She challenges nonprofit leaders to "look beyond their walls" to identify ways to "build a cohesive and inclusive community that embraces all its people." Rob Johnston, former president of the Leader to Leader Institute, told me that he considers the practiced capability of collaboration, networking, and coordination one of his three most important leadership qualities of leaders in the twenty-first century. He elaborated:

> When an organization is focused on quality, as it should be, it recognizes it can't and shouldn't try to do all things—that the customers in the world we live in require the attention of more than one specialist. The best way to serve our customer is to coordinate with other nonprofits that are serving the rest of that family, to work with local government to facilitate outreach, for example. It means doing the work in ways that may not always be within your organizational control but will ultimately provide better and more significant services to those who need them.

The foregoing are excellent examples of manifestations of organizational soul—organizations transcending artificial boundaries for the purpose of a cause or ideal beyond the organization's sense of self.

Moving from the macro (organizational) level to the individual leader level, Csikszentmihalyi (2003) provides a framework for actions that are soul-based. "At the human level, curiosity, empathy, generosity, responsibility, and charity are some of its noteworthy manifestations" (p. 145). The most familiar example of soul in action, he states, is "when a person devotes attention not just to selfish interests, or even to material goals in general, but to the needs of others, or to the cosmic forces that we assume must rule the universe" (p. 145).

A myriad of authors on leadership have properly emphasized the vital importance of vision. Vision is a means of articulating soul, for an organization's vision extends beyond the interests of a few to wider goals, the "anticipated evolution of an organization that has become conscious of its own potentialities" (Csikszentmihalyi, 2003, p. 147). Vision extends the focus beyond the present or the self to a desirable future that does not yet exist. The capacity of the leader to guide the development and articulation of a vision that does something to benefit others (what nonprofits are in business to do) and achieves alignment of the individuals within the organization to that vision is a manifestation of soul leadership (if done with a positive and beneficial intent). As described and illustrated by Riggio, Bass, and Orr in Chapter Five, the transformational leadership model is a worthy guide for leaders seeking to develop an environment of meaning or soul in their nonprofit organizations. The essence of transformational leadership, evolving out of the research of leadership scholars (Burns, 1978; Bass, 1985, 1998; Avolio and Yammarino, 2002), Riggio, Bass, and Orr tell us, is a leader "who not only inspires commitment to a vision or cause but also develops, or 'transforms,' followers to reach their highest potential and to take on the responsibilities of leading the organization toward its mission."

In research involving visionary and successful business leaders conducted by Csikszentmihalyi (2003, p. 157), five traits emerged as most important in their attitude toward life—attitudes that framed their soul-based leadership to an expanded state beyond vision:

1. Unbounded optimism—this involves a positive attitude toward the future and a basic belief in the overall good of human beings. This optimism often involved a commitment to a cause or a calling to something greater than oneself.
2. Strong belief in the importance of integrity—an "unwavering adherence to principles on which mutual trust can be based" (Csikszentmihalyi, 2003, p. 156).
3. A high level of ambition coupled with perseverance—giving them strength and endurance in dealing with hardship and assuming challenging tasks or undertakings.
4. A constant curiosity and desire to learn.
5. Empathy for others and a sense of mutual respect.

The application of these principles of soul-based leadership will be explored next.

Applying the Principles of Soul-Based Leadership

Unbounded optimism for a nonprofit leader with a passion for the organization's mission and cause seems like a no-brainer. But what's behind this seemingly simple principle?

Cristina Regalado, vice president for programs with the California Wellness Foundation, provided her perspective on this subject in response to my inquiry regarding the most important qualities for leaders of nonprofit organizations. Regalado has firsthand knowledge of the challenges and demands of grassroots organizations; she has, throughout her career, been a champion for social change, working through and with a multitude of diverse organizations dealing with complex racial, cultural, gender, and class issues in a dynamic and multicultural region, Southern California.

Regalado, in her description of the work environment within which the nonprofits she knows best operate, stressed the importance of congruence, for the leader, among optimism, drive, and the leader's own personal vision of what social change needs to occur through the organization's mission and vision. Her perception is that one of the reasons people burn out is the lack of balance between the care of one's self and the fulfillment of one's work or passion. As she put it, "There has to be something deeper—a spiritual calling or moral drive that sustains the leader over time." Due to the "rapidly devolving environment with dwindling resources, nonprofits are in crisis—on a weekly basis!" Leaders, she emphasizes, must have their own source of sustaining power. "It provides a compass to where they are heading—a clear vision that inspires others to get them engaged."

Rob Johnston, former president of the Leader to Leader Institute, described the necessary focus, for nonprofit leaders, on mission and customers. "Nonprofit organizations have to have clarity about why they are in business, why they do what they do and who they serve by doing that. The nonprofit leader is the one who has to carry the primary responsibility to assure that the organization develops that clarity, with board, staff, and customers. When an organization has clarity, it can be assured that it doesn't waste its efforts and resources; then it can further its mission." K. M. Thiagarajan upholds this position in Chapter Four, describing how the mission serves as the driving force for microcredit, self-help groups in rural Indian villages.

Integrity is a powerful yet fragile word—powerful in all that it encompasses; fragile because it can be damaged or destroyed in a moment of bad judgment, indiscretion, or thoughtlessness. As Joanne Ciulla reminds us in Chapter Six, "The most important source of power for a nonprofit leader is the ability to gain the respect, trust, and loyalty of others. . . . The difference between the morality of leaders and everyone else is that the ethical failures and successes of leaders are magnified by their role, visibility, power, and the impact of their actions and behavior on others." Take the example of William Aramony, former president of United Way of America. His errors of professional judgment and personal indiscretions in the early 1990s, which sent him to prison, tarnished the reputation of an entire national network of local agencies. It has taken years for many local United Ways to regain full public trust, even though the former president's role and actions were far removed from the local agencies. The national organization continues its quest for account-ability and standards designed to respond to public trust issues. The new standards have been designed to show donors clearly how their money is used, ensure that the funds are used wisely, and require that local United Ways report overhead and pro-gram costs accurately and consistently (Williams, 2003). The new standards also re-quire local United Ways to conduct and submit to the United Way of America a periodic "self-assessment" of their management, governance, decision making, and community work for review by a special committee.

As critical as integrity is as a leader interacts with external constituents, it is equally crucial to the leader's interaction and relationship with internal con-stituents. Frances Hesselbein defines it in Chapter One as "a matter of how to be, not how to do. In the end, it is the quality and the character of the leader that de-termines the performance, the results." Integrity can also be framed by the words *transparency, authenticity, integration, coherence,* and *caring*—"a sense of connection, at a minimum with the people who are engaged in the work, ideally with the people who will be affected by the work" (Csikszentmihalyi, 2003, p. 161). Integrity in a leader can be measured by the consistency of the leader's actions and behaviors across situations, congruence with beliefs and personality, and the conviction of his or her values—what and who the leader is.

Ambition coupled with perseverance is another indispensable quality in a leader. Ambition in this sense is founded in achieving quality, having the highest-quality product, and performing at the highest possible level. Ambition, however, is also a personal attribute of the leader; it is based on the belief that one should never be satisfied with the present state of things, that one must always stretch to reach beyond where one is.

Perseverance, tenacity, a never-say-die attitude, are also key attributes of a leader—never giving up when confronted with obstacles. It is often reflected in en-ergy and stamina, integrating passion, enthusiasm, and vigor on the job—walking the walk and talking the talk.

Also essential in a leader are *constant curiosity and the desire to learn.* Richard Hughes, a director with the Center for Creative Leadership, focused in our talks on the ability to keep learning and having a sense of curiosity as key characteris-tics for the leader of the twenty-first century. He explains, "The conditions within which you are trying to nurture and grow your organization aren't stable; people in organizations are changing and more diverse. The leader needs to learn at a personal level but also be savvy enough to build systems to have those in your organization learning on a continual basis."

Csikszentmihalyi (2003) expands on that concept: "The calling of visionary leaders includes a sense of incompleteness, of wanting to go beyond the boundaries of what is known. Their favorite mode of being is becoming, which reveals itself in a wide-ranging curiosity, an openness to all kinds of experiences" (p. 163). Regalado provides another perspective: "A leader needs a self-reflective quality; being humble enough to assess where he or she is going and can accept criticism and either improve or move out of the way so the organization can respond to the need for change. Such leaders have the sustaining power to be effective—they can explore and work across different lines—race, culture, class, and sectors. The ability to learn and be flexible, expanding one's horizons, gives the effective leader the edge."

The dictionary defines *empathy* as "the capacity for participation in another's feelings or ideas." It is crucial for leaders to believe that their actions are benefiting their employees, their customers, the community, society, and the environment, and the most effective and soul-based way of being certain of that is having empathy (Csikszentmihalyi, 2003).

Being empathic extends to involving as well as to motivating people. For a leader, having empathy means putting oneself in another's shoes; it also involves respect—for peers, customers, and subordinates. It can affect, for example, how work groups are brought together and function, as explored by Pearce, Yoo, and Alavi in Chapter Thirteen. Designing evaluation methods to improve the organizational effectiveness as discussed and illustrated by Stewart Donaldson in Chapter Sixteen falls within this area.

Empathic leadership involves emotional intelligence. Daniel Goleman (1998) frames emotional intelligence in two sets of competencies: personal (self-awareness, self-regulation, and motivation) and social (empathy and social skills). Empathy is the key element of social competence, which Goleman describes as a competency to determine how one handles relationships. Hughes feels that the challenge of motivating other people to do great work is a key in nonprofit leadership. "Most people want to be engaged in work that has a noble purpose and is meaningful. They want to contribute to something greater than themselves. In a nonprofit, you have a greater opportunity to create that linkage." Goleman contends that emotional competence is central to leadership—to getting others to do their jobs more effectively. "A leader's strengths or weaknesses in emotional competence can be measured in the gain or loss to the organization of the fullest talents of those they manage" (Goleman, 1998, p. 32). Leadership is about building effective, empathic, and trusting relationships.

Conclusion

"Few will have the greatness to bend history itself, but each of us can work to change a small portion of events, and in the total of those acts will be written the history of this generation."

In "Challenge Is the Opportunity for Greatness," Kouzes and Posner (2003) suggest that the challenges faced in this current period of unprecedented change provide the opportunity for great leadership to emerge, based on the historic evidence of great leadership evolving during times of great challenge. The editors of *Leader to Leader*, the publication in which the article appeared, while acknowledging the opportunities, admonish the reader that "still there are actions we can take to help leadership flourish. One of the most important things leaders do is set the example, thus making intangible leadership qualities visible in action" ("From the Editors," 2003, p. 2).

It is likely that the majority of people in leadership positions in our country's nonprofit organizations will not achieve the greatness to "bend history itself," as Kennedy put it. However, as he noted, "each . . . can work to change a small portion of events" within the organization he or she leads and the systems (community, regional, national, or international) of which the organization is a part.

"And in the total of those acts will be written the history of this generation." This generation of nonprofit leaders has an opportunity to set the example for the other sectors in our county's democratic system. In Chapter One, Frances Hesselbein quotes Peter Drucker as he described the role of the social sector in this new century: "It is in the social sector that we find the greatest innovation, the greatest results in meeting human needs. And what we will do as a sector will determine the health, the quality, and the performance of the twenty-first-century society." Hesselbein states in response: "The greatest challenge of this nonprofit century is to provide the leadership, the competence, and the management that will determine the quality and the performance of the twenty-first-century society."

The challenges abound. The opportunities are limitless. The leaders who will transform organizations and lead innovation, who will provide the greatest results, and whose acts, combined with those of other leaders in the social sector, will write the history of this generation, will be the leaders who create gratifying places to work. They will lead with soul.

References

Avolio, B. J., and Yammarino, F. J. (eds.). *Transformational and Charismatic Leadership: The Road Ahead*. Greenwich, Conn.: JAI Press, 2002.

Bass, B. M. *Leadership and Performance Beyond Expectations*. New York: Free Press, 1985.

Bass, B. M. *Transformational Leadership: Industrial, Military, and Educational Impact*. Mahwah, N.J.: Erlbaum, 1998.

Bolman, L. G., and Deal, T. E. *Leading with Soul: An Uncommon Journey of Spirit*. (rev. ed.) San Francisco: Jossey-Bass, 2001.

Burns, J. M. *Leadership*. New York: HarperCollins, 1978.

Csikszentmihalyi, M. *Good Business: Leadership, Flow, and the Making of Meaning.* New York: Viking Press, 2003.

Ellsworth, R. R. *Leading with Purpose: The New Corporate Realities.* Stanford, Calif.: Stanford University Press, 2002.

"From the Editors." *Leader to Leader,* 2003, *28,* 2–3.

Goleman, D. *Working with Emotional Intelligence.* New York: Bantam Books, 1998.

Kouzes, J. M., and Posner, B. Z. "Challenge Is the Opportunity for Greatness." *Leader to Leader,* 2003, *28,* 16–28.

O'Neill, M. *Nonprofit Nation: A New Look at the Third America.* San Francisco: Jossey-Bass, 2002.

Tocqueville, A. de. *Democracy in America.* New York: Knopf, 1945. (Originally published in 1835.)

Williams, G. "United Ways Agree to New Accountability Measures." *Chronicle of Philanthropy,* January 23, 2003. [http://philanthropy.com/free/update/2003/01/2003012301.htm].

NAME INDEX

A

Adams, J., 113, 114
Akers, J., 73
Alavi, M., xxiii, xxvii–xxviii, 180–199, 273
Albanese, R., 187
Alutto, J. A., 187
American Red Cross, 66, 175
Ammons, D., 67
Anderson, D., 23
Anderson, L. A., 23
Antle, R., 78
Antonakis, J., 53
Aramony, W., 58–60, 72, 73, 74, 273
Argyris, C., 155
Arnould, R., 86
Arroyo, G. M., 55
Arsenault, P. M., xxiii, 252–264
Arthur, M. B., 51
Atwater, L., 261
Austin, J. E., 152
Avolio, B. J., 49, 50, 52, 53, 183, 184, 185, 186, 220, 223, 228, 229, 252, 272

B

Baer, D., 163
Barger, N. J., 256
Bartlett, C. A., 221
Bass, B. M., xxiv, 44, 49–61, 183, 184, 185, 186, 220, 222, 223, 272
Bastian, A., 107
Beeson, J., 103
Benjamin, B., 253, 254, 255, 261
Bennis, W., 5, 155, 225
Bentler, P. M., 188
Berghuis, J. P., 166
Bertrand, M., 86, 97
Betz, N. E., 259
Bezos, J., 14
Bickman, L., 244
Bikson, T. K., 181, 186
Birckmayer, J. D., 241
Black, F., 84
Bolman, L. G., 270
Bonaparte, N., 10
Bowen, W. G., 61n.2
Boydell, T., 253
Brickley, J. A., 86

C

Brinckerhoff, P. C., 29–30
Brown, B. M., 103
Brown, P., 255
Brown, R. B., 103
Bruhl, L., 107
Bryant, J., 56–57
Bryman, A., 264
Buehler, J. W., 168
Burbridge, L. C., 81
Burns, J. M., 44, 49–50, 113, 158, 182, 220, 222, 223, 229, 272
Bush, G. W., 13, 14
Byant, J., 56–57

C

Cambron, L., 104
Cantor, N., 169
Carlos, J. (King), 70
Carroll, L., 10
Carver, J., 103
Cass, R. H., 267
Catania, J. A., 168
Chambré, S. M., 168
Chang, L., 183, 186
Chang, W., 172

SUBJECT INDEX

Numbers in italics reference pages with Exhibits, Figures, and Tables.

A

AARP (American Association of Retired Persons), 104
Ability bias and wages, 81
Absenteeism, Board meeting, 122
Accountability of nonprofit organizations, 227; and effectiveness, 26, 248; and ethical conduct, 25–27; program services share of expenses, 82, *83*, 84; three basic requirements of, 25
Accounting profession reputation, 13–14
Action: moral, 64–66, 67, 273; social, 160. *See also* Causes, social
Adulteries, 72
Advocacy and lobbying, 33–34
"Age of social transformation," 19
AIDS volunteerism, 168–170
Alliances: among sectors, 7–9, 24; betterment, 24; empowerment,

24; forming strategic, 24–25, 27, 149
Altruism, 65–66, 67, 269
Ambiguity, tolerance of, 11
Ambition and perseverance, 274
America, the leadership crisis in, 12–13
American Society for Training and Development (ASTD), 103
Archetypes, succession: historical, 113–114; matrix of, 108, *109*, 110, 112–113; and scenarios, 110–112; some common, 112–113; universal Jungian, 107–108
Army Leadership Field Manual, 5
Asking for funds, fear of, 143–144
Assessment: accepting a new model for, 257–259; leadership, 255–256; measurable goals of, 260, 262; the mental model of, 256–259; old versus new traditions in, 258–259, *258*; scales for TL, 223. *See also* Leadership assessment
Assessment plan: individual leadership, 260–262, *263*; methods and strategies, 260–262, *262*

Assumptions: choices not, 133–135; exploring, 21; and individual leadership development, 260–261
Audits, 26

B

Baby boomer leaders, the departure of, 104, 106
Banking, social investment, 40–53, 56–57
"Bathsheba Syndrome," 71–72
Bhagavad Gita, 106
Black power, 14
Board chair, 119, 140–143; and the executive director, 141–142; kit for a, *142*
Board members: assessing the capabilities of, 125–126, *127*; contract for, 139; expectations of, 137, 138, 140; full disclosure by, 138; as funders and donors, 21, 121–122; key knowledge areas for, *127*; key responsibilities and duties of, *139*; letting go of difficult, 145–146;

Printed in the United States
138886LV00006B/11/P